HOWARD & MASCHLER ON FOOD

HOWARD & MASCHLER ON FOOD

Elizabeth Jane Howard

Fay Maschler

Michael Joseph – London

First published in Great Britain by
Michael Joseph Limited
27 Wrights Lane, London W8
1987

British Library Cataloguing in Publication Data

Maschler, Fay
Howard and Maschler on Food.
1. Cookery, International
I. Title   II. Howard, Elizabeth Jane
641.5   TX725.A1

ISBN 0-7181-2722-6

Typeset in Ehrhardt
by Wilmaset, Birkenhead, Wirral
Printed and bound in Great Britain by
Billings and Son, Worcester

for
Jane's daughter, Nicola Starks,
and
Fay's mother, Mary Coventry

Acknowledgements

Cooking is a magpie business. Inspiration, guidance and facts are gleaned from so many sources: relations, friends, chefs and cookery book writers. It will be clear from the references throughout the text with which cookery writers our sympathies lie, but we should like to thank the following, to whom we owe a great debt of gratitude: Elizabeth David, Jane Grigson, Marcella Hazan, Madhur Jaffrey, Richard Olney, Claudia Roden. As acknowledged in the text, recipes have also been inspired by Victor Gordon, Anton Mosimann, the Roux brothers, Delia Smith, Fortune Stanley and Alice Walters.

Cooking at home can be a lonely business and we should like to thank Lily Uniacke and Hazel Short, both of them loyal and marvellous collaborators in the kitchen.

Contents

Introduction

A moratorium on cookery books is not a bad idea: there are enough. If anyone wants to devote his or her life to making only recipes that incorporate peanut butter or learn from scratch the finer points of cuisine, there is a book available that instructs. There are, of course, various books dealing with 'occasions' but they assume them to be optimistic ones: Engagement Party, Golden Wedding, Hunt Breakfast, etc. This book recognises those highpoints and caters for them (see the chapter on New Year's Eve, for example), but also includes the lowpoints that need fuelling (see the chapter on Abandoned Man, a godsend to anyone suddenly obliged to cope for himself, or herself).

Everyone who cooks has a repertoire, but frequently life demands that he or she cooks outside it. This book is the collected experience of two people who have come to see cooking as an indispensable skill for living, a necessary aptitude if you are going to get by, or get through the occasions that life throws in your way, be they the dinner when you know your guests are likely to be greedy – or dull –, the meal you want to prepare for an invalid, or, on a happier note, a prospective loved one, a supper the day you or your friends move house, or a picnic, or the day you are desperately short of time. It is designed to deal with the pure sociability of food – the ways in which it can be used to please, to impress, to lure; as a weapon, as a last resort, as an expression of power or love. The chapters accommodate cooks with limited resources, with pressures of time, the rich, the young, the put upon, and the eccentrics. Naturally, chapters overlap as our index will indicate; the one on vegetarian cooking, for example, would have relevance to the one on cooking when you are hard up.

We make the following assumptions. 1: That the reader understands the fundamentals of cooking, although we do provide a certain amount of basic information – such as how to make mayonnaise, for example.

Indeed it would be *possible* for an intelligent beginner to start with this book, but the book was not designed for beginners. 2: That you have, on the whole, the kitchen equipment that you need and can afford. Many books set out the most alarming array of *batterie de cuisine*, but as one of the best cooks we knew made his fantastic meals with three dented old saucepans and a cooker endearingly called 'The New Suburbia' whose oven door had a fairly large hole in it, we will simply remark that we regard a food processor as indispensible, that one of us gets frantic about knives being razor sharp and the other is set upon steamers that will take anything from a large fish or bird to a quantity of vegetables.

Neither of us cooks metric, infinitely preferring ounces and pounds. We have provided the metric equivalent, but if you have the choice, we recommend that you follow our preference, since there is never an *exact* translation of ounces to grams; but whichever you do, we assume that you will take instructions about quantities seriously. This is also the place to make the time-honoured point about reading right through a recipe before you do anything else about it.

1 *Foolproof Dinner*

There was a halcyon time when the even comparatively less-well off could afford to entertain friends in a restaurant. Victorians (think of Mr Pooter) ate out on occasion and food that is now in the luxury class was generally available. Oysters will never be 9d a dozen again, nor sirloin of beef 8½d a lb, or, indeed – including inflation – anything like it. If we want to entertain our friends, we have to cook at home. This is fine for many people: even if they don't like the day to day drudgery of cooking family meals, they enjoy preparing the odd – more festive – meal for friends.

But not everyone feels like that. Some people really hate cooking because they find it so anxious, unpredictable and difficult; the idea of making a three-course dinner for friends where everything is timed right fills them with terror, and they know that the evening holds no pleasure for them. The pleasure of their guests is consequently much reduced. Apart from waiting till starving while the potatoes get cooked, or chewing their way through half-raw ones, the anxiety of their hostess is contagious: the kinder guests may find themselves in the kitchen attempting to advise about a separated sauce, a sunken soufflé or burned pastry while the others sit soaking up quantities of drink – bad for them and expensive for you – and longing for something simple and immediate, like ham sandwiches.

The point of entertaining your friends is to *see* them – a spot of mutual enjoyment is what you are aiming at. So the more nervous you are of providing the food, the more necessary it is that your dinner should be foolproof: at least half an hour before your friends are due, you should have done it all, should be feeling relaxed and expectant – be looking forward to the evening.

Obviously, the main aim is for you to have done your cooking well in advance, when making mistakes won't be such a big deal. But also, your confidence will steadily increase if you concentrate upon making a few things well. For the acutely nervous, we suggest that you practise beforehand, but all the dishes below should be foolproof if you follow directions *precisely*. (Perhaps it is worth saying here, that a great many cooks who are nervous and make mistakes *don't* read a recipe carefully. Read it right through and make sure that you understand it before you begin.) It doesn't matter if your repertoire is small, provided that everything you make is pleasant to eat; indeed, you could get famous for your fish pie or your treacle pudding – people may end up by flocking for miles, their mouths watering with nostalgic greed. The most noticeable characteristic of a failed dish, however, is its failure – the fact that you've explored another avenue that has turned out to be a cul de sac will neither comfort nor impress your guests.

Right; when you have read the recipes below, decide which ones you want to make and then do a careful shopping list without ever assuming that you have got any ingredient without checking. We suggest that you start by making your pudding before your hands become tainted by onion or garlic.

Artichoke Soup

Kipper Fillet Salad

Salade Niçoise

Fish Pie

Lancashire Hot-Pot

Oxtail Stew

Polish Beetroot

Glazed Carrots

Peas French Style

Puréed Vegetables

Treacle Sponge

Butterscotch Sauce

ARTICHOKE SOUP

Serves 6

2 lb/1 kg Jerusalem artichokes	*2 pints/1.25 litres chicken stock*
1 large onion	*nutmeg*
1 oz/30 g butter	*salt and pepper*
1 tablespoon oil	

Scrub and cut up the artichokes; you need not peel them, but clean them thoroughly.

Peel and chop the onion. Heat the butter and oil in a pan and fry the onion until it begins to turn colour. Add the artichokes and stir gently to get them coated in the onion mixture. Add half the stock by degrees and let it come to the boil, making sure with a wooden spoon that nothing has stuck to the bottom of the pan. Then add the rest of the stock and simmer until the artichokes are soft. Pass the mixture through a mouli (or liquidise if you prefer, but this tends to make too suave a texture), season with some grated nutmeg, pepper and salt.

Reheat for serving. If liked, this soup can be served with a dollop of soured or fresh cream.

KIPPER FILLET SALAD

Nowadays, it should be possible to buy kipper fillets undyed with Brown FK. Seek them out for their more genuine flavour and to support the anti-additives lobby. In the heyday of kipper fillet salad, enthusiasts would remark that it was almost as good as smoked salmon. It is nothing like smoked salmon, but nevertheless excellent in its own right. Use the best olive oil you can find for the dressing.

Serves 4

8 kipper fillets	*2 tablespoons lemon juice*
1 large onion, peeled and sliced into thin	*4 tablespoons olive oil*
rings	*freshly-ground black pepper*

Rip the silvery skin off the kipper fillets and then slice the flesh on the diagonal into strips about ¼-inch/0.6 cm wide. Place them in a shallow dish and scatter half of the larger onion rings on top. Pour on the lemon juice and turn the fillets and onion in the juice. Leave in the fridge or a cool place for a few hours, occasionally stirring the kipper around.

Drain off the juice, pour on the olive oil, scatter about the remaining onion rings – you then have differing textures of onion – and grind on black pepper lavishly.

Serve with thinly sliced brown bread and butter.

SALADE NICOISE

There are many variants of this and we are not sticking to the classical recipe, but suggesting ingredients we find good. This is a first course that is better in summer months as it depends upon new and small vegetables.

Serves 6

1 lb/500 g new potatoes
8 oz/250 g small french beans
1 lb/500 g young, small broad beans
8 oz/250 g smallest peas you can get
½ cucumber
1 red, and *1 yellow pepper (green will do if you can't get the others)*
small bunch of radishes
bunch of spring onions

1 lb/500 g tomatoes
1 fennel root
1 tin anchovy fillets or *one tin of tuna fish, whichever you prefer – or both*
parsley
fresh basil – if you can get it
chives – easy to grow yourself
fresh French tarragon
8 oz/250 g black olives

Cook the potatoes; they will need to be scraped for this dish in order to look nice. Put them in boiling salted water and boil gently; be careful not to overcook them.

The french beans and podded broad beans should be steamed until they are *al dente* (crisp, but tender, which should take only about 5 minutes). Shell the peas, but use them raw.

The cucumber should be diced, rather than sliced. Leave the skin on; it makes cucumber more digestible as well as looking pretty. Slice the peppers into thin strips. Clean and trim the radishes and spring onions.

Skin the tomatoes by dipping them into near boiling water for half a minute and then peeling off the skins. Wash and then slice the fennel as thinly as possible.

If you are using anchovies, open the tin and drain the fillets well. Then cut them into pieces about 1 inch/2.5 cm long. With tuna, you take it out of the tin, drain and flake.

Chop the herbs and put them in the fridge in a jam jar covered with cling film.

Put all the ingredients except the herbs into the largest serving bowl you have, reserving some olives, radishes and some of the red and yellow peppers for garnishing.

Then make a French dressing as follows:

1 level dessertspoon salt
1 level dessertspoon sugar
1 level dessertspoon mustard powder

a heavy screwing of black pepper
3 tablespoons tarragon vinegar
¼ pint/150 ml best olive oil

Put all the dry ingredients into a small mixing bowl and combine with a fork. Add the vinegar and stir until everything has dissolved. Add the oil and beat thoroughly. Pour over the salad and mix gently but very thoroughly. If you don't feel that there is enough dressing (test it by tasting) make some more – it is very much a question of preference. Arrange the garnish on the salad's surface.

Just before serving, sprinkle over the fresh herbs.

FISH PIE

Serves 6

12 oz/375 g fresh haddock or cod (buy a middle section, not a tail)
12 oz/375 g smoked haddock (try to buy Finnan haddock)
¾ pint/475 ml milk
1½ lb/750 g potatoes
milk and butter for the potatoes

1 oz/30 g butter
1½ oz/45 g flour
juice of ½ lemon
salt and black pepper
8 oz/250 g fresh prawns
2 hard-boiled eggs, sliced
1 tablespoon chopped fresh parsley

Turn on the oven to 190°C/375°F, Gas 5.

Put the fish in an ovenproof dish large enough to hold it in one layer. Pour over the milk, plus about ½ pint/300 ml of water. The fish should be more or less covered. Bake in the oven for about 20 minutes or until the fish flakes away easily from the skin and bones. Boil the potatoes and, when cooked, mash with plenty of butter and hot milk, and season with salt and pepper. It is not advisable to use left-over potatoes as it spoils the texture.

In a heavy-bottomed saucepan, make a roux with the butter and flour. (You put in the butter and the moment it has melted, add the flour, stirring until the mixture is smooth and comes away from the pan.) Stir in enough of the fish poaching liquid to make a consistency of double cream. Add the liquid by degrees, stirring all the time and you won't get lumps. Season with lemon juice and salt and pepper.

Carefully fold in the flaked fish, the prawns, the hard-boiled eggs and the parsley. Put into a pie dish and cover with the mashed potato. Plough the potato with a fork. Dot with butter and return to the oven for 30 minutes, or until the potato is lightly browned.

LANCASHIRE HOT-POT

Making this dish in a straightforward manner is not so much to contribute to its foolproof quality, but to its homeliness and correctness. Some talk of adding bacon or carrot or mushrooms to the assembly, but we like a down to earth meat-and-potatoes approach. Lamb's kidneys, however, are essential to add richness to the gravy. Another essential is a crusty brown layer of potatoes, so if necessary, turn up the oven a little for the last half-hour of cooking.

Serves 4–5

2 lb/1 kg lamb chops (neck or best end)	*½ lb/750 g potatoes, peeled and sliced*
seasoned flour	*salt and freshly-ground black pepper*
2–3 lamb's kidneys	*1 bay leaf*
4 onions, peeled and sliced	*butter or dripping*

Turn on the oven to 150°C/300°F, Gas 2.

Trim the obvious fat from the chops, melt that fat in a frying pan, flour the chops and brown them gently. This step improves the colour and texture of the gravy. Put the chops into a pot – a round-bellied earthenware pot is traditionally used. Trim the kidneys of any fat or gristle and chop them into pieces. Layer the kidneys, onions and potatoes on top of the chops, seasoning as you go along, adding the bay leaf and finishing with a layer of overlapping slices of potato. Add ¾ pint/475 ml of water. Brush the top surfaces of the potatoes with butter or dripping, season with salt and pepper and cover with a lid.

Cook for 1½ hours, then remove the lid, turn up the oven a little and cook some more until the potatoes are brown and crispy.

OXTAIL STEW

Serves 4–6

4 lb/2 kg oxtail (get the butcher to cut it in pieces for you)
2 oz/60 g flour
salt and black pepper
2 tablespoons sunflower seed oil
1 small head of celery
1½ lb/750 g carrots

2 lb/1 kg onions
2 bay leaves
3 cloves
3 pints/1.8 litres beef stock (beef cubes will do – but there is nothing like beef stock)

Turn on the oven to 170°C/325°F, Gas 3.

Cut as much fat as you can from the pieces of tail. Roll the pieces in flour that you have seasoned with pepper and salt. Fry them gently in a pan with oil until the oxtail is thoroughly browned on all sides. As they are done, put the pieces into a large pan or stewpot. Add all the vegetables, cleaned and sliced, together with the bay leaves and cloves. Scatter any remaining flour on top of the meat and and vegetables. Then add the stock.

Cover the pot and stew in the oven for about 3 hours, or until, when you test the meat, it will come away easily from the bone. When it is cooked, remove the lid, allow it to cool and then put it into the fridge overnight.

The next day, you should be able to skim off any fat that has come to the surface. If the liquid seems thinner than you like, add a flat tablespoonful of flour scattered over the top of the dish before you warm it up. This is also the moment to check the seasoning. The oxtail will need about 1½ hours to complete its cooking, again in a slow oven, 170°C/325°F, Gas 3.

This stew – like many stews – is better made the day before you eat it, and the more fat that you can remove from the pan before the final cooking the better.

POLISH BEETROOT

Serves 6–8

2–3 lb/1–1.5 kg cooked beetroot	*black pepper*
3 oz/90 g butter	*2 tablespoons wine vinegar*

Turn on the oven to 150°C/300°F, Gas 2.

Peel and grate the beetroot. Place it in a buttered, ovenproof dish with knobs of butter. Grind on a liberal quantity of black pepper (far more than you would usually put on things: beetroot has an unique capacity for absorbing pepper). Add the wine vinegar, then put it in the oven to heat. After 15 minutes or so, take it out and give it a good stir to mix the butter and vinegar well with the beetroot. Put the dish back into the oven until you are ready to serve.

GLAZED CARROTS

For some reason, adding sugar and butter to the cooking water for your carrots can allow you to be insouciant about timings as the carrots never seem to disintegrate finally, however wildly and lengthily you boil them. What seems like an impossibly subtle process – that of having carrot pieces cooked at the time the water has evaporated and the butter and sugar caramelised – is, in fact, easy. Cooked this way, carrots become luxurious and so partner well the frugality sometimes implicit in stews.

Cumin and carrots have great affinity, so should you stock cumin seeds or know where to buy them (any competent supermarket or oriental grocer); do use them.

Serves 6

2 lb/1 kg carrots (old ones work very well	*1 tablespoon brown sugar*
* in this recipe)*	*1 heaped teaspoon cumin seeds or*
1½ oz/45 g butter	* chopped fresh coriander or parsley*

Peel the carrots. Cut them as follows: in half across, then stand the halves on the flat round surface and quarter them vertically. You end up with batons, nicer than fat circles reminiscent of institutional food.

Put them in a sturdy saucepan, add water to cover by about ½ inch/ 1.25 cm, and the butter and sugar. Set to simmer. After the carrots have simmered for about 15 minutes, turn up the heat and start to reduce the liquid. Your aim is to drive off the water and oblige the sugar and butter to form a shiny glaze; watch carefully at the end that the glaze does not burn.

Scatter the cumin seeds in a small heavy-bottomed frying pan and put on a high heat (with no fat) for a minute or two, stirring with a wooden spoon, until a spicy smell comes off them. Scatter onto the carrots and serve. Or, if you are using coriander or parsley, sprinkle that on.

PEAS FRENCH STYLE

This recipe transforms frozen peas into a thing of delectation. Try to buy what they call *petits pois* rather than the larger garden variety. With frozen peas, the frost provides almost enough liquid.

If you use fresh peas, remember that 1 lb/500 g of fresh peas gives you probably less than ½ lb/250 g of podded peas, so buy accordingly, and buy them as young as possible or they will resemble bullets. You must add a little more water for fresh peas.

Serves 4

1 lb/500 g frozen petits pois	*a few fresh mint leaves if available*
1 small Dutch lettuce	*1 teaspoon white sugar*
4 spring onions	*salt and freshly-ground black pepper*
1 oz/30 g butter	

Put the peas into a heavy-bottomed saucepan. You can, and should, cook them from frozen. Trim any damaged leaves from the lettuce. Use your judgement about whether the other leaves should be washed. Often hothouse (Dutch) lettuces are disturbingly dirt-free. Slice the pristine leaves into ribbons about ¼ inch/0.6 cm wide. Clean the spring onions, trimming off the base and most of the green part, leaving about 1½ inches/3.75 cm green. Wash and slice lengthways so that you have long, thin pieces. Mix the lettuce and onions with the peas.

Add the butter cut into pieces, mint if you have it, the sugar and a pinch of salt and pepper. Put in 1 tablespoon of water just to get the thing going (more if fresh peas are being used). Cover and place over a medium heat. When the liquid that forms comes to the boil, lower the heat and simmer for about 15 minutes with the lid at an angle so that some of the liquid can evaporate.

Test the peas for tenderness and boil off any remaining liquid but leaving a thin buttery sauce to which the silkiness of the lettuce will have contributed.

PUREED VEGETABLES

Puréed vegetables, that once highly fashionable garnish, are ideal for a dinner which is carefully planned because they can be made in advance and either kept hot or re-heated in a double saucepan. A food processor is invaluable and even the most elliptically-involved cook should consider the purchase of one. The alternative is a mouli-legumes or the task of pushing the vegetables through a sieve. If the last is what you decide to do, make sure to overcook the vegetables to the point of craven malleability.

Most root vegetables respond well to this method of preparation but cooked sprouts, whizzed in a food processor, make an excellent purée and since left-over sprouts are not unknown, e.g. after Christmas lunch, it is worth keeping this in mind. Should you have garnished them with peeled chestnuts, include them too.

The recipe below will work well for parsnips, celeriac, carrots, swedes (which will need lavish buttering) and leeks.

Serves 6

2 lb/1 kg root vegetables (see above), peeled and chopped into pieces measuring about 1½ inches/3.75 cm square
3 oz/90 g butter

1 tablespoon cream or top of the milk
a pinch of grated nutmeg
salt and generous amounts of freshly-ground black pepper

Boil the vegetables until they are well and truly tender. Drain them in a careless way so that they are waterlogged rather than absolutely dry. Put them into the bowl of a food processor or the goblet of a liquidiser with the butter, cream and seasonings, and whirr to a purée. You may need to do this in batches. Put the purée into the top of a double saucepan over simmering water. Taste for seasoning, adding more if necessary and keep hot until you need it.

If you are using a sieve or mouli-legumes, push the vegetables through, place the purée in a pan and, over a low heat, stir in the butter, cream (or milk) and seasonings.

TREACLE SPONGE

The only trick about this recipe is allowing enough time for the pudding to steam and being around to check on the water level so that it does not boil dry. The actual preparation takes only minutes, particularly if you use a food processor.

Serves 4–6

2 tablespoons golden syrup
grated rind and juice of 1 lemon
1 oz/30 g fresh breadcrumbs
4 oz/125 g butter
4 oz/125 g caster sugar

2 eggs
5 oz/150 g self-raising flour
a pinch of salt
milk

Mix the syrup with the lemon juice, stir in the breadcrumbs and put this mixture over the bottom of a lightly-buttered 3-pint/2 litre pudding basin. Cream the butter with the sugar and the lemon rind, add the beaten eggs, and stir in the flour which you have sifted with a pinch of salt; then add the milk, a spoonful at a time, until you have a batter that drops reluctantly from a spoon. Pour into the pudding basin, and tie on a cover of foil or greaseproof paper.

Place the bowl in a saucepan that will hold it comfortably. Add boiling water to about half-way up the bowl and steam, covered with a saucepan lid, for about 2 hours, checking the water level from time to time.

Remove the foil or greaseproof paper, place a large plate over the basin and turn the basin over. The pudding will come out easily. Serve with custard or more syrup heated and sharpened with more lemon juice.

BUTTERSCOTCH SAUCE

It is quite possible now to buy high quality ice-cream made with proper ingredients rather than whale fat and emulsifiers. New England ice-cream is one variety that we would recommend, and this recipe for a luxurious sauce, particularly suited to vanilla ice-cream, was given to us by Bill Blackburn, the founder of the company.

Serves 6–8

4 oz/125 g butter
8 fl oz/250 ml single cream
6 oz/180 g soft brown sugar

2 tablespoons brandy
4 drops pure vanilla essence (not the ersatz kind)

Melt the butter in a double saucepan or over a very low heat. Add the cream and blend together, then stir in the sugar; cook gently for about 30 minutes. Add the brandy and vanilla essence, stir and remove from the heat – the sauce will thicken as it cools.

This recipe makes a considerable amount, but any left-over sauce can be stored for a few days in a screw-top jar in the fridge.

2 Dîner à Deux

Food plays many roles in life: the fundamental one of simply fuelling, but beyond that it is also used to bribe, to honour, to placate, to harass, to slight, to cherish, to repair and – to seduce. Early on in most romances, food plays a central part. The first time someone prepares a meal for a loved one, or a prospective loved one, is often the first time that that person has spent a protracted length of time in the cook's home. Making a meal takes some of the heat out of the scenario and also lends a backdrop of touching sights – as so many movies over the years have reminded us – of the heroine with a dab of flour on her nose, the hero coming to the rescue with some invaluable tip or a bottle of wine and so forth. Men cooking can tug at the heartstrings effectively, as anyone who has seen Jack Lemmon straining spaghetti through a tennis racket in the film *The Apartment* will know.

For the purposes of this chapter devoted to a *dîner à deux*, we are supposing that it is not an impromptu meal, a merry fry-up or taking pot luck, but a planned event. Someone has come into your life, and the next canny move would seem to be to entertain them deliciously and let them glimpse a side of you of which they were perhaps not fully apprised. We are talking about concealed virtues like imagination, well-judged extravagance, simplicity, knowing how to deal with a scallop.

There are most definitely foodstuffs that are sexy and foodstuffs that are banal. This perception does not have to be taken to the point of absurdity, as so often it is, so that seductive food has to be representational, e.g. phallic leeks or the moist crevasses of oysters, but whilst a lobster does seem romantic, mince does not. That the one costs a good deal more than the other is a point but not the whole point. Food for a candlelit dinner – and however much you subscribe to fashionable up-lighting or the halogen bulb, candles cast a glow so flattering that it would be foolish not to take advantage of them – should be neat, easy to eat with grace and style. Mince might well dribble down your chin.

When a meal is deliberately designed for two, and more numbers would rob it of its aim, then items like the aforementioned lobster are particularly apt. Wild duck divides neatly. A rack of lamb has just the right amount of cutlets to feed two, one slightly more greedy than the other. True piggishness is not catered for in these recipes as lovers' minds should be slightly abstracted and certainly not wholeheartedly fixed on their stomachs. There will be time later for roistering scenes based on *Tom Jones* or naked greed when you are greedily naked.

From the dishes that follow it would be possible to assemble a meal that can be prepared entirely in advance, but from our experience it is often quite useful to have something to jump up to attend to. It can fill a lull in the conversation, or give you a moment to pull your thoughts together, or check your profile. If the meal is going well and you wish to prolong it, and also bring out some other bottle, then a savoury is worth part-preparing.

Presentation is important for a *dîner à deux*. It is worthwhile having the table laid before your guest arrives and to polish glasses and silver so that they do sparkle in the candlelight. Flowers, leaves, ribbons and so forth can all do their work, but whilst you may not want to exaggerate, making it look too much like a put-up job, you also don't want to be scrabbling around looking for clean napkins at the last minute. This is the moment, by the way, for large cotton or linen napkins, not the paper variety.

A last word of warning on the tricky business of sentimental entertaining: implicit in the event is a lack of familiarity with the other party, so be original but not too outrageous with the food, generous but not reckless so that if during the cheese course you realise you have made the most frightful mistake, it is not going to take you weeks to restore your bank balance as well as your emotional one.

Quantities can usually be doubled quite safely if you want to use one of the recipes for 4 people.

Devilled Almonds	Scallops with Leeks
Gulls' Eggs or Quails' Eggs	Cold Wild Duck
Asparagus	Rack of Lamb with Herb Crust
Oyster Stew	Hot Lemon Soufflé
Oeufs en Cocotte à la Creme	Instant Berry Sorbet
Gravad Lax	Scotch Woodcock

DEVILLED ALMONDS

8 oz/250 g almonds with their skins on   *2 teaspoons sea salt*
1 tablespoon olive oil   *good pinch of cayenne pepper*

Turn on oven to 120°C/250°F, Gas ½.

Put the almonds in a bowl. Pour on boiling water and after a minute or two drain into a sieve. The skins should now slip off fairly easily. Dry the nuts, then coat them in the oil. Spread on a baking tray. Sprinkle on the salt and cayenne pepper and bake for about 2 hours until they are a light golden colour. Cool and store in an airtight tin.

GULLS' EGGS OR QUAILS' EGGS

It is now no longer possible to buy plovers' eggs, a very seductive egg, because they may no longer, by law, be gathered. However, in the early summer you can buy the eggs of black-headed gulls which are almost as good. With their greeny-blue shells freckled with brown they look very attractive piled into a china dish or rush basket. They are sold hard-boiled. Serve them with celery salt and cayenne pepper and thinly sliced brown bread and butter. To make more of a meal of them, you could also serve mayonnaise.

Quails' eggs are available fresh throughout most of the year. If you buy them raw, boil them for just 1 minute. You can also fry or poach quails' eggs which make very dainty dishes; fairy food. Make a 'nest' of lightly-dressed mustard and cress and perch the quails' eggs upon it. Soft-boiled, they are also good served in a manner similar to the way the Connaught Hotel treats them: in a pastry boat, on a purée of mushrooms and covered by a light hollandaise.

ASPARAGUS

Asparagus is one of those items that is symbolically sexy, the fat white French ones presumably more so than the thin green English variety which, in its truly weedy state, is referred to as sprue. It is important not to overcook asparagus. If you don't have a tall thin pan so that the tender asparagus heads can stay above the water and just steam, try steaming the whole vegetable. However you cook it, start testing for 'doneness' after about 9 minutes as you do not want your asparagus floppy . . .

1 lb/500 g of asparagus is plenty for two people. As well as considering a hollandaise sauce, melted butter or a vinaigrette as an accompaniment, here are some other ideas for dipping sauces.

BROWNED BUTTER AND SOFT-BOILED EGG

3 oz/90 g butter   *salt and freshly-ground black pepper*
2 eggs

Melt the butter and cook it just beyond melted, i.e. let it start to turn brown but take it off the heat just as it reaches a nutty colour. Do not let it burn. Prepare the eggs softly boiled, that is for 3 minutes. Place each egg in an egg cup and cut off the top. Mix salt and freshly ground black pepper together. The form is: each person dips an asparagus spear by turn into the browned butter, the soft egg yolk and the heap of salt and pepper.

PARMESAN AND MIMOSA

2 hard-boiled egg yolks   *salt and freshly-ground black pepper*
2 oz/60 g freshly grated Parmesan cheese
   (not from a packet)

Push the egg yolks through a sieve – they now resemble mimosa blossom. Mix with the Parmesan and season with salt and pepper. Serve the asparagus with a little melted butter and this mixture in which to roll the tips.

RED PEPPER PUREE

The colour of this is a lovely contrast to green asparagus.

2 red peppers   *1–2 anchovies*
1 clove garlic, peeled   *a pinch of sugar*
asparagus water   *salt and pepper*

Char the peppers by turning them under the grill. Put them immediately into a polythene bag to steam for 5 minutes. The skin can now be scraped off easily. Remove all the seeds and pith and cut into squares. Boil with the garlic in water (the asparagus water if you have already cooked the asparagus and are planning to serve them cold). When the peppers are tender, liquidise together with the garlic clove and the anchovies, and with just enough of the water to make a purée. Season with sugar, salt and pepper. Don't make this sauce too far ahead as it tends to separate.

OYSTER STEW

We know a man who invariably employs this dish in his seductive dinners. He has legendary success, which may be to do with the recipe, the touching sight of a man cooking, or just him. It is possible, and indeed preferable for reasons of energy and cost, to make this stew using frozen Japanese oysters which are obtained in Oriental supermarkets. They have good flavour and obviate struggling to prise open shells, probably stabbing yourself and sitting through dinner with an unattractive plaster on your thumb. Take the precaution of discovering whether your guest is allergic to oysters.

Savoury crackers, for example cream crackers or saltines, are the correct accompaniment.

4 shallots, peeled and finely chopped	*16–20 frozen oysters*
3 oz/90 g butter	*½ teaspoon salt*
12 fl oz/375 ml milk	*white pepper* or *paprika*
4 fl oz/125 ml double cream	*chopped parsley*

To make it into a bisque: *2 egg yolks*

Use a heavy-bottomed pot that later you can surround with water in a larger pot, i.e. a double saucepan or a *bain-marie*. Sauté the shallots gently in the butter until they are softened. Bring the water for the double saucepan arrangements to a simmer. Into your sauté pan put the milk, cream, oysters, salt and pepper. Cook slowly over, or surrounded by, water until the oysters float, whereupon the stew is ready. Check the seasoning, sprinkle with parsley and serve.

To make this into an even more wickedly rich dish, it can become a bisque: beat two egg yolks in a bowl and slowly add a few spoonsful of the oyster stew liquid. Whisk until foamy. Return this to the stew, mix gently, and heat through without boiling until slightly thickened.

OEUFS EN COCOTTE A LA CREME

½ oz/15 g butter
2 tablespoons double cream

2 fresh free-range eggs
salt and black pepper

Turn on the oven to 180°C/350°F, Gas 4.

Warm 2 cocottes (small round fireproof dishes) and put them in a baking tin half full of hot water, with a small knob of butter in each one. When the butter has melted, paint it up the sides of cocotte. Bring half the cream to the boil and then put it into the cocottes. Break the eggs and place one in each cocotte. Season and put the rest of the butter in small knobs on top. Put the tin in the oven and bake for between 5 and 7 minutes: the whites should be set, but only just and the yolk should be creamy. Just before serving, spoon over the top the rest of the cream, which should be cold.

This is not the classic way of making this dish, but we have found the contrast between the cold cream and the hot egg particularly delicious.

GRAVAD LAX

This is not a dish for a sudden romance as it requires at least 24 hours' marination in the refrigerator. If, however, you are plotting a meal with someone special in mind it is an ideal first course. Large quantities of a luxurious ingredient, e.g. salmon, are always romantic and this process of pickling it in sugar and salt works equally well with the cheaper farmed salmon, so make plenty and serve it in thickish chunks rather than the skimpy thin slices favoured by restaurants.

1 tail piece of salmon weighing 1½–2
   lb/750–1 kg
1 heaped tablespoon sea salt
1 rounded tablespoon sugar

1 teaspoon coarsely-ground pepper
1 rounded tablespoon dillweed (chopped if
   fresh)

For the sauce:

mayonnaise (preferably home-made) into
   which you mix:
1 tablespoon German mustard

1 teaspoon sugar
1 teaspoon dillweed
dash of vinegar

Bone the fish which will give you two kite-shaped pieces. If you haven't found a tail-piece, a small salmon or salmon trout will do, in which case clean, bone and behead it.

Mix together the salt, sugar and pepper. If you wish, moisten with a little brandy. Put some of the mixture plus a third of the dillweed into a dish that holds the fish quite snugly.

Lay on it the first piece of fish, skin-side down. Spread on more pickle, more dillweed and sandwich with the other piece of fish, skin-side up. Scatter on the remaining pickle and dillweed. Cover with a double layer of aluminium foil and then a weight – tins or a brick. Leave in the fridge for at least 24 hours, but no longer than 3 days, turning the fish occasionally.

To serve, drain from the pickle, remove the skin, slice generously and accompany the fish with the sauce described above, some rye bread or hot boiled new potatoes.

SCALLOPS WITH LEEKS

Fresh scallops, which are becoming increasingly easy to find, are the perfect lovers' meal; nourishing, unfattening, delicate and quick to cook. Forget any idea of bedding them down in mashed potato and instead try this method adapted from a recipe of the three-star Michelin chef, Roger Vergé.

4 thin or 2 fat leeks
1 oz/30 g butter
6–8 scallops
5 tablespoonsful of the white wine you have chosen for the meal

a squeeze of lemon juice
3 tablespoons double cream
salt and pepper
fresh parsley

Trim the leeks and clean them really thoroughly, sacrificing outer layers until you are sure that no grit lurks. The root must be taken off and most of the green part. Cut them in half lengthways and then into narrow strips, (about $\frac{1}{4}$ inch/0.6 cm long). Melt $\frac{1}{2}$ oz/15 g butter in 4 tablespoons water in a small saucepan and cook the leek strips until tender, about 15 minutes. Set the saucepan on one side but keep warm.

Cut each scallop in two horizontally, but leave the corals whole. Remove the thin, dark intestine and the little muscle which would toughen. Melt the remaining butter in a pan, sauté the scallops for seconds and then add the wine. Bring to the boil and simmer for 2 minutes. Remove the scallops and keep warm with the leeks.

Reduce the scallop liquor by boiling it vigorously. Add the cooking juices from the leeks, plus a squeeze of lemon juice. Boil again until you are left with about 4 tablespoonsful of liquid. Add the cream, boil briefly, and season.

Arrange the leeks and scallops prettily on a warmed plate. Pour over the sauce and scatter chopped parsley on top.

COLD WILD DUCK

1 plump wild duck, dressed	*1 small onion*
2 small oranges	*salt and pepper*
2 oz/60 g butter	*4 thin strips streaky bacon*

Turn on the oven to 200°C/400°F, Gas 6.

Wipe the insides of the duck with a damp cloth. Grate the rind of one orange and squeeze the juice. Cut the other orange into thick rounds.

If you have a chicken brick, we have found this ideal; if not, then a *small* earthenware dish or baking tin will do. Put half the butter into the dish and heat it until the butter melts. Put the orange slices into the dish. Rub the duck breasts with the rest of the butter, and put the onion – quartered if need be – inside the bird. Rub the grated orange rind onto the buttered breasts, season with salt and pepper and then cover with the bacon.

If you are using a chicken-brick, put on the lid: if not, cover the dish with aluminium foil. Roast in a hot oven for 30 minutes; then remove the lid or foil, baste the bird, and cook for another 20 minutes. This last cooking will vary a little in time depending upon the size of the bird; your aim should be to have the bird slightly pink, but not running with blood when you prick it. After taking the duck from the oven, allow it to cook in its juices for a little while. You can then strain off the fat, and use the remaining liquid in a Cumberland-type sauce if liked, but since one eats such a bird largely with the fingers, it is very good without any sauce.

This is best cooked the morning of the day you are going to eat it, and not refrigerated. Watercress can also be eaten with the fingers and is a good accompaniment.

RACK OF LAMB WITH HERB CRUST

Rack of lamb is also called *carré d'agneau* or you could ask your butcher for best end of neck trimmed for roasting. The meat should be chined, meaning the backbone is split, and 2–3 inches/5–7.5 cm of clean bone should protrude from the cutlets. Remove the skin and most of the fat before coating the meat and roasting it. One best end of lamb will give 2–3 cutlets each for two people, so it makes a perfect intimate dinner.

1 clove of garlic, peeled
salt and pepper
1 tablespoon mellow mustard (Dijon or
  something sweeter if you prefer)
2 tablespoons fine breadcrumbs

2 tablespoons chopped fresh herbs – try to
  include both parsley and thyme,
  perhaps a few leaves of mint and finely
  chopped sprigs of rosemary
lemon juice
a knob of softened butter
1 rack of lamb

Turn on the oven to 230°C/450°F, Gas 8.

Crush the garlic with the salt and mix with the mustard. Stir in the breadcrumbs and herbs, a squeeze of lemon juice and the softened butter – enough to give a spreading consistency. Spread the mixture between the cutlets, on the ends and over the trimmed fat. Place on a rack in a roasting tin and cook for 20–25 minutes which will give a crisp crust and pink meat. If you prefer your meat well done, cook for 5 minutes or so longer. Let the meat rest in a warm place for 5 minutes before serving.

If you are cooking this when broad beans are first in season, serve a dish of baby broad beans, which you have boiled, skinned and re-heated in a little butter. In winter, a puréed vegetable (*see* page 20), would go well. Serve a fruit jelly, for example redcurrant or quince, either home-made or produced by a reputable firm or a Women's Institute stall.

HOT LEMON SOUFFLE

This recipe, taken from Elizabeth David's *French Country Cooking*, is so quick and simple that you can leave it until the end of the meal to judge whether, indeed, you want a pudding at all or find your sweet times elsewhere. Pessimists, however, could prepare it up to a point, i.e. beating the yolks of the eggs with the sugar and lemon juice beforehand

and whipping the whites at the end of the meal just before you pop it into the oven.

4 eggs, separated   *juice and rind of 1 lemon*
3 tablespoons caster sugar

Turn on the oven to 200°C/400°F, Gas 6.

Beat the yolks of the eggs with the sugar and lemon rind and juice for several minutes. Butter a 1½-pint/1-litre soufflé dish. Whisk the egg whites until they stand in firm peaks. Fold the lemony mixture in with a light hand. Pour into the soufflé dish and cook for about 12 minutes.

INSTANT BERRY SORBET

This elegant idea was suggested by Prue Leith and exemplifies both her sympathetic approach to the home cook and the constraints of serving restaurant food. Any new, or even well-worn partner, will not fail to be impressed by the effective simplicity of this dessert and the immediacy of flavour in the fruit. Soft fruit such as raspberries and strawberries work well, but there is no reason not to use redcurrants, blackcurrants or even, more magically, whitecurrants.

Either buy frozen fruit or freeze fresh fruit, but make sure it is thoroughly frozen before you start. Add sugar to one-third the weight of the fruit, which is the proportion which makes the sorbet successful. You might also like to squeeze in a little lemon juice to tone down the sweetness.

12 oz/375 g frozen strawberries or   *4 oz/125 g caster sugar*
* raspberries*   *juice of ½ lemon*

Note: this recipe is predicated on the ownership of a food processor; a liquidiser will work but you will have to do the fruit in batches.

Empty the frozen fruit into the bowl of the food processor. Sprinkle the sugar on top and leave for about 20 minutes, until the fruit is beginning to soften around the edges. Turn on the motor and whizz, either using a pulse button or switching on or off, until you have a purée the consistency and temperature of sorbet.

Add lemon juice to taste and whizz again. Serve immediately or freeze until it is wanted.

SCOTCH WOODCOCK

Some think this the best of all savouries, others might put forward the case for a roasted snipe on toast, but ingredients for this assembly are more easily available.

2 slices toast, trimmed of crust, about 3"
× 2"/7.5 × 5 cm in size,
well-buttered
6 anchovy fillets or if you prefer, use 1
heaped tablespoon finely-chopped
cooked ham

salt and freshly-ground black pepper
2 egg yolks
2½ tablespoons double cream
½ oz/15 g butter

Turn on the oven to low to keep the toasts hot.

Arrange the toasts in a small ovenproof serving dish. Pound the anchovy fillets, mixing in a little pepper and spread them on the toasts (or do the same with the ham). Keep them warm in the oven.

Beat together the egg yolks and cream and season with salt and pepper. Melt the butter in a small, thick-bottomed pan, stir in the egg and cream mixture and stir over an extremely low heat until it begins to thicken. Don't let it scramble. Pour over the toasts and serve immediately.

3 Budget Dinner Party

Two do not live as cheaply as one and six do not eat as cheaply as two, but finance need not be a deterrent to entertaining – except in the realm of drink where you must tactfully impress on your guests that they should contribute. 'Bring a bottle' may conjure up visions of tawdry parties where you spent a good deal of time sitting on the stairs, but there is no rule that the bottle of wine should not be a good one and for you, the host, there is the added pleasure of an element of surprise and the enjoyment of something you have not thought about, made decisions about and trailed out to purchase.

The 'bringing' ethic can also successfully be extended to food in the shape of one course where the considerations of novelty and the feeling of being entertained in your own home are even more relevant. Somehow, not having to make, say, a dessert or a first course or even a salad, lightens the burden of a dinner party immeasurably, and removes a little of the responsibility for its success. However, this ploy, it must be said, only works well among good friends who have the same points of view about cooking. If you have a secret horror of aspic, your evening would be off to a disastrous start should a guest arrive proudly clutching a jellied savoury tomato mould filled with Russian salad. It could happen.

Food that is cheap to buy is often expensive in terms of the time taken to prepare it. This is a truism that gets bandied about and like many truisms has little substance. Some cuts of meat may take hours to cook but you do not have to be sitting beside them while they do, and if you are wondering how much the electricity is costing to have the oven on, then probably a dinner party is too perilous an undertaking at the moment. Many seemingly drawn-out tasks, including making bread, only require brief bursts of activity from the cook. Indeed, making your own bread can, for hardly any financial outlay at all, make people feel cherished, almost spoiled. To achieve the same effect practically instantaneously, you can knock up some Oat Cakes or Water Biscuits to accompany cheese and salad.

What is and what is not expensive food changes over the years as demands fluctuate and fashions alter. Where once butchers would practically give away offal, they now sell it at a premium price to Arab restaurants and shrines of haute cuisine. Chicken, once a dish for special occasions, has become the bore of butchers, though the maize-fed and free-range varieties can be diverting. Vegetables always strike us as good value, particularly root vegetables whose price never seems to shoot through the roof, and one of the great bargains of all times is the potato. A positive outcome of being obliged to think in terms of a budget is that you are likely to do something interesting with, for example, potatoes. This can prove much more delicious and unusual than a hunk of meat or fillet of fish.

For a dinner party on a shoe-string, it is important to avoid the obvious cheap items like the symbolic (of shoe-string) spaghetti or the worthwhile Shepherd's Pie. These have their own, valuable role in everyday life but are too familiar for a festive evening. Fresh pasta with an interesting sauce does not come into the Spaghetti Bolognese category. Abandoning the usual three-course formula, with the most important course being the middle one, is a wise tactic. A substantial and relatively unusual first course, e.g. Curried Parsnips served with poppadums and a cucumber raita, means that you can follow with something very simple, perhaps just some mussels – still a bargain – and your guests will feel in no way short-changed. Indeed, what must be avoided is a lot of stodge which makes everyone feel got at and apt to dwell on the fact that it is usually the rich who are also thin.

The following recipes are ideas around which you might build a meal, using salads and fresh fruit and affordable cheeses, like ricotta, for some of the courses. In other words, it would not be our intention that you start with a Mussel and Potato Salad, move on to the Breast of Lamb Stuffed with Spinach and Kasha, and end with the Marlborough Tart. That might be a fairly cheap dinner but it would not be cheerful.

Lentil Soup

Brown Rice Salad with Anchovies
  and Pimento

Warm Mussel and Potato Salad

Hoummous

Smoked Haddock Soufflé

Breast of Lamb Stuffed with Spinach
  and Kasha

Feuilleté of Kidneys

Chicken Liver Risotto

Curried Parsnips

Rösti

Gujerati Carrot Salad

Marlborough Tart

Pierre Martin's Apple Tarts

Brandy Snaps

Oat Cakes

Water Biscuits

Devils on Horseback

Sardines on Toast

Welsh Rabbit

LENTIL SOUP

Serves 4

a ham bone (you can usually get this for   *salt and pepper*
  about 50p from a delicatessen)   *knob of butter*
12 oz/375 g green or *brown lentils*
  (soaked for an hour in cold water)

If there is any fat left on the ham bone, cut it off. Put the bone and lentils
into a pan with 2½ pints/1.5 litres of cold water and cook gently until the
lentils are tender. Remove the bone, and pass the lentils through a mouli
or liquidise, and then return to a clean pan. Season with salt and pepper
and a good knob of butter.

(This soup is also good with a handful of chopped sorrel if you can get
it, or grow it.)

BROWN RICE SALAD WITH ANCHOVIES AND PIMENTO

Serves 4

8 oz/250 g brown rice   *1 tin anchovy fillets*
2 red peppers (green or yellow will do,
  but red looks prettier)

Dressing:

2 tablespoons olive oil   *salt and black pepper*
juice of 1 lemon

Wash the rice in a hand sieve with cold water. Then boil it in salted
water until it is cooked; brown rice takes longer than refined rice –
usually between 20 and 25 minutes. While you are cooking the rice, heat
your grill – first covering the grill pan with aluminium foil. Cut the
peppers into flat strips, removing all seeds and undue pith. Lay the strips
skin-side up on the grill pan and grill until the skin is black and can be
easily removed. Then cut the strips into small rectangles.

Make a dressing with the olive oil, a level teaspoonful of salt, the juice
of a lemon and a plentiful screwing of black pepper. Put the rice into a
bowl while it is still warm, but not hot and mix in the dressing
thoroughly. Add the peppers and the anchovies – drained of their oil
and cut into small pieces. This dish can be garnished with either fresh
chopped coriander or, if you cannot get that, fresh chopped parsley.

WARM MUSSEL AND POTATO SALAD

Mussels remain one of the most reasonable forms of interesting protein and this dish, which is a felicitous combination of textures and flavours, benefits in that it not only economises on mussels but in the time it takes to clean them, since you need fewer to serve many.

Serves 6

2 lb/4 kg waxy potatoes
2 quarts/2.3 litres mussels
1 glass white wine
6 shallots or *spring onions, cleaned and chopped*

parsley – some chopped, some in sprigs
black pepper
6 fl oz/180 ml well-seasoned vinaigrette

Boil the potatoes in their skins. When cooked, peel and slice them. While they are cooking, scrub the mussels thoroughly, remove any barnacles with a sharp knife and pull away the 'beard' that protrudes from one side. Discard any cracked or open mussels or any that you can push sideways, which indicates that they are full of sand.

Put the cleaned mussels, wine, shallots, some parsley sprigs and some freshly ground black pepper into a large pan, put over a high heat, cover and bring the liquid to the boil; remove the mussels as soon as they open, discarding the shells.

Put the mussels in a dish to cool and strain the hot cooking liquid over the potatoes. Drain the potato slices when they are not quite cold, mix them with the mussels and trickle on enough vinaigrette to moisten well. Arrange in a shallow dish and garnish with the chopped parsley.

HOUMMOUS

A quarter of a pound/125 g of chick peas makes a surprising amount of hoummous. The Cypriot restaurant variety often contains too much *tahina* (sesame paste) whose tacky texture can take over. This recipe is deliberately low on *tahina*, so add more if you like it. Serve with hot pitta bread and perhaps a few thin slices of aubergine, salted, left to sit, blotted, floured and quickly fried in vegetable oil to a crisp.

Serves 4

4–6 oz/125–180 g chick peas, soaked overnight	*2 tablespoons* tahina
juice of 1 large or 2 small lemons	*2 fat cloves garlic, crushed*
	salt

Garnish:

1 tablespoon olive oil	*ground cumin (optional)*
1 teaspoon cayenne pepper	

This recipe can be made by hand or by using a mouli and would probably be all the better for it, but a food processor makes it the work of minutes and if you don't over-process, you will retain a desirable slightly rough texture.

Put the soaked chick peas into fresh water and bring to the boil. Simmer for about 1 hour or until they are tender. It is hard to over-cook chick peas. Drain, but reserve some of the water. Put the chick peas in the bowl of the food processor with 1 tablespoonful lemon juice, 2 tablespoonsful of the cooking water, the *tahina* and crushed garlic. Whizz to a purée and taste. If it needs more lemon juice, use this to thin the consistency. If not, use more cooking water until you have a fairly thin paste. Taste for salt.

Pour the hoummous into a pretty serving dish. Mix the oil with the cayenne and dribble it on in a pretty pattern. To complete the Persian carpet effect, make lines or streaks of ground cumin.

SMOKED HADDOCK SOUFFLE

Of all fish soufflés, we think this is the best because the soufflé process tends to have a slightly deadening effect on flavour but gutsy smoked haddock pulls through. Also, the process of cooking the fish in milk gives you a flavoured stock for the soufflé base. The best smoked haddock is Finnan haddock, properly cured, not dyed, and sold on the bone. Try to get this. Because a contrast in textures is desirable with soufflés, a garnish of crunchy, deep-fried sprigs of parsley is a nice idea.

Serves 4

8 oz/250 g smoked haddock	*4 eggs separated + 1 extra white if that*
½ pint/300 ml milk	*is easy*
2 oz/60 g butter	*2 tablespoons grated hard cheese*
2 tablespoons flour	*freshly-ground black pepper*

Either in the oven or on top of the stove, simmer the fish in milk, plus enough water to just cover it for about 10 minutes or until it flakes easily. Remove the fish; skin and bone it if that is pertinent. Strain its cooking liquid into a measuring jug.

Turn the oven to 200°C/400°F, Gas 6 and put a baking sheet on the oven shelf you are going to use. Melt the butter in a fairly large saucepan. Add the flour and cook, stirring, until you have a smooth paste. Add the haddock milk slowly, stirring until you have a thickish roux. You will probably need almost ½ pint/300 ml of liquid. Let it bubble a few minutes to cook out the taste of flour. Remove from the heat and beat in the egg yolks one by one. Stir in the flaked fish, 1 tablespoonful of cheese and some black pepper. Butter a soufflé dish and dust with the remaining cheese.

Beat the egg whites in a large clean bowl until they hold stiff peaks. Fold a quarter of the egg whites gently into the haddock mixture to lighten it. Now fold that, still with a light touch, into the remaining egg whites. Turn into the soufflé dish. With a knife, make a circular indentation in the mixture about 1½ inches/3.75 cm from the edge of the dish, which should result in a cottage loaf effect. Put the soufflé in the oven, and immediately turn the heat down to 190°C/375°F, Gas 5. Cook for about 30–35 minutes or until well risen, golden brown and not too wobbly, though a slightly sloppy centre is desirable.

BREAST OF LAMB STUFFED WITH SPINACH AND KASHA

The most important thing here, in order to avoid any jibes about cheap cuts, is to spend time removing practically every scrap of fat from the lamb breasts and, if you have time, the bones; though this is not essential. Dedication and a small sharp knife will do it. Kasha is roasted buckwheat and is available at health food stores and enterprising shops.

Serves 4–6

2 breasts of lamb	*1 lb/500 g fresh spinach or 1 packet*
mustard powder	*frozen leaf spinach*
salt and pepper	*4 oz/125 g kasha*
1 onion	*1 egg*
olive oil	

Turn on the oven to 220°C/425°F, Gas 7.

Season the breasts of lamb enthusiastically with mustard, salt and pepper and roast them skin-side up in a hot oven for about 20 minutes or until the skins look brown and appetising. It is important to the look and texture of the finished dish. You could also cook them under a large grill. Turn the oven down to moderate; 180°C/350°F, Gas 4.

Peel, finely slice and sauté the onion in a little olive oil until it is golden. Trim and wash the fresh spinach and cook it in the water that clings to the leaves. Drain firmly and chop. Or cook the frozen spinach according to the packet instructions, drain and chop. Mix the spinach with the onion.

Put the kasha into a saucepan. Break in the egg; cook gently stirring all the while until the grains are coated with the egg. Add boiling water to come just above the grains, season with salt and, with the lid firmly on, cook the kasha for 15 minutes or until tender but still nutty. Check from time to time to see if more water is needed.

Place one breast of lamb, skin-side down in a clean roasting pan. Cover with a layer of spinach. Cover the spinach with the kasha. Place the other lamb breast, skin-side up on top. You now have a sandwich. Roast your lamb sandwich for 30–45 minutes, depending on how long was the first cooking. Serve in slices which you cut at the table.

FEUILLETE OF KIDNEYS

Frozen pastry is a perfectly respectable commodity and using it one can fashion delicious containers that 'stretch' whatever is your main ingredient, be it a luxury vegetable like asparagus or seafood or meat. Kidneys are not, in any case, expensive and whilst they are good, no one wants to eat masses of them. They are, therefore, a particularly suitable passenger for this carriage.

Try to buy fresh lamb's kidneys – amenable butchers will sometimes tear them directly from the carcasses.

Serves 4

6 lamb's kidneys	¼ pint/150 ml chicken stock
1 8-oz/250 g packet frozen puff pastry	1 egg yolk
2 oz/60 g butter	2 tablespoons double cream
2–3 shallots or 1 onion, peeled and finely chopped	1 generous dessertspoon Dijon mustard salt and freshly ground black pepper
1 clove garlic, peeled and finely slivered	
1 tablespoon sherry vinegar or wine vinegar	

Trim the kidneys of any gristle or membrane and winkle out the fatty core, leaving the kidneys whole. While you cook the puff pastry in the shape you fancy and according to the instructions on the packet, start on the sauce.

Melt the butter and gently sauté the kidneys for about 5 minutes. You want them to stay a little pink in their hearts. Remove them and keep warm. Sauté the onion or shallots and garlic until softened. When the shallots are golden, add the vinegar and bubble fiercely (a splash of Madeira or port would only improve matters). Add the stock and then simmer for about 15 minutes.

Beat the egg yolk and cream in a small bowl. Add 2 tablespoonsful of the stock to the mixture. Return this, well combined, to the stock and cook over a low heat until it is thickened. Stir in the mustard and seasoning, and heat through. Slice the kidneys, add them to the sauce and warm through gently.

Split the pastry horizontally, place the bottom half on the serving dish, pour on the kidney mixture, then cover with the top of the puff pastry. Serve at once.

CHICKEN LIVER RISOTTO

Serves 6

2 large onions	a pinch of ground coriander
3 peppers (preferably one of each colour)	1 lb/500 g brown rice
1 lb/500 g chicken livers	2 oz/60 g walnuts
12 oz/375 g mushrooms	1 small bunch of parsley
butter	black pepper
sunflower seed oil	

The good thing about this dish is that you can prepare it all beforehand, and then heat it up – gently in a slow oven.

Put whatever dish you want to serve your risotto in (ovenproof with a lid) beside the stove. Chop the onions and peppers. Trim all greeny, yellow bits from the livers and chop them roughly – not too fine. Peel and slice the mushrooms. Next, set a large pan of cold water on the stove to boil for rice. Sauté the onions in ½ oz/15 g butter and 1 dessertspoon of oil. When they are softened, add the peppers and cook until the peppers are just *al dente*. Strain the vegetables from the pan and put into the ovenproof dish; leave as much liquid behind in the pan as you can. Put the mushrooms in the pan; you may find you need more oil for them, but use as little as possible – a non-stick pan helps this. Fry the mushrooms lightly, adding black pepper and a good pinch of ground coriander. Add the mushrooms to the ovenproof dish.

By now, the water for the rice should be boiling. Just before adding the rice, add a teaspoonful of salt – this will raise the temperature of the water and help the rice to come to the boil quickly. Brown rice takes far longer than white to cook – the length of time depends upon the variety of rice used – and you should start testing after fifteen minutes: it must not be over-cooked as it has to stand being re-heated. Test it not by squeezing it between finger and thumb, but with your teeth.

While the rice is cooking, sauté the chicken livers. The mushrooms will have made a good deal of liquid – this can be added to the main dish if liked. Start the chicken livers in a clean pan with the minimum of butter. They should be cooked until they are just pink on the inside. Then they too should be put into the ovenproof dish.

When the rice is cooked, carefully drain it and then stir it into the big dish so that everything is well mixed up. Chop up the walnuts and stir in. Just before serving, add the parsley, chopped roughly.

CURRIED PARSNIPS

If you haven't already done so, this would be the moment to visit an Oriental supermarket or grocery shop and stock up on Indian spices in their whole form. They are cheaper this way, keep better and can be

ground as needed. A cheap electric coffee grinder kept for this purpose
is a sensible investment.

Serves 4

1 lb/500 g parsnips	*1 scant teaspoon black mustard seeds*
1 oz/30 g butter	*1 dried red chilli*
1 tablespoon vegetable oil	*1 teaspoon ground turmeric*
1 teaspoon cumin seeds	*salt and pepper*
1 teaspoon coriander seeds	*lemon juice*
½ teaspoon fenugreek	*finely chopped parsley* or *fresh coriander*
the seeds of 5 cardamon pods	*or watercress leaves*

Peel the parsnips and cut as if you were making chips; in half
horizontally, then quarter vertically. Heat the mixture of butter and oil in
a frying pan on which you can fit a lid. When the oil is hot, add the
cumin, coriander, fenugreek, cardamon, mustard seeds and chilli and
stir-fry until the seeds begin to pop, which they quickly do. Add the
turmeric and stir again. Now put in the parsnips and turn in the spices
until the parsnip pieces are coloured. Add two tablespoonsful of warm
water and cook, covered, testing frequently and adding more water a
little at a time if the mixture begins to stick. Continue cooking until the
vegetable is tender, which should take 10 to 15 minutes.

Squeeze on a little lemon juice, season and garnish with chopped
parsley.

So good is this that it can be a meal in its own right with the
accompaniments of Basmati rice, poppadoms and plain yoghurt.

Note: If you cannot find all the spices, don't abandon the recipe, just
use your imagination. Having said that, it should be pointed out that
turmeric is essential for the colour and the flavour.

ROSTI

The essence of this dish is its simplicity and the care you take in putting
it together. Amusing ideas like tossing in a handful of chopped ham, a
tablespoonful of peas or even some grated cheese should be resisted.
The counsel of perfection is to parboil the potatoes for 7 minutes, drain
them and allow them to cool overnight in the fridge. This makes a

difference to their texture which makes the difference to the finished dish, but if it is not possible just try to cook the potatoes until nearly done somewhat ahead of time.

Rösti makes a superb accompaniment to simple grilled or roasted meat or poultry and we have even dined on it by itself with just a salad to follow.

Serves 3–4

1½ lb/750 g large potatoes
1 tablespoon vegetable oil

1 oz/30 g butter
salt and pepper

Grate the parboiled potatoes using a coarse grater. Heat the oil and butter in a 9-inch/22.5-cm diameter non-stick frying pan, or one more or less that size. Spread the grated potatoes evenly in the pan without pressing them down too harshly. Sprinkle with salt and pepper. Find a plate that will fit over the potatoes and cook them gently for 10 minutes.

Turn the Rösti out of the pan by putting a wooden board or similar over the plate and pan and turn the whole thing over. You should now have a potato cake sitting neatly on the plate ready to be sliced. You could slip the Rösti back in the pan to fry what was the top side, but we like the contrast of crisp and soft that results from the original method.

GUJERATI CARROT SALAD

This recipe of Madhur Jaffrey's is delicious and moreish. The nuttiness of black mustard seeds (available at Oriental grocers) tones well with the inherent sweetness of carrots.

Serves 4

1 lb/500 g carrots
1 tablespoon lemon juice
sea salt

2½ tablespoons vegetable oil
1 tablespoon black mustard seeds

Clean, peel and grate the carrots, then toss in a bowl with the lemon juice and salt. Heat the oil in a small frying pan, add the mustard seeds and wait for a few seconds until they begin to pop. When they do, pour the contents of the frying pan onto the carrots and mix well.

This salad is equally good as a first course or as a vegetable accompaniment.

MARLBOROUGH TART

Serves 6

8 oz/250 g puff pastry (bought or made: *6 oz/180 g brown sugar*
   that's up to you)   *4 egg yolks*
6 oz/180 g butter   *2 oz/60 g mixed peel, chopped small*

Turn on the oven to 200°C/400°F, Gas 6.

Line a 10in/25 cm flan tin with pastry and put in the fridge. Mix butter, sugar and the egg yolks in a double saucepan very thoroughly until the sugar is melted. Put the chopped peel onto the pastry and pour the mixture over it. Bake in the oven for about 30 minutes.

This tart can be served hot or cold.

PIERRE MARTIN'S APPLE TARTS

The phenomenally economical thing about these delicious tarts is that one apple will make four of them. Use a crisp dessert apple such as Cox's or Laxton's and do not be tempted to load the pastry with more than one layer of paper-thin slices, albeit overlapping ones, as they will not cook in time. This restaurateur's dream, as far as profits are concerned, was first tasted at Lou Pescadou, Pierre Martin's Brasserie/ Restaurant in the Old Brompton Road in London. It is imperative that the tarts are cooked in an extremely hot oven, and that you work quickly to prevent the apples browning.

Serves 6

1 8-oz/250 g packet frozen puff pastry,   *caster sugar*
   defrosted   *loosely whipped cream*
1–2 dessert apples   *if affordable, a splash of Calvados*
butter

Turn on the oven to 240°C/475°F, Gas 9.

Roll out the defrosted pastry very thinly. Cut out rounds using a tea saucer as a guide. Place these on a wetted baking sheet (oddly enough pastry rises crisply in a damp atmosphere). Peel the apple(s), cut very thin slices and lay them on the pastry rounds in slightly overlapping pieces. Dot each tart with about a teaspoonful of butter and sprinkle with caster sugar. Cook for 15–20 minutes or until the pastry has risen and is crisp.

Serve immediately with the whipped cream, and a splash of Calvados if you have it.

BRANDY SNAPS

Serves 6

4 oz/125 g sugar
4 oz/125 g butter
4 oz/125 g Golden syrup (see page 105 for measuring tip)
4 oz/125 g plain flour

1 tablespoon ground ginger
juice of ½ lemon
½ pint/300 ml cream flavoured with real vanilla essence and ground ginger, whipped

Turn on the oven to 180°C/350°F, Gas 4.

Melt the sugar, butter and syrup in a double saucepan, add the sieved flour, ginger and lemon. Stir well. Then, in teaspoonsful, put the mixture on a non-stick baking sheet, placing the dollops well apart as the mixture will spread widely. Put in the oven and bake until golden brown, about 8–10 minutes.

Remove from the oven, leave to cool for a few moments and then roll each piece round the handle of a wooden spoon. (This is not difficult: the secret is to get the mixture exactly at the right temperature; too soon and it will not stay rolled; too late and it will become rigid and crack.) Lay each rolled snap onto a wire rack to cool.

You can then fill them with whipped cream, but we think it nicer to serve the cream separately in a bowl. That way the snap doesn't get sodden by the cream, which tends to happen in 2 or 3 hours.

OAT CAKES

1 oz/30 g lard or dripping
1 lb/500 g medium oatmeal plus extra
   for the rolling process

½ teaspoon bicarbonate of soda
½ teaspoon salt

Turn on the oven to 150°C/300°F, Gas 2.

Melt the chosen fat (bacon fat is good) in ½ pint/300 ml hot water. Mix the oatmeal in a bowl with the bicarbonate of soda and salt. Make a well in the oatmeal, pour in the melted fat and water and mix with a knife to a fairly moist dough. Dust a surface with oatmeal and roll out the dough, using plenty of oatmeal to prevent any sticking. Cut in rounds with a pastry cutter.

Bake for about 20 minutes on an ungreased baking sheet, turning several times, until the oatcakes are crisp and golden.

WATER BISCUITS

8 oz/250 g plain flour
½ teaspoon salt
1 teaspoon baking powder
2 oz/60 g butter or margarine

sea salt and/or *poppy seeds* or *sesame*
   seeds or *caraway seeds (depending on*
   the cheeses these will accompany)

Turn on the oven to 150°C/300°F, Gas 2.

Sift the flour, salt and baking powder together. Rub in the butter or margarine conscientiously and add enough water to make a firm dough. Roll out thinly on a floured surface. Prick all over with a fork and cut out circles with a large scone cutter or a tea cup. Sprinkle with whatever seed you choose or just sea salt. Bake on a lightly-oiled baking sheet for 20 minutes or until crisp and faintly brown.

These are best served almost straight from the oven. If you make them ahead of time, store in a tin with a tightly fitting lid, and crisp in a low oven when you need them.

DEVILS ON HORSEBACK

Unexpected courses provide a luxury of their own. After a light meal, a savoury is a great treat and a reason to keep going with the wine and wit.

On the Russian Doll principle of cooking, this version of Devils on Horseback is fun. For 4 people, take 8 large prunes and pour boiling water over them. Leave for half an hour and then simmer them in this liquid until tender. When cool, carefully stone the prunes and stuff them with the sort of olive that, in its turn, has been stoned and filled with pimento.

Take a half-rasher of thinly sliced bacon for each prune. Stretch and flatten it and wrap it round the prune. Set on a baking tin and bake in a hot oven until the bacon is crisply cooked – about 10 minutes. Let each Devil on Horseback ride on a piece of thin, hot buttered toast.

SARDINES ON TOAST

Serves 4

Skin the contents of a tin of sardines, and take out the backbones. Mash the sardines with a teaspoonful of juice from a jar of cocktail onions (or press some onion in a garlic press), 1 oz/30 g of butter, a teaspoonful of Dijon mustard and 2 teaspoonsful of red wine vinegar. Cut some toast into suitable squares, spread them with the sardine mixture and put them under the grill for a few moments.

A little chopped fennel is good on top.

WELSH RABBIT

Correctly, Welsh Rabbit is made on the principle of fondue, with the cheese being slowly melted into brown ale with butter and seasoning and the whole being poured over toast. This is a simpler way that can be prepared ahead of time. However, Worcestershire sauce should still be served. The correct way to apply it is to press a knife criss-cross fashion into the hot cheese and shake on the sauce so that it dribbles into the runnels.

For 4 people, grate 4 oz/125 g of Cheddar and mix with a little butter and a little beer to a spreadable paste. Season with black pepper and made mustard. Spread onto buttered toast and grill.

4 Dull People

'The capacity of human beings to bore one another seems to be vastly greater than that of any other animal. Some of their most esteemed inventions have no other apparent purpose; for example, the dinner party of more than two, the epic poem, and the science of metaphysics.' Some entertaining that, for one reason or another, is thrust upon you makes one empathise deeply with H. L. Mencken's view.

We have all been faced with those evenings where the cooking seems so much more fun than the prospect of the arrival of the guests. The sister of one of the authors once gave her an apron bought in Los Angeles which she is often tempted to wear to open the door to guests. It says on it, 'Who invited these tacky people anyway?' which, when tired and frazzled and consumed with doubts about the meaning of life, is a thought which flits through the mind of even the most munificent hostess.

And, on the whole, if this is how you feel, it will be because somebody else, not you, has initiated the event. Why invite people if that is how you feel you might be thinking. But that is a naïve response, dear reader. Entertaining, the noun, has its own stringent by-laws, one of which is that it often bears very little relation to entertaining, the adjective. Duty dinners, business contacts, family and in-law coddling, return matches, can all conjure the prospect of a dreary evening. However, we have to add here that frequently, almost uncannily frequently, a dreaded evening turns into the jolliest of occasions. Conversely, you can invite six people celebrated for their wit and charm and needle-sharp intelligence and the evening can be a complete frost, so furious and sulky is each one to find someone else telling jokes or looking devastating.

But given that you suppose that the lunch or dinner is going to need kindling, that it is not going to be an affair of spontaneous combustion, the following ideas will help to what we believe is known as break the ice.

Many of them involve the participation of the eaters, and if conversation flags, and new topics are elusive, they can always resort to squabbling over whose piece of beef it is skating round the fondue pot.

Stilton Soup   Individual Crème Brûlées
Lettuce Packets   Baked Alaska
Tacos   Chocolate Mousse Cake
Lamb Cutlets in Filo Pastry   Iced Camembert
Fondue Bourguignonne

STILTON SOUP

This rich soup makes an impressive start to the meal. You may think it is a dubious notion, but it is actually delicious. Beth Coventry who serves it at Green's Champagne Bar in Duke Street, St James's, in London, says that Americans love it and ask for the recipe. So if you are having dull Americans to dinner . . .

Serves 4

2 oz/60 g butter
1 onion, peeled and finely chopped
1 fat clove garlic, peeled and chopped
2 stalks celery, de-stringed and diced
1½ oz/45 g flour
1 teaspoon ground coriander
½ chicken stock cube, crumbled

8 oz/250 g Stilton cheese, broken up
  with a fork
½ pint/300 ml milk
1 sherry glass of port
pepper
2 tablespoons double cream (optional)

Melt the butter and cook the onion, garlic and celery very gently – just let them soften. Stir in the flour and cook for a minute or two to lose any raw taste. Add the ground coriander and the crumbled stock cube. Add the milk and when the mixture is smooth, add enough water to achieve a consistency of thin cream – something in the region of 1½ pints/1 litre. Simmer for 15 minutes. Add the crumbled Stilton and, off the heat, beat the soup with a whisk. Add the port, mix again, grind on some black pepper, taste for seasoning and whisk in the cream. Re-heat, but gently, since the soup must not be allowed to boil.

Serve with wholemeal toast.

LETTUCE PACKETS

Alongside the illusion of healthiness, there is an 'involving' quality about this dish, helpful if conversation is limping. Each guest takes a lettuce leaf, adds a spoonful of the pork mixture, makes up a parcel as neatly or as messily as they are capable and proceeds.

The recipe below is a simplified version of a Chinese idea, but once you have grasped the concept you will be able to improvise with your own mixtures. Cooked root vegetables diced finely, spiked with chilli, is one thought.

Serves 4

2 tablespoons vegetable oil or lard, according to preference	2 tablespoons dry sherry
12 oz/375 g minced pork	3 tablespoons chicken stock (from a cube will suffice)
salt	½ cucumber, diced
sugar	½ tablespoon cornflour, whisked into 2 more tablespoons stock
1 tablespoon chopped onion	2 teaspoons sesame oil (optional)
1 teaspoon grated fresh root ginger	1 Iceberg lettuce or Webbs Wonder, the leaves separated, washed and dried
4 stalks celery, de-stringed and diced	
1 tablespoon soya sauce	

Heat the oil or lard (the latter gives a more unctuous effect) in a large frying pan or wok. When hot, add the pork. Sprinkle with a good pinch of salt and a teaspoonful of sugar and stir-fry for 2 or 3 minutes or until there is no trace of pink in the meat.

Add the onion and ginger; stir-fry for 2 minutes. Add the celery, soya sauce, sherry and stock. Fry for 1 minute, then add the cucumber and cook until it is heated through but still crunchy.

Give the cornflour mixture a stir to create a cloudy liquid and pour onto the meat. Stir-fry for 1 minute. Finally glaze the meat by dribbling on the sesame oil (or a little vegetable oil if that is all you have to hand).

Serve on a heated dish with the lettuce leaves stacked on a separate plate.

TACOS

Like the Lettuce Packets, this is another involving course. The taco shells (which you buy in a packet made by the company Old El Paso since they taste all right and it is difficult, if not impossible, to buy *masa harina* to make your own) are filled first with spiced beef and then garnished with various sauces and substances. Each taco that a guest assembles can differ a little from the one before. If you are feeding serious numbers, then you might consider offering a variety of meats, for example shredded cooked chicken or fried crumbled sausage of a spicy variety as well as the beef.

Serves 6–8

2 onions, peeled and finely chopped	*a hefty pinch of chilli powder* or *1 small*
2 cloves garlic, peeled and finely chopped	*green chilli de-seeded and finely*
2 tablespoons vegetable oil	*chopped* or *1 teaspoon chilli sauce*
2 lb/1 kg minced beef	*soya sauce*
2 teaspoons ground cumin	*salt and pepper*
2 teaspoons dried oregano	*a pinch of sugar*
	1 packet Old El Paso taco shells

Fry the onion and garlic in the vegetable oil. Add the minced beef and stir until browned. Season with cumin, oregano, chilli and a dash of soya sauce. Season with salt, pepper and a pinch of sugar. Add a cup of water and simmer for 20 minutes.

Heat the taco shells for 2–3 minutes in a moderate oven.

Prepare bowls of:

shredded lettuce	*an avocado mashed with a peeled, seeded*
grated hard cheese	*and diced tomato and seasoned with*
yoghurt or *soured cream*	*lemon juice, salt, pepper and chilli*
Salsa Cruda (see page 57)	*sauce*

Offer the taco shells with the minced beef and the garnishes.

LAMB CUTLETS IN FILO PASTRY

This is made on the same principle as Beef Wellington, the dull person's favourite dish, but we think it better as it is somewhat easier to get the timings right; the pastry puffed and golden, the meat cooked but rosy pink.

Filo pastry, available at Cypriot bakeries and some delicatessens and supermarkets, is a great conversation piece so long as you conceal its origins and just look faintly smug as though rolling out paper-thin dough is something you do every day. If you fail to find filo pastry, use defrosted frozen puff pastry, rolled out thinly.

It is important to buy small, neat cutlets, well trimmed of fat and with a long bone protruding. Inform the butcher that you want best end cutlets prepared in the French style.

Serves 4

1 oz/30 g butter or 1 tablespoon
   vegetable oil
1 Spanish onion, peeled and finely
   chopped
2 cloves garlic, peeled and finely chopped
4 oz/125 g mushrooms, wiped clean and
   finely chopped

1 tablespoon chopped parsley
salt and freshly-ground black pepper
1 8-oz/250 g packet frozen puff pastry
   (defrosted) or 8 oz/250 g filo pastry
8 best end of neck lamb cutlets
1 egg beaten with a pinch of salt

Turn on the oven to 220°C/425°F, Gas 7.

Heat the butter or oil and sauté the onion and garlic until softened. Add the mushrooms and stir around until cooked. Mix in the parsley and season enthusiastically.

If you are using puff pastry, roll it out thinly and cut into 8 triangles, each one just large enough to wrap around the meat. If you are using filo pastry, cut strips about 5 in/12.5 cm wide, one for each cutlet, and brush on one side with oil or melted butter. Cover strips with a damp tea towel to keep the pastry pliable.

In the cleaned out sauté pan, seal the chops quickly in a little more oil or butter. Remove, let any fat drain off, and then season the meat. Drain off any liquid from the onion/mushroom mixture. Put a heaped teaspoonful into the centre of each pastry triangle or at one end of your filo pastry strip. Place a cutlet on the stuffing and, with the puff pastry, pinch the pastry around it making a firm seal and aiming for the look of a three-cornered hat. With the filo pastry, wrap it loosely round the meat rather as if you were bandaging it. Brush the pastry with the egg wash. Place the parcels on a wet baking sheet and cook for 15 to 20 minutes, or until the pastry is flaky and golden.

Serve with redcurrant jelly.

FONDUE BOURGUIGNONNE

For this you need a fondue set with a burner to keep the oil hot or you could use an electric frying pan. The long-handled slender forks that come with fondue sets are useful but not imperative; ordinary forks will do. Use good quality meat as it is subject to very brief cooking. Serve a selection of sauces from the ideas given below in small bowls and bake small potatoes in their jackets for 45 minutes to hand round afterwards as a vehicle for left-over sauces.

8 oz/250 g steak per person (rump or sirloin)

1 litre vegetable oil or if you wish to add some flavour, substitute butter or olive oil for one-third of the quantity

Cut the meat into bite-sized pieces and pile up attractively in two dishes. Make a selection of the sauces below:

AIOLI

Crush 3 cloves of garlic and stir into 2 egg yolks. When that is well blended, add 1 teaspoonful made mustard. Slowly begin to add vegetable oil, drop by drop, stirring all the while until the sauce thickens and the emulsion seems reliable. Add more oil (in total about 8 fl oz/250 ml) until you have a sauce with the consistency of ointment. Flavour with salt, pepper and a squeeze of lemon juice.

AVOCADO SAUCE

Purée the flesh of an avocado with a little oil, lemon juice, salt, pepper and a dash of chilli sauce. If you wish, thin with 2 heaped tablespoonsful natural yoghurt.

SALSA CRUDA

2 large ripe red tomatoes, skinned and finely chopped
1 onion, peeled and finely chopped
2 small green chilli peppers de-seeded and cut into fine threads

1 tablespoon chopped fresh coriander or substitute parsley
a pinch of sugar
1 tablespoon oil
1 dessertspoon red wine vinegar
salt and pepper

Mix all ingredients together and leave at room temperature.

PARSLEY SAUCE

4 fl oz/125 ml vegetable oil
2 tablespoons white wine vinegar
1 teaspoon mustard

1 clove garlic, peeled and crushed
4 oz/125 g parsley, finely chopped
salt and pepper

Mix the oil and vinegar and seasonings and stir in the parsley, adding more if necessary to obtain a cohesive sauce.

REMOULADE SAUCE

8 fl oz/250 ml mayonnaise
2 oz/60 g chopped gherkins
1 tablespoon capers, finely chopped
2 hard-boiled eggs, finely chopped

1 teaspoon chopped tarragon – if
    available
1 dessertspoon chopped parsley and/or
    chives
salt and pepper

Mix together thoroughly.

SATAY SAUCE

1 onion, peeled and finely chopped
1 tablespoon vegetable oil
finely chopped chillis or chilli sauce to
    taste

6 oz/180 g crunchy peanut butter
1 teaspoon sugar
juice of ½ lemon
1 tablespoon soya sauce

Fry the onion in the oil until golden. Add some finely chopped chilli or ½ teaspoon chilli sauce, the peanut butter, about 6 fl oz/180 ml water and the sugar. Stir well and simmer until you have a thick mixture. Stir in the lemon juice and soya sauce and taste for further seasonings, if any.

CHINESE DIPPING SAUCE

4 tablespoons soya sauce
2 tablespoons rice vinegar (available from
    Oriental grocers) or use 1 tablespoon
    sherry plus 1 tablespoon vinegar
a good pinch of sugar

1 fat clove garlic, peeled and crushed
1 dessertspoon sesame seeds, lightly
    roasted in a dry frying pan
2 spring onions, very finely chopped

Mix all the ingredients together. Threads of fresh root ginger, if you have some, can be added.

YOGHURT MINT SAUCE

1 small tub Greek (strained) yoghurt
salt and pepper

1 dessertspoon mint sauce base (not jellied
    mint sauce)

Mix together.

Guests spear a piece of meat, cook it to their liking in the bubbling oil and dip it into their choice of sauces, which should first be spooned onto their plates to avoid a messy ending.

INDIVIDUAL CREME BRULEES

Serves 6

1 pint/625 ml double cream
1 tablespoon caster sugar: if you keep a
jar of caster sugar with a vanilla pod
in it, use it; if not use 1 vanilla pod,
split, or a few drops vanilla essence

4 egg yolks
more caster sugar for the brûlée

Butter 6 cocotte dishes, and turn on the oven to 140°C/275°F, Gas 1.

Put the cream and sugar (plus pod or essence) in the top of a double saucepan and heat to scalding point. Remove from the heat, and pour in the egg yolks in a thin stream, stirring vigorously all the while. Remove the pod if you were using one, and strain the mixture into the buttered cocotte dishes. Put the dishes in a baking tin half full of warm water and bake in the oven for half an hour or until the custard is just firm. Leave to cool, and then put in the fridge.

Before serving, heat the grill, sprinkle caster sugar $\frac{1}{8}$ inch/0.3 cm thick over the top of the custards and grill until caramel-coloured. Remove. A few minutes later, the caramel will have cooled and should be like very thin glass.

BAKED ALASKA

You can count on the fact that there will always be someone thrilled and startled to find that a dessert can come out of the oven and yet still have firm ice-cream at its centre. The trick is to cover the sponge base and the ice-cream lavishly with meringue so there is no crack to let the heat through, and to have the oven well pre-heated, so that the meringue crisps quickly.

Serves 6

1 layer of sponge cake – home-made or
bought
¾ pint/475 ml good quality vanilla ice-
cream
fresh soft fruit in season

3 egg whites
salt
6 oz/180 g caster sugar
2 tablespoons brandy or rum, if you want
to flame the pudding

Put the cake on an ovenproof serving dish. Cut up the ice-cream and arrange in one layer, leaving about ½ inch/1.25 cm sponge cake around the edge. Put in the freezer for 1 hour.

Turn on the oven to 230°C/450°F, Gas 8.

Arrange your choice of soft fruit, e.g. raspberries, blackberries, peaches or currants, on the ice-cream. Whisk the egg whites with a pinch of salt until stiff. Whisk in 2 tablespoonsful of the sugar and continue until you have glistening snowy peaks. Carefully fold in the remainder of the sugar. Spoon the meringue over the fruit, ice-cream and cake leaving no patch uncovered. Bake in the oven for about 3 minutes or until the tips of the meringue are browned.

CHOCOLATE MOUSSE CAKE

This is a recipe from Joscelyn Dimbleby, Queen of Puddings. She has said that friends of hers have said that they have never tasted a better pudding than this. When you tell people it is made with no flour at all, even guests on dull diets will tuck in, disregarding the inclusion of chocolate, sugar and cream. Make the cake ahead of time and keep it chilled in the fridge. In summer, fill it with soft fruit such as raspberries, strawberries and currants; in winter, stew dried apricots, peaches, or pears, sharpening them with a little lemon juice in the syrup.

Serves 6

6 oz/180 g plain chocolate (try to get Chocolate Menier)
5 eggs
6 oz/180 g caster sugar

12 oz/375 g fruit (see above)
8–10 fl oz/250–300 ml double cream
icing sugar

Turn on the oven to 180°C/350°F, Gas 4. Brush two 8-inch/20 cm sandwich tins with oil and put a disc of greaseproof paper in the bottom of each.

Break the chocolate into small pieces and put over a pan of hot, but not boiling water. Stir occasionally until it melts.

Separate the eggs, putting the yolks into a large basin and the whites in a smaller basin. Add the sugar to the yolks and whisk thoroughly together until the mixture is pale in colour and fairly thick in consistency. When the chocolate has melted, remove from the heat and whisk it into the egg yolks and sugar. Whisk in 2 tablespoonsful of very hot water to soften the mixture. Whisk the egg whites until stiff and then fold gently, but thoroughly into the chocolate mixture with a metal spoon. Pour the mixture into the prepared sandwich tins and bake for 15–20 minutes, until firm to a light touch in the middle. When you take them out they will sink down a bit – do not worry about it. Cool, and then let get completely cold in the fridge for at least 1 hour or overnight.

Have a large round plate ready. Loosen the edges of the cake with a knife. Turn out one cake onto the round plate, and remove the paper. Spread the fruit over the cake (if it is fresh fruit, you may want to sprinkle it with caster sugar). Beat the cream until stiff and spread it over the fruit. Turn out the second cake and then turn it onto the cream so that the crackly baked surface is on top.

Before serving, sprinkle icing sugar through a sieve over the cake and decorate with any spare fresh fruit.

ICED CAMEMBERT

This recipe dates from the Thirties. The combination of cold cheese and hot biscuits is a good one. Look on page 48 for the recipe for home-made Water Biscuits and Oatcakes and make one or other as the accompaniment.

Serves 6

1 Camembert cheese – it should be ripe but not 'humming' with ripeness
¼ pint/150 ml single cream

¼ pint/150 ml double cream
salt and pepper
cayenne pepper

To serve:
crushed ice
few sprigs parsley

hot biscuits (see above)

Pare the rind from the cheese, wasting as little as possible. Mash the cheese with the single cream using a fork, or you could whizz it in the food processor or liquidiser. Beat the double cream until it just holds its shape and fold in the cheesy mixture. Season to taste with salt, black pepper and cayenne. Freeze in a shallow dish until firm, but not rock hard.

Set a serving dish in crushed ice. Slice the camembert, and arrange on the dish with sprigs of parsley. Hand hot biscuits separately.

5 *Ladies' Lunch*

In the bad old days, ladies' lunches were regarded with patronising indulgence by the male sex and with various feelings ranging from anxiety to boredom by the lunch goers. One of us, old enough to remember those times, can recall that it was a way for bored middle-class women, who were not allowed by their husbands to engage in any profession or work, to pass the time between shopping at Daniel Neal for their children and running the First Aid classes for the Red Cross.

They were also a part of the old London Season: mothers met at lunch to plan the dinner and cocktail parties surrounding the dances, and the debutantes met to go over the fun and games of the night before. We can be fairly sure that the food on these occasions was either dull – nursery food but with smaller helpings – or downright awful, on the premise that if something was nasty enough you would not eat very much of it and so preserve your figure. One such lunch can indeed be remembered, where all three courses were some kind of (different) mousse or pâté, dun-coloured and running the spectrum of taste between cheesy face flannel to saccharine-flavoured lemon. The middle course defied description until one more outspoken guest described it as near mouse paste. Food to toy with, you might say.

People mind more about what they eat these days and the only two things that have changed about ladies' lunches is the (almost) universal desire not to become fatter as a result, and the more serious fact that instead of sending for cook after breakfast and ordering the meals – in the Thirties that was regarded as a terrible chore – you have to do it all yourself. Two courses should suffice, and simplicity and the minimum of last-minute cooking should be the keynote on the principle that you ask women to lunch with you because you really like them and actually want to talk to them.

Gazpacho   Egg Mousse
Watercress Soup   Spinach Soufflé with Anchovy Sauce
Caesar Salad   Pigeon Breasts
Delancey Salad   Hot Fruit Salad
Korean Egg Bundles   Iced Coffee Granita

GAZPACHO

This dish, practically a liquid salad, is not only palpably good for you but must have an almost minus quantity of calories. There is much discussion over what is and what is not an authentic gazpacho. This is not. In fact, the recipe emanates from Fire Island in New York, but it is so good that authenticity seems suddenly irrelevant.

Serves 4

14 fl oz/435 ml tin, bottle or carton good quality tomato juice

2 green peppers, cleaned and roughly chopped

4 tomatoes, skinned and quartered

2 cloves garlic, peeled

1 stalk celery, trimmed

1 large or 2 small cucumbers, roughly chopped

1 egg

2 fl oz/60 ml olive oil

4 fl oz/125 ml wine vinegar

a pinch of salt

a pinch of cayenne pepper

Garnishes:

1 green pepper, cleaned and finely chopped

2 hard-boiled eggs, finely chopped

1 Spanish onion, peeled and finely chopped

2–3 slices of bread, cubed and fried in olive oil until golden

Using small amounts of tomato juice, blend together the first six ingredients in the list. Pour into a bowl, thin with 4 fl oz/125 ml more tomato juice and stir in the oil and vinegar. Season with salt and cayenne pepper. Decide on the consistency of soup that you like, and add more tomato juice if necessary. Chill thoroughly.

Just before serving, prepare the garnishes and serve them in small bowls beside the soup for people to help themselves.

WATERCRESS SOUP

Serves 4

1 large onion

2 bunches watercress

1 oz/30 g butter or 1 tablespoon sunflower seed oil

1½ pints/1 litre good chicken stock

salt and pepper

Peel and chop the onion finely. Wash the watercress and chop roughly. Melt the butter or heat the oil in a pan. Add the onion and cook gently for a few minutes, adding a little salt to make the onions sweat. Add the watercress, and cook, stirring, for two minutes, then add the stock.

Simmer for half an hour, then pass through mouli, liquidise or whizz in the food processor. Return to the pan, and season.

Note: With soups, there is always the choice between using a hand mouli or liquidising: the latter is quicker, but the former produces a more interesting texture.

CAESAR SALAD

The method below is for the 'classic' Caesar salad, made famous by a restaurateur in Tijuana in the Twenties. It may strike you as simplistic, but its restraint is what makes it so good, provided you take no short cuts in the preparation. Success depends on the last-minute coming together of the constituent parts.

Serves 4 as a first course

1 large Cos lettuce or *2 smaller ones*
juice of ½ lemon
2 oz/60 g Parmesan cheese, freshly grated
2 eggs

white bread from a proper loaf
Worcestershire sauce or 1 tin anchovies
2 fat cloves garlic
olive oil
salt and freshly-ground black pepper

Pick over the lettuce and use only the unblemished leaves. Wash them, dry them thoroughly and put in a plastic bag in the refrigerator.

Towards the time of serving, assemble all the other ingredients, squeeze the lemon half, grate the Parmesan if you have bought it in a lump, and set water to boil for the eggs. Trim the crusts from three slices of bread and cut into cubes. Open the anchovies if you are using them; Worcestershire sauce is, apparently, authentic.

Crush the garlic into 3 tablespoonful olive oil and fry the croûtons (bread cubes) in this, turning and stirring the while to ensure they are evenly browned. Place the lettuce in a large salad bowl and add 2 tablespoonful olive oil. Toss to coat the leaves. Sprinkle on some sea salt and freshly-ground black pepper and toss with another tablespoonful of olive oil – imagine you are a Mexican restaurateur.

Pour on the lemon juice, a couple of splashes of Worcestershire sauce (or the drained and chopped anchovies) and break in the yolks of the eggs which you have plunged into boiling water for just one minute. Toss once. Sprinkle on the Parmesan. Toss again and add the croûtons which should first be drained on kitchen paper. Serve immediately.

DELANCEY SALAD

Serves 6

1 lb/500 g fresh prawns
1 bunch watercress
12 oz/375 g mushrooms

½ large cucumber
1 box mustard and cress
2 avocados

For the dressing:

1 teaspoon salt
1 teaspoon sugar
freshly-ground black pepper

2 tablespoons olive oil
1 tablespoon tarragon vinegar

This salad can all be prepared beforehand, except for the avocado which should be added just before serving.

Peel the prawns. Wash and roughly chop the watercress, peel and slice the mushrooms, cut the cucumber into thick slices and chop into pieces. Cut the cress from its box. Combine all the ingredients in a large salad bowl. Before serving, halve the avocados and scoop out pieces with a teaspoon.

Dress the salad in the following manner: Scatter the salt over the salad and mix. Add the sugar and mix. Add several good screws of black pepper and mix. Add 2 tablespoonsful of best olive oil and mix. And finally, 1 tablespoonful of tarragon vinegar and mix. Italians very often dress salads in this manner and the result is very fresh and appealing. Naturally you may want to adjust the ingredients of the dressing to suit yourself. Taste the salad in any case to see whether more of anything should be added.

KOREAN EGG BUNDLES

This recipe, taken from Madhur Jaffrey's *Eastern Vegetarian Cooking*, is a dainty dish fit for ladies. Rectangular egg pancakes are cut into thin strips and the strips tied into bundles with blanched spring onions. It is the dipping sauce that makes the dish.

Since, unless you are Korean or Japanese, you are unlikely to have a rectangular frying pan, use a 6-inch/15-cm omelette pan or non-stick frying pan and be prepared either for some waste or curvy sticks.

Serves 4–6

5 large eggs
2 teaspoons vegetable oil

12 spring onions, trimmed and washed
2 teaspoons salt

For the sauce:

4 tablespoons Japanese soya sauce
2½ tablespoons rice vinegar
1 teaspoon sugar
1 tablespoon very finely sliced spring
  onion

1 clove garlic, peeled and crushed
1 teaspoon sesame seeds, roasted and
  lightly crushed

Beat the eggs but not to a froth. Put 1 teaspoonful of oil into the frying pan. Spread it around and heat it over a medium-low heat. When hot, pour in half the beaten eggs. Turn heat to low and cover loosely (with aluminium foil, if necessary). Cook for 5–6 minutes or until the bottom of the pancake is no longer soft. Ease a spatula under the pancake and turn it over. Cook the other side for 2–3 minutes or until it, too, is firm. Remove the pancake. Add another teaspoonful of oil to the frying pan and make the second pancake the same way. Allow both pancakes to cool, then cut them into strips that are about 2½ inch/6 cm long and ¼ inch/o.6 cm wide.

Bring 2 quarts/2.3 litres of water to a rolling boil in a 4-quart/5-litre pot. Add the salt. Put the spring onions, bulbs first, into the water; like spaghetti, the upper ends of the spring onions will have to be eased into the water as they soften. Boil rapidly for 2 minutes. You may have to hold the spring onions down with a spoon so they stay submerged. Drain the spring onions in a colander and rinse immediately under cold running water, then pat them dry. Split each spring onion lengthways into two or more strands by first cutting the bulb with a knife and then tearing upwards.

Now put four egg strips together to form a neat bundle. Place the bulb end of the spring onion strip on the centre of the bundle and then wrap round and round over it. Tuck the end of the strand underneath the binding. It will hold. Make as many bundles as you can this way. Arrange bundles prettily on a round or rectangular platter. If not to be eaten immediately, cover with cling film and refrigerate for a few hours. Mix together the sauce ingredients and serve in small bowls for dipping.

EGG MOUSSE

Serves 6

6 hard boiled eggs
3 tablespoons mayonnaise
⅝ packet of gelatine
2 tablespoons of light stock

6 anchovy fillets
2 tablespoons cream, whipped
fresh parsley and, if possible, fresh
  coriander

Chop the eggs and mix with the mayonnaise. Dissolve the gelatine thoroughly in the stock (the best way of doing this is to put it in a small bowl in a saucepan of boiling water and stir with a fork), and add to the mixture. Chop the anchovies finely and add. Finally, fold in the cream, put the mixture into a cold mould, and put into the fridge. Turn out before serving, and garnish with parsley and/or coriander.

SPINACH SOUFFLE WITH ANCHOVY SAUCE

The way to serve this dish is to bring the soufflé to the table, whereupon your friends will 'ooh' and 'aah' as people invariably do when confronted by a soufflé. Boldly thrust a spoon down into the centre and pour in the hot anchovy sauce, keeping the rest to serve separately. Any dryness or monotony in the soufflé will be obviated by the tingling, creamy anchovy.

Serves 4

1 lb/500 g spinach
3 oz/90 g butter
3 tablespoons flour
½ pint/300 ml milk
4 oz/125 g double cream cheese

1 oz/30 g Parmesan cheese grated
  (optional)
salt and freshly-ground black pepper
4 eggs, separated
1 tin anchovies
¼ pint/150 ml double cream

Turn on the oven to 190°C/375°F, Gas 5.

Wash the spinach leaves, trim off any hard stalks and cook, in only the water which clings to the leaves, until it is tender. Drain in a colander and when it is cool enough, squeeze it with your hands to get it as dry as possible, and then chop it finely.

Melt 2 oz/60 g of the butter, stir in the flour to make a roux. Slowly add the milk until you have a thick smooth sauce and then beat in the cream cheese, bit by bit. Add the Parmesan if you are using it. Stir in the spinach and season quite vigorously. Let it cool a little and then beat in the egg yolks one by one.

This can be done ahead of time. When ready to cook, whisk the egg whites until stiff. Fold about a quarter of them into the mixture to lighten it, then the rest with an even gentler hand. Pour into a buttered soufflé dish and bake for 25–30 minutes.

To make the sauce, briefly soak 5–6 anchovy fillets in warm water and then pat them dry. Melt the final 1 oz/30 g butter, add the fillets, stir around until they break up and then pour in the cream. Bring to the boil, give a quick bubble and serve.

PIGEON BREASTS

Contrary to many pigeon recipes, lightning cooking of the pigeon flesh gives far better results than long stewing. Even if you are nervous about techniques like boning or, indeed, dealing with raw meat at all, do not be afraid of the notion of removing the pigeon breasts from the carcass. They scoop off easily and neatly. The skinny legs and the carcass are then used for the stock.

Serves 6

1 pigeon per person
olive oil
lemon juice or *wine*
salt and pepper

ground ginger
1 teaspoon arrowroot
port or *red wine*

Vegetables for stock:

1 carrot
1 onion, stuck with a clove
1 stalk celery
bay leaf

3 cloves of garlic per person trimmed but
   unpeeled
peppercorns

Using a sharp, cunning little knife, take off the pigeon breasts by working the knife between the flesh and breast bone; they practically slide off. Trim any gristle or skin that overhangs the 'supreme'.

Mix together some olive oil, a little lemon juice or wine, and salt and pepper. Turn the breasts in this and leave to marinate. Use the carcasses and vegetables to make the stock, adding some peppercorns and the garlic cloves. Simmer for as long as time allows, up to 1½ hours. Strain the stock and put aside the garlic cloves. Continue to boil the stock until it is well reduced. You want only a couple of tablespoonsful per person. Mix the arrowroot with a little port (or red wine) and stir it into the stock to make it glossy.

Remove the pigeon breasts from the marinade. Sprinkle with a little ground ginger and some black pepper. Grill the breasts under a moderate heat for a few minutes on each side and then leave to rest under the switched-off grill for 10 minutes.

To serve prettily, slice the breasts across, and fan out the slices on a warmed plate. Surround with the sauce. If you like garlic (after cooking in the stock, it will now be mild and nutty), sauté the cloves briskly in a little butter and serve alongside.

HOT FRUIT SALAD

This recipe comes from Elizabeth David's *Summer Cooking*. She says that it is important to use red gooseberries – not green ones – and also that one must stick to the proportions.

Serves 6

1 lb/500 g red gooseberries	*sugar*
4 oz/125 g redcurrants	*8 oz/250 g raspberries*

Stew together gently for 5 minutes (without water) the gooseberries, redcurrants and sugar. The sugar has to be used in quantities depending upon how sweet or sharp you like your summer fruit: start with 2 tablespoonsful and add more if you feel the fruit needs it. Add raspberries and cook for a further 2 minutes. Serve very hot with fresh thick cream; the cream should be served separately, so that those who don't want it may have the fruit by itself.

This recipe can also be adapted, using loganberries instead of the gooseberries, and blackberries instead of the raspberries. Redcurrants are desirable for both dishes.

ICED COFFEE GRANITA

A granita should not be smooth like a sorbet but composed of fine-grained frozen crystals, in this case of strong coffee. It makes an excellent finish to a lunch. True coffee lovers eat an iced coffee granita whilst drinking a cup of hot espresso. The coffee should preferably be made in an Italian Moka coffee pot, the kind where hot water is forced up from the bottom of the pot through the coffee and into the top. For preference, use freshly-ground high roast continental beans.

Serves 4

¾ pint/475 ml of strong coffee   *double cream, freshly whipped (optional)*
2 tablespoons sugar, or more to taste

Pour hot coffee into a jug and dissolve the sugar in it. Taste for sweetness but do not make it very sweet as sugar weakens the flavour. Pour the coffee into metal ice cube trays from which you have removed the grids, or similar containers. When the coffee is cold, put the trays into the freezer and leave for 15 minutes, then stir the contents to break up the ice crystals and to turn the mixture sides to middle. Repeat the operation 15 minutes later and after that stir regularly until you are ready to serve it. It will take up to 3 hours in total to freeze properly.

Serve in individual glasses with whipped cream as an optional topping.

6 Abandoned Man

A man accustomed to being cooked for is a helpless thing. Abandoned by his cook, either temporarily or permanently, his first instinct is to find someone else to make his meals. This conditioned response may be because women, from his mother onwards, have not only spoiled him, but woven an air of mystery around cooking. They have whispered of barding and basting and double boilers. Like cats, they have spat at frying pans to test the heat or, in apparent ungovernable rage, flung strands of spaghetti at the wall to see if they would stick. The whole performance, from the shopping that seems to require arcane and distressingly female talk – phrases like a pound of skirt or a bag of Desirées – to choosing the one dish of the thirty available, that in some talismanic way his cook will have decreed the only one suitable, could have made a man craven in the kitchen.

On the other hand, he may just have been arrogant and idle or simply not interested. But friends will soon tire of providing for him and he must turn to the fridge and stove and think conscientiously about cooking for himself and for others, because nothing is more lowering than too many solitary meals, and a man left to cook for his children will find they grow fractious on uninterrupted junk food.

Men who cook, particularly those new to the activity, want to make dishes that either have the quality of immediacy, or ones where alchemy in the oven will transform them. Men, on the whole, are not good at diddling about waiting for one thing to happen before proceeding with the next. For this reason, a stew which can be left alone to cook for hours and requires no cosseting is a favourite. Most men, even abandoned ones, believe it improves with keeping and that it can be jazzed up with curry powder and raisins towards the end of its life. This is not so, although the sauce of a stew does mellow when it is cooked on one day, heated up and eaten the next.

Fundamental Beef Stew
Steak Tartare
Hamburgers Chic or Childish
Kidneys en Pyjama

Baked Potatoes with Soured Cream
  and Caviar
Salad Dressing
Omelette Soufflé au Grand Marnier

FUNDAMENTAL BEEF STEW

This recipe contains the basic steps of any stew or casserole, i.e. preparing the meat, sealing it and browning it, adding flavourings and spices, making a stock and, where appropriate, thickening or reducing the sauce. Once the steps have been understood, they can be applied to any resilient cut of meat or tough game bird or fowl. Beef, especially the cheaper cuts, is particularly suitable for stewing, and the first recipe serves as a good model for all stews. Details in flavouring must be followed to avoid any risk of a school dinner result but they can of course be varied according to whim.

Serves 4 (Quantities can be doubled easily)

2 lb/1 kg stewing beef – referred to at the butcher's as braising steak or stewing steak
1 tablespoon flour
1 teaspoon ground ginger
salt and freshly-ground black pepper
1 oz/30 g butter

2 tablespoons olive or vegetable oil
2 medium-sized onions, peeled and chopped
4 carrots, peeled and chopped
1 pint/625 ml Guinness or red wine
1 tablespoon soya sauce
2 cloves garlic, peeled
4 strips of orange rind

Turn on the oven to 170°C/325°F, Gas 3.

Trim any obvious fat from the meat and cut the meat into cubes about 1½ inch/4 cm square. Pieces on the large side emerge looking appetising rather than bitty. Spread the flour on a plate. Sprinkle it with the ginger, a good pinch of salt and eight turns of the pepper mill – if you have no pepper mill, substitute two pinches of pepper and buy one. Coat the meat lightly with the flour which, when you come to fry the pieces, will help them brown and provide a foundation for the sauce.

In a large frying pan, or cast-iron casserole, melt the butter in the oil and let them get hot. The oil stops the butter burning at the temperature it normally would. Fry the onion and carrot until they take on a colour. Remove them either to an ovenproof dish or onto a plate if you are cooking in a cast-iron pot.

Brown the meat carefully on all sides. This is an important step which, if done half-heartedly, will spoil the colour of the finished product. Don't cook for more than about 4 minutes, or the meat will begin to seize up. Take out the meat and add to the vegetables. Pour off any fat remaining in the pan before adding the Guinness or red wine and the soya sauce. Stir vigorously with a wooden spoon, scraping all the crusty bits off the bottom of the pan into the liquid. Bring to the boil. Pour onto the meat and vegetables (or return them to the pan). Add the garlic cloves which you have flattened with the blade of a knife, and the orange rind. This flavour gives a lift to the stew and blends with beef particularly well. Tangerine rind works too.

Cover the casserole and place in the oven, and leave to cook for 3–4 hours. Or part cook it one day and finish the next. If the liquid is at all copious when you come to serve the dish, pour it off and boil vigorously to reduce. The meat should not be swimming – just lying back – in the sauce. Taste the sauce and add more salt or pepper or perhaps a pinch of sugar if you have cooked with a ropey red wine. Pour back on the meat.

Triangles of fried bread are an easy and appropriate accompaniment to beef stew – or any stew – as they provide a desirable crunch.

To Fry Bread: Cut slices diagonally to give two large triangles and then cut each in half again so that one slice of bread gives you four triangles. Heat 1 tablespoonful of vegetable oil plus 1 tablespoonful butter in a frying pan until hot but not smoking. Lay in as many slices of bread as the pan will accommodate. Fry until they are brown and crisp on the base (lift up to look), turn over and fry the other side. Drain on kitchen paper.

STEAK TARTARE

Abandoned men do not feel threatened by mince. It is agreeably malleable and requires no cutting or trimming. It also doesn't resemble the beast from whence it came.

An ideal meal for two, or even one, poor pet, is Steak Tartare. It is important that this is made from high quality beef with little fat, and if there is no mincer or food processor in the house, the best tactic is to buy porterhouse, rump or sirloin steak. Having thus pleased the butcher by your largesse, ask him to mince it. Then proceed as follows.

Serves 2 as a main course, 4 as a first course

8 oz/250 g minced or finely chopped (e.g. in a food processor) steak
1 small onion or 2 shallots, very finely chopped
1 dessertspoon capers

3–4 anchovy fillets
Worcestershire sauce or Tabasco
1 tablespoon olive oil
salt and pepper
egg yolks (optional)

There are two approaches to this. One is to serve a patty of the raw
chopped meat for each person with, alongside, small mounds of finely-
chopped onions, capers and anchovies; the oil, Worcestershire sauce or
Tabasco and seasoning should be close by. Each person mixes up the
meat according to preference. The other approach is to do the mixing
first. One school of thought is that steak tartare is raw meat and should
taste of meat. Another attempts to disguise that stark fact.

Therefore, for a main course, it is probably better served on a D.I.Y.
basis. For a first course, mix it first, going easy on the capers which can
be overwhelming.

Steak tartare is often served with a raw egg nestling on top, but we
think olive oil in the mixture is preferable and would make the heart beat
a little more healthily. Black bread goes well with the dish.

HAMBURGERS CHIC OR CHILDISH

Less marvellous mince can be turned into hamburgers which, made
according to the following method incorporating a tip known so far only
to few, can be served to adults and children with equal success.
Children, conditioned by fast food chains, will stipulate a sesame seed
bun. Others might prefer the simple pan sauce described below.

Serves 4

1 lb/500 g minced beef	*pepper*
1 egg yolk	*coarse sea salt*
1 large onion, finely chopped (optional)	

Mix the meat with the egg yolk, onion if you fancy it, and pepper – but
no salt. Shape the mixture into four or six patties depending on the
thickness preferred. Sprinkle sea salt generously into a thick-bottomed
frying pan, preferably made of iron. When the pan is hot and the salt
practically jumping, sear the hamburgers on both sides. You need no fat
in the pan. A tasty crust will form, a pleasing contrast to the yielding, and
if you like it that way, slightly rare centre. Children usually prefer the
hamburgers cooked further to a consistent grey/brown.

Serve the burgers in a bun or make a sauce as follows: clean out the
excess salt from the pan but leave the juices which will have come from
the burgers. Shake in a teaspoonful of plain flour and stir around quickly

until it browns. Add single or double cream and stir until you have a pale brown sauce. Taste for seasoning and serve separately. You may also use soured cream or, if on a health kick, yoghurt.

KIDNEYS EN PYJAMA

Kidneys en Pyjama is absurdly simple and the name will find favour with a lonely chap. By now the butcher should have become a friend and can be persuaded to rip kidneys still encased in their suet (fat) from lamb carcasses. If not, this dish requires not so much skill in preparation as in shopping, since kidneys in their suet are not available everywhere.

Serves 2

4 even-sized potatoes, not too large   *Dijon mustard*
a little oil   *salt and pepper*
4 lamb's kidneys encased in their own fat

Turn on the oven to 200°C/400°F, Gas 6.

Wash the potatoes, dry them, rub them with a little oil and sprinkle them with salt. Put them on the middle shelf of the oven, two on each side. Put the kidneys in their fat in a baking tin and place it on the same shelf in the oven. Leave for 1 hour.

Trim any remaining fat away from the kidneys which are now perfectly cooked, having been self-basted throughout the hour. Split open the potatoes, or take a slice off the top of each one and scoop out a hole. Place a teaspoonful of Dijon mustard, then a kidney in each potato. Add a dribble of the hot fat, a little salt and pepper, and serve.

BAKED POTATOES WITH SOURED CREAM AND CAVIAR

If you only have potatoes in the house, buy a jar of Danish lumpfish roe (or caviar if you can run to it) at the late-night delicatessen, plus a carton of soured cream. Bake the potatoes as in Kidneys en Pyjama and, when cooked, split them open and serve with the soured cream, caviar and perhaps a small jug of melted butter; a seductive meal.

SALAD DRESSING

The problem of serving vegetables with a meal, which involves feats of timing that the newcomer cook might shy from, can be avoided by serving a salad. A mixture of green leaves is both the simplest and the nicest – forget those terrible English salads with tomato quarters, beetroot, cucumber and hard-boiled egg jostling one another in the bowl – but it stands or falls on its dressing. A vinaigrette should be freshly made, not shaken in a bottle like a can of emulsion paint. It will taste subtly different every time but that is only an advantage.

It is worth purchasing the best ingredients: extra virgin olive oil, wine vinegar, sea salt, freshly-ground pepper. The ratio of oil to vinegar should be about 4 or 5 to 1 and it is best to dissolve the salt first in the vinegar before stirring in the oil. Crushed garlic, powdered mustard and fresh herbs can be added to taste. Dress the salad just before it is to be eaten.

OMELETTE SOUFFLE AU GRAND MARNIER

It is unlikely that an abandoned man, having managed to make one or two courses, will feel like making dessert. It is possible nowadays to buy exotic fruits, excellent sorbets and reasonably good patisserie that will stand in. However, if the meal itself has been purchased at the delicatessen and has been served cold, the following will redeem any flatness. It is a culinary ace up a man's sleeve.

Serves 2

2 eggs
2 heaped dessertspoons caster sugar

2 tablespoons Grand Marnier (or other liqueur)
½ oz/15 g butter

Separate the eggs, putting the yolks in one medium-sized bowl, the whites in another. Add the sugar to the yolks and mix well. Stir in the Grand Marnier. This can be done before dinner. Just before you want to eat dessert, whisk the egg whites until they stand in peaks. Fold in the yolk mixture. Heat the butter in an omelette pan until it is foaming, then pour in the egg mixture and, after a few minutes, attempt to turn the whole thing over. It won't work but that doesn't matter. It simply gives more delicious crisp sugary cooked brown surface to eat. Wait another minute or two and serve.

7 After-Theatre Supper

Because most plays, concerts or operas start at a time that makes it impossible, or anyway unappealing, to eat beforehand, there is nearly always a moment when, during a dull monologue or less than perfectly sung aria, your thoughts turn to food. When they do, it is comforting to know that something has been prepared; that you are not reliant on restaurants which are invariably hazardous late in the evening. Also, should the performance give rise to combative discussion, as all good performances should, then it is helpful to be at home where no waiter is going to interrupt your most trenchant observation with 'Who's the vichysoisse?'; for a waiter's timing in this respect is always perfect.

Back home, hungry and thirsty, it is possible to have a drink instantaneously and with the first course ready and waiting, to eat fairly immediately, two conditions restaurants frequently fail to fulfil. You, the host, will not want at this point to tie on a pinny and start flurrying around, so it is vital that, apart from easy tasks like heating a soup or grilling a brochette, the work is all done.

Supper is a word we use advisedly. Even though you have been deprived of food, if not drink, for the past three hours or so, it is late and would be a mistake to consume a heavy dinner. The least appetising after-theatre meal we know was one of roast beef and Yorkshire pudding timed to be perfect at approximately the end of Act Two. By the time the play was over and the members of the party had taken themselves across London to eat it, stern dry meat and rigid batter was the none too festive greeting.

The recipes below have been designed as menus: the one with Kedgeree more suited to winter, the one featuring Cold Turbot composed with summer in mind.

There are also suggestions for simply an array of dishes, similar to a Greek or Middle Eastern *meze*, from which people can help themselves as they wish. We feel that this is a particularly agreeable form of eating. It promotes relaxation and strolling. When you have been sitting, pinned to your seat for some time, you do not wish to be stuck with what may well turn out to be another drama, albeit a domestic one. Also, the sight of a spread of food is a cheering one. With the help of a food processor, it is now easy to make interesting dips and also items like fish pâté. The recipes for a *meze* in this chapter can be embellished with Humus from BUDGET DINNER PARTY and practically any of the salads listed in the index. Chicken Wings, vigorously seasoned, then fried or grilled, can be prepared at the last minute and are a welcome hot addition.

Naturally, the ideas contained in this chapter are equally well suited to other forms of entertaining, but the concept of an after-theatre supper or, indeed, an after-cinema supper, seems an important one to sustain and promote. With the ticket prices the way they are, it makes an evening of entertainment and eating financially conceivable. Making a meal is also a welcome way of rewarding the purchaser of the tickets.

Borscht

Grilled Peppers

Ceviche

Kedgeree

Turbot with a Mild Aioli

Brochette of Lamb's Kidneys and
  Chorizo Sausage

Barley Salad

Fennel, Radish and Cress Salad

Fruit Tart

Black Treacle Jelly with Cream

Apple Purée

Ideas for a Meze:

Dolmades

Tabbouleh

Queensberry's Cod's Roe Pâté

Aubergine Pâté

Green Bean Salad

Tomato Salad

Fruit Kebab

BORSCHT

Serves 6

1 lb/500 g uncooked beetroot – it is best
   if you can procure them with the
   leaves on – peeled
2 onions
2 large tomatoes, skinned
2 carrots
2 stalks celery
1 lemon

3 pints/1.8 litres beef stock (if you can
   make your own stock from shin of beef,
   this is desirable; failing that, you can
   make an acceptable soup with beef
   cubes)
a little wine vinegar
salt and pepper
8 fl oz/250 ml soured cream

Clean and dice all the vegetables. Prick the lemon all over with a fork, then put the vegetables and lemon in a pan with the stock and simmer until cooked. Pass through a mouli or liquidise. Add the vinegar, salt and pepper to taste. Chill. Serve with a large dollop of soured cream on top.

GRILLED PEPPERS

If you are making this dish as the only hors d'oeuvre, you will need one large pepper per person; if you are using it as part of an array of hors d'oeuvre dishes, half a pepper per person would do.

Serves 6

3 large peppers – one of each colour
   would look prettiest
2 tablespoons olive oil
1 tablespoon tarragon vinegar

½ teaspoon salt
½ teaspoon sugar
freshly-ground black pepper
fresh parsley

Quarter the peppers and remove all the seeds. Flatten the strips even if this means slightly breaking them. Put the strips, skin side up, under a hot grill, and grill until they are black and blistering. Then skin the peppers carefully. You may need to return odd pieces to the grill, so don't turn it off.

Arrange the peppers in a flat dish and pour over them the amalgamated mixture of oil, vinegar, salt, sugar and black pepper. Garnish with parsley. This is good eaten with hot pitta bread or crisp french rolls.

CEVICHE

The main point of this recipe is that the fish should be as fresh as possible.
Monkfish, turbot, halibut, even fresh haddock or cod can be used.

Serves 2

2 fresh green chillies
1 small piece of fresh root ginger
4 limes (if unavailable, use 3 lemons)
1 onion
8 oz/250 g white fish (see above)

1 tablespoon olive oil
a small pinch of cayenne pepper
1 good sprig fresh coriander (optional, but
    nice if you can get it)
salt and freshly-ground black pepper

First of all, prepare the vegetables. De-seed the chillies and cut them into
strips like matchsticks, only thinner; cut the root of ginger in a similar way.
The rind of the limes or lemons should also be cut into matchsticks, and
the juice squeezed. The onion should be very finely chopped.

Put the fish with all these prepared ingredients in a shallow dish,
together with the oil, cayenne and finely chopped coriander. Leave in a
cool place for at least 3 hours, turning the fish occasionally. It should
end up looking milky – as though you had cooked it.

Before serving, season with salt and black pepper.

KEDGEREE

Kedgeree, the anglicised version of the Indian dish of rice and lentils
called *khichri*, is altogether an amenable dish. The constituent parts can
be prepared some time before assembling and, once assembled, the dish
can be cooled and then successfully re-heated in a double saucepan. For
the purposes of after-theatre eating, it would be a good idea to hard-boil
the eggs while you are heating up the otherwise completed kedgeree,
then chop them and scatter on just before serving. Try to buy Finnan
haddock on the bone; it is infinitely preferable to the dyed fillets.

Serves 4–6

12 oz/375 g smoked haddock
milk to cover the fish (approx.
    1 pint/625 ml)
8 oz/250 g rice (preferably Basmati)
1 tablespoon vegetable oil

2 oz/60 g butter
2 onions, peeled and thinly sliced
1 dessertspoon ground turmeric
salt and freshly-ground black pepper
3 eggs, hard-boiled

Turn on the oven to 180°C/350°F, Gas Mark 4.

Put the haddock in an ovenproof dish, add enough milk to come level with the top surface of the fish and cook for about 20 minutes, until the fish flakes easily. Strain off and reserve the fish-flavoured milk, then remove the skin and bones. Cook the rice using your preferred method. In the oil and butter, fry the onions until golden. Add the turmeric, season and cook gently, stirring, for a few minutes.

Add the haddock and rice, and season; mix gently until the rice is coloured a rich saffron yellow. Use some of the milk to moisten the mixture and more butter if you want richness. Taste for seasoning and be generous with the pepper. Scatter the dish with chopped hard-boiled eggs.

TURBOT WITH A MILD AIOLI

Serves 6

2 lb/1 kg turbot or *other firm white fish (haddock is very good)*

3 shallots or *a bunch of spring onions*
½ cauliflower

Court bouillon:

1 onion
1 lemon
1 large carrot

1 bay leaf
8 peppercorns
1 glass white wine

Aioli:

1 fat clove garlic (or more depending on preference)
2 egg yolks

½–¾ pint/300–475 ml oil – half olive and half vegetable
salt and pepper
lemon juice

In a pan large enough to hold the turbot in one piece, put the court bouillon ingredients. Put in the trimmed fish, and add cold water until the fish is covered, just. Bring the pan slowly to the boil and when it has reached boiling point, give it one or two definite bubbles, cover the pan and turn off the heat. Let the fish become completely cold in its liquid by which time it should be perfectly cooked.

Make the aioli by mixing the crushed garlic into the egg yolks. Slowly start to add oil, mixing with a wooden spoon. As each bit of oil is incorporated, add some more. When you have a definite stable-looking emulsion you can add the oil with a freer hand. Season with salt, pepper and lemon juice.

Flake the fish and fold it into the mayonnaise with the shallots which should have been peeled and finely sliced into crescents (or the spring onions, cleaned and chopped) and sprigs of cauliflower which should have been boiled for no more than 4 minutes. Pile the mixture into a pretty dish. The recipe given for Grilled Peppers (*see* page 81) goes well with this dish.

BROCHETTE OF LAMB'S KIDNEYS WITH CHORIZO SAUSAGE

This recipe was invented for a barbecue, but it works almost as well using a domestic grill the richness of the *chorizo*; (a spicy paprika-red Spanish sausage available in delicatessens) offsetting the compact quality of kidneys. Assemble the dish on stainless steel or wooden skewers and grill when you return from the theatre.

Serves 4–6

8–10 lamb's kidneys	*8–16 fresh sage leaves* or, *if*
1 lb/500 g chorizo sausage	*unobtainable, 8 bay leaves*
1 Spanish onion or *3 shallots*	*vegetable oil*
	salt and freshly-ground black pepper

Chop the kidneys into three and remove any gristle and the hard core. Chop the sausages into lengths slightly shorter than 1 inch/2.5 cm. Peel the onion or shallots, quarter and separate the layers so you have pieces roughly the size of the meat. Thread the skewers alternating the kidneys and sausage and interspersing them with onion and the occasional sage or bay leaf. Dribble oil rather scantily onto them.

When the time comes for the main course, grill the skewers fiercely, for a total time of about 8 minutes, turning frequently. Season with salt and pepper.

Serve with Barley Salad (*see* next recipe) and lemon quarters to squeeze over.

BARLEY SALAD

Victor Gordon, author of *The English Cookbook*, is keen to revive the use of barley in forms other than barley water. It has a good taste, a distinctive texture and is full of goodness. The snag about barley is the cooking time needed. A pressure cooker can reduce it or you can blanch it with three successive kettles of boiling water, allowing it to soak 3 minutes in each water before being drained ready for the next. This is Victor Gordon's recipe.

Serves 4–6

7 oz/200 g pot barley
4 tablespoons olive oil
4 tablespoons sunflower seed oil

salt and freshly-ground black pepper
4 tablespoons chopped parsley
4 spring onions or *2 shallots*
lemon juice to taste

Boil the barley in salted water – it could take up to 3 hours without the blanching described above. Take it off the heat when it is yielding, but still slightly *al dente*. Drain it patiently, removing as much water as the absorbent cereal will allow.

Put the barley into a salad bowl. While it is still hot, add the oils, pepper and a little salt; mix well. When it has cooled down to tepid, add the parsley and chopped spring onions or shallots. When it is cold, add the lemon juice gradually, tasting until you have the right acidity. 'Much nicer than boring old rice salad, this stands comparison with the cracked wheat salads of Levantine cooking.'

FENNEL, RADISH AND CRESS SALAD

Serves 4–6

1 large fennel root
1 bunch radishes
1 tablespoon olive oil
juice of 1 lemon

½ teaspoon salt
pepper
2 boxes cress

Slice the fennel as thinly as possible, and trim and slice the radishes horizontally in thin rounds. Mix in a salad bowl with a dressing of oil, lemon juice, salt and pepper. Before serving, add the cress and toss the salad well.

FRUIT TART

Serves 4–6

5 oz/150 g butter
8 oz/250 g plain flour
salt
1 egg yolk

2 large cooking apples
4 large tablespoons apricot jam
juice of ½ lemon

Rub the butter into the flour thoroughly; add a pinch of salt. Make a well in the centre of the flour: mix a little water with the beaten egg yolk and add to the flour until you have a soft dough; you may not need all of the egg, so add it by degrees. Roll out the pastry and line a buttered 10-inch 25-cm tart tin or dish. Put this in the fridge for at least 2 hours.

Turn on the oven to 180°C/350°F, Gas 4. We find it better to bake the pastry blind, which means putting some butter beans on a piece of foil into the tart to hold down the centre of the pastry. Bake until the tart is a pale biscuit colour, then take out and cool, turn off the oven. While it is baking, you can prepare the fruit.

We are suggesting apples because they are obtainable all the year round, but of course a wide variety of fruit could be used.

Peel, core and quarter the apples and then cut them into thin slices and lay between two damp cloths. Do use a stainless steel knife for this.

Make the apricot glaze as follows: put the jam with 2½ fl oz/75 ml water into a pan, bring gently to the boil and cook for 5 minutes. Add the lemon juice, stir and cook again until the glaze just drops from the spoon. When the tart is cool, remove the butter beans, and paint glaze all over the bottom of the pastry; this helps to prevent the juice from the fruit soaking into the pastry.

Turn on the oven to 150°C/300°F, Gas 2. Lay the apple pieces slightly overlapping round and round until you have entirely covered the tart. Paint generously with more glaze and return to the oven for about 20 minutes. Serve cold.

BLACK TREACLE JELLY WITH CREAM

Serves 4–6

4 oz/125 g black treacle
2 lemons

¾ packet gelatine
½ pint whipped cream

Put the tin of treacle in a saucepan of boiling water so that it becomes easy to pour. Squeeze the lemons. Dissolve the gelatine in a bowl with a little hot water, stirring it with a fork until it is thoroughly melted. Pour black treacle into a pint jug, add the strained lemon juice, gelatine and as much hot water as necessary to fill the jug. Stir the mixture well and pour into a shallow dish and, when cool, put into the fridge.

Serve with whipped cream.

APPLE PUREE

This is a very simple pudding, but light and refreshing.

Serves 4–6

2 lb/1 kg cooking apples	*3 oz/90 g unsalted butter*
3 oz/90 g brown sugar	*a pinch of ground cinnamon*

Peel, quarter and core the apples, making sure that there is no core left. Put the quarters into an enamel pan with about 2 tablespoonsful of water – just enough to stop them sticking before they start to exude their own juice – and the sugar. Stew very gently until soft. Then add the butter and let it melt into the purée, and finally add the pinch of cinnamon.

Put the purée into a large bowl and beat with an egg whisk until smooth. (You can put it in the food processor, but the texture is mysteriously not the same and, in our view, inferior.)

This should be eaten cold – with whipped cream or yoghurt if liked.

IDEAS FOR A MEZE

DOLMADES

This can either be absolutely delicious or taste like a wet school mackintosh down which school lunch has dribbled. To achieve the first effect, you need either fresh young vine leaves or small ones put up in brine or tins, good olive oil, fresh lemon juice, pine kernels and no meat in the mixture. We are adamant on that point.

The quantities below would serve 8–10 people as part of a buffet, but dolmades keep well and are hardly worth making in a small quantity.

olive oil
2 large onions, peeled and chopped
6 oz/180 g Basmati rice
2 oz/60 g pine kernels
a handful of currants

parsley, chopped
a few fresh mint leaves
salt and freshly-ground black pepper
30 vine leaves
2 lemons

In about 4 tablespoonsful olive oil, gently fry the chopped onion until soft and slightly tinged with colour. Wash the rice, swirling it round to float off any starch. Drain and add to the onions, stirring it round until it glistens. Add a cup of water, the pine kernels and currants and bring to the boil. Simmer gently until the water is absorbed. It is not necessary for the rice to be completely cooked. Mix in a handful of finely-chopped parsley and a few mint leaves, chopped. Season with salt and pepper, and allow to cool.

If you are using tinned or packet vine leaves, rinse them well and blanch for 5 minutes in boiling water. If you have fresh leaves, cut out the hard part of the stalk and blanch in boiling water for at least 5 minutes. Drain them on tea towels.

Lay a spoonful of stuffing near the base of a leaf. Fold in the sides and roll into a neat parcel, but not too tight as the rice will swell in the cooking. Squeeze the parcel gently in your hand to seal the envelope. Put any spare leaves in the bottom of a large shallow pan with a lid. Place the stuffed leaves on top with the join of the parcels downwards. Pour on 4 tablespoonsful olive oil, the juice of 1 lemon and enough water to bring the liquid level with the dolmades. Weight them down with a plate and simmer with the lid on gently for about 1 hour, checking from time to time that they have not dried out, but you should end up with the water absorbed and the little parcels shining with oil.

Cool and then remove carefully to a large pretty plate, and if you think they need more lemon, squeeze on the juice of the other lemon.

TABBOULEH

This Middle Eastern dish actually improves by being made some time ahead, as it gives time for the flavours to permeate the bulghur (sometimes called burgul, but otherwise known as cracked wheat). It is important to use the kind that looks like tiny grains and not an English variety that is flaky. Good delicatessens and health food shops will stock it. It is one of these gratifying dishes that is both good for you – think of the iron and vitamin C in the parsley – and delicious.

Serves 4–6

4 oz/125 g bulghur
1 bunch spring onions, cleaned and finely chopped
2 large tomatoes, skinned, de-seeded and finely chopped
3 tablespoons finely chopped fresh mint, (use less mint if dried)

3 oz/90 g fresh parsley, washed and finely chopped
3 tablespoons lemon juice
3 tablespoons olive oil
salt and freshly-ground black pepper
crisp lettuce leaves or *radicchio for serving*

Pour cold water onto the bulghur and leave to soak for 20 minutes. Drain in a sieve and then squeeze with your hands to remove the water completely. Put in a bowl, add the spring onions and mix very thoroughly, crushing the onions slightly. Add the chopped tomato, mint, parsley, lemon juice, oil and salt and pepper to taste. Mix and try a spoonful to see if you wish to emphasise any flavour.

Serve heaped onto a pretty dish with the lettuce leaves served alongside to be used as scoops or wraps.

QUEENSBERRY'S COD'S ROE PATE

The Marquis of Queensberry evolved this recipe and it is far superior to most of the pink emulsions that go by the name of taramasalata. The important point is that the roe should be mixed with a fork and not in a food processor, which breaks up the eggs and creates a paste. Serve it, as they do at Green's Champagne Bar & Restaurant in London's Duke Street, St James's, in white china egg cups with triangles of brown toast alongside and a lemon section for squeezing on.

Serves 4

8 oz/250 g moist smoked cod's roe (bought as a piece)
3 fl oz/90 ml high quality olive oil

fresh lemon juice
freshly-ground black pepper

Scrape the roe from its skin and membrane using a sharp little teaspoon. Discard any hard pieces. Put the roe into a bowl and add the oil slowly, mixing all the while with a fork. Squeeze in lemon juice to taste and add a good deal of freshly ground black pepper, but no salt.

AUBERGINE PATE

Serves 6

2 large aubergines
1 clove garlic
1 medium-sized onion
1 tablespoon chopped parsley

3 tablespoons olive oil
juice of 1 lemon
salt and pepper

Bake or grill the aubergines until soft – about half an hour. Then scoop out the insides and combine the flesh in the food processor with the other ingredients. Put into shallow bowls.

GREEN BEAN SALAD

Serves 6

1½ lb/750 g french beans (the younger
    and smaller, the better)

Dressing:

2 teaspoons caster sugar
1 teaspoon mustard powder
1 teaspoon salt
black pepper

1 small clove garlic, crushed
1 tablespoon tarragon vinegar
3 tablespoons best olive oil

Make the dressing first so that it has time to dissolve and settle. Mix all the dry ingredients and garlic with the vinegar. Then add the oil and mix very thoroughly.

Tail the beans but leave them whole. If you have a big enough steamer, this is the best way to cook them. If not, put them into a pan one-third full of boiling salted water and boil gently until the beans are just *al dente*. Drain thoroughly and then put into a serving bowl. Let them cool a little, but while they are still warm, pour over the dressing to which you have given a last minute stir, and mix well.

The garlic can be omitted if it is unpopular, but this would be a pity.

TOMATO SALAD

This is a simple dish, but it is often so carelessly made that its pleasure is spoilt. We know that tomatoes have largely lost their personality, but occasionally it is possible to come across a variety that has some taste left. If you feel as gloomy as we do about the likelihood of this, here is a way to make them taste slightly more.

Blanch tomatoes first by dropping into boiling water for 1 minute. Tomato skins are utterly indigestible. When you have skinned them, cut them in fine slices with a serrated knife, keeping all the juice that runs out. Lay the slices in a flattish dish; sprinkle with a pinch of salt and rather more caster sugar and leave them for an hour or two. Meanwhile, mix one part vinegar to two parts of olive oil, add sugar and salt and generous screwings of black pepper. Add any juice left from the cutting and pour over the dressing. If you have chives, cut a large bunch into small pieces and scatter thickly. If you don't have chives, use 2 or 3 spring onions chopped very finely.

Before serving, baste the tomatoes with the dressing and the extra juice that they will have made.

FRUIT KEBAB

Because you are making these in advance, sprinkle them lavishly with lemon or lime juice and wrap the dish you lay them on in cling film, tightly sealed. Chill in the refrigerator. The fruit you use will depend on what is in season, so the recipe below is a guideline only. Currants or pomegranate seeds can punctuate the skewers and the more exotic the fruit, usually the better. Slender wooden skewers, the kind sold for satay, are the best.

Serves 4–6

½ pineapple
1 apple or *1 pear*
1 small bunch grapes
½ melon, shaped into balls or cubes
1 mango

8 oz/250 g strawberries
2 kiwi fruit, peeled and thinly sliced
1 starfruit, thinly sliced
fresh lemon juice or *lime juice*

Should you want to flame the kebabs:

granulated sugar

2 tablespoons Cognac or *Grand Marnier* or *other fruit-based alcohol*

Prepare the fruit in pieces as much the same size as possible, but using the grapes whole – or halved if they have big seeds – and strawberries whole or halved depending on size. Thread a selection of fruit onto each skewer. Sprinkle with lemon or lime juice, paying special attention to apple or any fruit that discolours in contact with oxygen. Cover with cling film and chill until needed.

If you want to flame the kebabs, sprinkle them with granulated sugar, and turn them quickly under a hot grill. Heat your chosen alcohol in a small pan. Pour onto the hot kebabs which have been arranged on a serving dish. Take quickly to the table and set the alcohol alight.

————————

8 Weekend Entertaining

The secret to successful weekend entertaining that does not leave you a wreck is *planning*. You really need to design all your menus on Wednesday so that you can shop either that day or on Thursday. If you leave the planning until Thursday or Friday, you may find that you simply cannot get some vital ingredient, or you may have to spend a disproportionate amount of time searching for such items as pheasant or hare even when they are in season. Not finding them may throw everything else out. We have tried to present you with a choice that both covers the seasons and enables you to do most of the cooking before your guests arrive. This means that you will spend most of Friday in the kitchen (how much depending upon the number of your guests), but it should leave you free to enjoy them when they *do* arrive.

The most relaxed way of dealing with breakfast is to have all ingredients for it laid out, and then to let guests boil themselves eggs if they want to and make toast as they require it. Home-made muesli and yoghurt, a large bowl of fresh fruit, a choice of jam and marmalade, coffee and various teas will do very well, but if you feel that a hot breakfast dish is *de rigueur*, you could make the Kedgeree from our AFTER-THEATRE SUPPER section.

Unless the weather is icy, we think a simple and light lunch is desirable: one main course followed by salads and a good cheese board. Dinner can then be the main thrust. A point about dinner is how many you are expected to provide. We think of weekends as beginning on Friday evening and ending some time on Sunday, but it is important to find out whether your guests intend staying for Sunday night supper or not. Whichever they do can turn out to be tiresome if you aren't prepared for it.

If guests are bringing children, it is advisable to keep some emergency food in the fridge or freezer. If they are too young for grown-up dinner you may, in any case, be giving them a separate, earlier supper. Food that is generally popular with children includes pasta, sausages, fish fingers, ham, hamburgers, cheese, bananas, ice-cream – all easy things to have available.

A word must be said about tea – the afternoon meal that used to be an integral part of English life, lurched out of fashion and is now creeping back. The less people have tea in their ordinary lives, the more they seem to love waking with a start from an afternoon snooze over the Sunday papers and finding themselves ambushed by a tea trolley reeking of hot crumpets and chocolate cake. If afternoon tea *happens* to people, they put up little or no fight, and *all* children need a good shot of carbohydrates by late afternoon. We have provided for this in the menu.

But food is not the only weapon in the armoury of the successful weekend entertainer. Comfort, enough privacy and freedom to choose how guests will spend their time are all important attributes. Remember that other people's houses nearly always seem colder than your own, so provide flexible warmth accordingly. Bedrooms and bathrooms should be places that can be lingered in. Electric blankets are one of the cheapest luxuries available. Do sleep occasionally in the spare room beds: if you find you have spent the night at what feels like the bottom of the Grand Canyon, or perched upon some padded toast-rack, it is time you got some new mattresses. Proper reading lights are also a priority. Our test is that you should be able to read a wartime Penguin in bed without strain. If you can't, then change the lighting. It is also deeply depressing for guests to open wardrobes and find them full of clothes you haven't yet sent to Oxfam. Some space and some decent coat hangers should be provided.

Do not have a lavatory whose flushing practices are so wilfully eccentric as to require desperate handwritten notices. Have it mended. Curtains should draw, taps should turn off; in fact, things should work in spare rooms much as you would expect them to do in the rest of the house. There is also a curious myth perpetrated by some hostesses to the effect that if you are only staying two nights in a place, you will need a much smaller bath towel and will hardly notice nylon sheets and pillows, the latter seemingly stuffed with an uninviting mixture of rubber and straw, and blankets better suited to a horse. Also, people over sixty tend to loathe duvets – it is kind to provide an alternative.

Apart from creature comforts, it is desirable to provide varied and good reading matter, flowers – even the tiniest vase with a few sprigs can give great pleasure – a bottle of water and glasses. Tins of biscuits are optional, but if you provide them, do *change* them at regular intervals.

Generally speaking, there are two aims about having people to stay – your enjoyment and theirs, but as these are remarkably interdependent, here for your side of it are a few stones you can turn.

Smoked Trout Pâté
Celeriac Remoulade with Anchovy
  Toasts
Egg and Spinach Pie
Chinese Noodle Salad
Crab Mousse
Fish Kebabs
Beth's Shepherd's Pie
Normandy Pheasant
Jugged Hare

Raj Chicken Curry
Bread and Butter Pudding
Toffee Sponge Pudding
Winter Fruit Salad
Brown Bread Ice-Cream
Mary Coventry's Coffee Cake
Panscones
Making Yoghurt
Muesli
Shipdham Marmalade

SMOKED TROUT PATE

Serves 4–6

2 smoked trout
4 oz/125 g unsalted cream cheese

juice of 2 lemons
freshly-ground black pepper

Take all the flesh from the trout and put into a liquidiser with the cream cheese and lemon juice. Season with freshly-ground black pepper.

This very simple pâté should be made at least 24 hours before it is to be eaten.

CELERIAC REMOULADE WITH ANCHOVY TOASTS

Some cookery books tell you to blanch grated raw celeriac, but in our experience, the only result of this is a subsequent watering down of the mayonnaise. What is important is to mix the celeriac into the mayonnaise immediately after the grating, to avoid it taking on a brown hue. The spirited flavour of anchovy toasts complements the creaminess of the celeriac well.

Serves 4

1 large celeriac

For the mayonnaise:

2 egg yolks
vegetable oil
2 dessertspoons Dijon mustard

a squeeze of lemon juice
salt and pepper

For the anchovy toasts:

1 tin anchovies
butter

slices of bread

Make the mayonnaise (a blender or food processor speeds things up) by dribbling the oil onto the well-beaten egg yolks until the emulsion thickens. Flavour it strongly with mustard, a splash of lemon juice, and salt and pepper.

Peel and then grate the celeriac and mix with the mayonnaise immediately, giving it no time to discolour. Taste and adjust the seasoning if necessary.

Mash 3 or 4 anchovies into about 2 oz/60 g butter. Toast slices of bread on one side, spread the untoasted side with the anchovy butter and put, anchovy butter-side up, under the grill until the butter is melted and the bread crisp. Cut into fingers and serve with the celeriac.

EGG AND SPINACH PIE

Serves 6

12 oz/375 g shortcrust pastry (see page 86)
1½ lb/750 g spinach
1 large sweet onion

1 tablespoon sunflower seed oil
12 oz/375 g Ricotta cheese
salt and pepper
6 eggs

For this dish you need a medium-sized pie dish of the kind that you would use for apple pie. Make the pastry, then reserving one-third for the top of the pie, line the bottom and sides of the pie dish and put it in the fridge.

Turn on the oven to 180°C/350°F, Gas 4.

Wash the spinach and cook it in the water that clings to the washed leaves. Chop it well, drain and leave to cool in a large bowl. Fry the peeled and finely chopped onion in oil until it is beginning to go brown. Mix the Ricotta cheese into the spinach, adding some salt and pepper. When thoroughly mixed, add the fried onion.

Now put this mixture into the pie dish, and in the mixture make 6 fairly deep indentations with your knuckles; each must be deep enough to accommodate an egg. Carefully break each egg into position. Roll out the remaining pastry fairly thinly and place on top of the pie. Score the pastry with a knife to mark the position of the eggs; each person should get one.

Bake in the oven for 25 minutes and serve hot.

CHINESE NOODLE SALAD

It is important to find the right noodles for this dish. They are called bean thread noodles and are obtainable at an Oriental supermarket or grocer. They need no cooking, just boiling water poured onto them. They will turn soft and transparent and have a unique slippery, sensual texture. They make a perfect summer dish.

Arrange the various garnishes to look aesthetically pleasing on top of the noodles and mix only at the time of serving. When you are in the Chinese supermarket, try to find a pack of wind-dried sausages, as their aniseedy flavour adds a special piquancy to the mixture.

Serves 4–6

8 oz/250 g bean thread noodles
1 dessertspoon sesame seed oil or
    vegetable oil
2 oz/60 g dried Chinese mushrooms
1 bunch spring onions
½ cucumber

8 oz/250 g cooked chicken, cut into fine
    strips or 8 oz/250 g steamed prawns,
    finely sliced or 4 Chinese wind-dried
    sausages, sliced on the diagonal and
    steamed or a combination of these

For the sauce:

2½ tablespoons soya sauce
1 tablespoon wine vinegar
1 tablespoon peanut butter
2 teaspoons sugar
1 teaspoon chilli oil

1 tablespoon dry sherry
2 tablespoons vegetable oil
1 fat clove garlic, finely chopped
salt and freshly-ground black pepper

Put the noodles into a large bowl and cover them with boiling water. Leave them for 5 minutes until they are soft and translucent. Drain well and toss in the sesame oil. Soak the dried mushrooms in hot water for 15–20 minutes or until they are tender; drain and cut into thin strips. Clean the spring onions and slice finely lengthways. Cut the cucumber into matchsticks. Prepare your chosen protein, but if using the sausage, steam it close to the time of serving.

Mix together the ingredients for the sauce, then toss the noodles in half the sauce and arrange them on a large flat serving dish. Place heaps of the garnish on top of the noodles and bring to the table in this manner. At the moment of serving, toss everything together with the remaining sauce.

CRAB MOUSSE

Serves 4–6

1 lb/500 g crabmeat
¾ pint/475 ml fish aspic (see below)
2 tablespoons mayonnaise
2 tablespoons double cream

1 teaspoon curry powder
1 teaspoon tomato purée
1 tablespoon lemon juice

Fish Aspic:

It is much better to make the fish aspic yourself and it's not at all difficult. Ask your fishmonger for the fish trimmings and you can also add the peelings from prawns if you happen to be using them for something else.

1 lb/500 g fish trimmings and scraps	*2 bay leaves*
¼ pint/150 ml white wine	*1 sprig of thyme*
1 onion	*2 sprigs of parsley*
1 carrot	*½ oz/15 g gelatine*

Put everything for the fish aspic except the gelatine into a pan together with 1¾ pints/1 litre water, and bring slowly to the boil. Simmer for 20 minutes, strain through muslin and return to the pan. Boil to reduce to ¾ pint.

Melt the gelatine in a little of the hot fish stock, then stir this into the rest of the stock and leave in a separate bowl until it is beginning to set.

Mix the crabmeat very thoroughly in a bowl. Add the mayonnaise and double cream, then add the curry powder, tomato purée and finally the lemon juice.

Stir this into the crab mixture, and put into a lightly oiled mould or dish, and place it in the fridge. When it has set, you can turn it out and garnish it.

FISH KEBABS

Serves 6

2 lb/1 kg firm white fish: we think turbot, halibut or monkfish are particularly good	*3 peppers – ideally one each of yellow, red and green*
12 oz/375 g small button mushrooms	*24 bay leaves*
2 medium-sized onions	*¼ pint/150 ml olive oil*
8 oz/250 g streaky bacon, cut finely	*juice of 1 large lemon*
	1 tablespoon crushed coriander seeds
	salt and pepper

You need to prepare each ingredient and lay it on a separate dish. Allow 2 skewers per person.

Chop the fish into 1-inch/2.5 cm cubes or as near that as anatomy will allow. Wipe the mushrooms with a damp cloth and plunge them in boiling water for a minute (this helps to stop them splitting when you skewer them).

Peel the onions and then ease off their outer skins, cutting them into pieces slightly larger than your fish pieces. Cut the bacon in 1-inch/2.5-cm length pieces. Halve the peppers, remove all the seeds, and cut into pieces the same size as the onion.

Now, skewer a piece of onion, fish, bay leaf, mushroom and pepper, easing each piece along the skewer. Continue until the skewer is full.

Make a marinade with the oil, the lemon juice, the crushed coriander, salt and pepper and put this in a large shallow dish long enough to accommodate the skewers. Lay the kebabs in it and roll them over gently until everything is coated. The kebabs can be left like that in the fridge overnight.

Turn the kebabs in the marinade once more before you grill them. They will need turning once under the grill, and should be grilled just long enough to cook the fish – about 10 minutes.

BETH'S SHEPHERD'S PIE

The best shepherd's pie is made with minced raw lamb. You can, of course, use left-over cold meat – the original intention of the dish – but it is unlikely, these days, that one has a big enough joint to have a couple of pounds of left-overs. You could use beef, but it tends to go into little pellets in an oily sauce whilst lamb manages to keep its unctuousness to itself. The mint is an important ingredient, naturally suited to lamb.

Serves 6–8

4 oz/125 g bacon, finely chopped
1 tablespoon olive oil
2 large onions
3 carrots
4 stalks celery
3 cloves garlic
2 lb/1 kg minced raw lamb
4 fl oz/125 ml milk
1 14-oz/440 g tin tomatoes

1 dessertspoon dried oregano
1 teaspoon ground cinnamon
1 tablespoon Worcestershire sauce
1 tablespoon chopped fresh mint
2 lb/1 kg potatoes (cooked and mashed
   with milk and butter)
2 oz/60 g Cheddar or Gruyère cheese,
   grated

Fry the bacon gently until the fat runs, then add the olive oil. Clean and chop the onions, carrots and celery, or shred all three in a food processor. Sauté the vegetables and finely-chopped garlic in the oil until softened. Stir in the meat and brown it carefully. Next add the milk and let it bubble away. This is always a good tip with mince as it lends a desirable sweetness. Whizz the tomatoes in a liquidiser or food processor, and add them to the meat together with the seasonings.

Simmer everything gently on top of the stove or in the oven (set at 150°C/300°F Gas 2) for at least 1 hour, preferably longer, then turn into a pie dish. Cover with mashed potato, sprinkle with grated cheese and heat through in the oven (set at 200°C/400°F Gas 6), or under the grill if the meat and potatoes are still hot. You can, of course, make the pie in advance, chill or freeze it, and heat through when wanted.

NORMANDY PHEASANT

This simple method of cooking pheasant results in a silky, luxurious dish, the cream and the apples doing the work themselves in melting down into a sauce. A nice accompaniment would be puréed Jerusalem artichokes, enthusiastically seasoned with freshly ground black pepper. If you wish to avoid using quantities of double cream, substitute fromage blanc or petit-suisse for half the amount of cream. For greedy guests, allow one pheasant for two people, although the richness of this dish means that you should be able to stretch one bird to three.

Serves 6

2 oz/60 g butter
2 tablespoons oil
2 plump pheasants
4 dessert apples, peeled, cored and sliced
4 tablespoons Calvados or 1 pint/625 ml
  dry cider, reduced by vigorous boiling
  to 4 tablespoons

½ pint/300 ml double cream or ¼ pint/
  150 ml double cream plus a
  petit-suisse or some fromage blanc
salt and freshly-ground black pepper

Turn on the oven to 190°C/375°F, Gas 5.

In half the butter and the oil, sauté the trussed pheasants (without their pork back fat, if provided) until golden on all sides. Remove from the pan and in the remaining butter and other pan juices, gently fry the apple slices.

Find an earthenware casserole or similar ovenproof dish with a lid that will hold the pheasants quite snugly. Place the apples in the bottom, and the pheasants on top. Add the Calvados or cider to the pan juices, bubble them a minute or two and then pour them on the pheasant.

Cover and cook in the oven for about 30 minutes. Remove the casserole from the oven, and add the cream. Season with salt and freshly-ground black pepper. If you are wanting to use less cream for health reasons, do as the French do and put a petit-suisse cheese inside the bird and pour in the smaller amount of cream.

Take this opportunity to turn the pheasants over, i.e., breast-side down. Return the casserole to the oven for another 15 minutes.

Place the birds on a warmed serving dish. Stir the contents of the casserole until well amalgamated, reducing the sauce, if necessary, by boiling for added thickness. Pour it round the pheasants, and serve.

JUGGED HARE

When you buy the hare, the blood should be kept. A hare is often sold with a bag over its head into which the blood has dripped. If the hare has been frozen, it will be in a sealed bag and the blood should also be contained in the bag. In either case, reserve the blood carefully; it is essential for the sauce. A medium-sized hare will serve 6.

Joint the hare and place in a marinade made as follows:

Marinade:

1 tablespoon redcurrant jelly	*1 teaspoon thyme*
3 fl oz/90 ml mushroom ketchup	*2 bay leaves*
1 onion cut into thin slices	*2–3 sprigs bruised parsley*
3 fl oz/90 ml port	*½ teaspoon allspice*
3 fl oz/90 ml medium sherry	*6 bruised peppercorns*
3 fl oz/90 ml good olive oil	

Melt the redcurrant jelly in the ketchup and add to the other marinade ingredients. Put the hare pieces in the marinade and leave for 24 hours.

Then assemble the rest of the ingredients which are:

4 oz/125 g bacon or pork fat	*1 bouquet garni*
2 medium-sized onions peeled and stuck	*½ teaspoon sea salt*
with 4 cloves each	*juice of 1 lemon and 1 orange*
2 stalks celery, diced	*2 pints/1.1 litres stock*
2 carrots, scrubbed and sliced	*1 wine glass of port*
6 peppercorns	*1 tablespoon redcurrant jelly*
1 teaspoon allspice	

Turn on the oven to 150°C/300°F, Gas mark 2.

Dry the hare pieces and fry them in bacon fat until brown all over. Then put them into a deep casserole with the vegetables, spices, bouquet garni, salt and fruit juices. Cover with the stock, cover the casserole tightly and cook in the oven for about 3 hours, or until the hare is perfectly tender (the time will depend upon the age of the hare).

Take out the hare pieces and then the onions and other vegetables. Thicken the gravy with enough *beurre manié* (1 oz/30 g butter to ¾ oz/20 g flour kneaded together with a fork) until the gravy is like thin cream. Allow it to boil, then set aside.

Add spoonsful of the gravy by degrees to the retained blood, then pour it gently into the remaining gravy, add the port and redcurrant jelly. Taste for seasoning – adding salt, pepper, redcurrant jelly or port until you like the flavour: it should be very rich and smooth.

At this point, you can choose whether you will bone the hare or simply put the pieces into a fresh casserole and pour sauce through a strainer onto them. We favour boning, as this makes the eating much easier for your guests, but the classic method is to leave the pieces intact.

We suggest serving this with mashed potatoes or noodles.

RAJ CHICKEN CURRY

With the publication of dozens of Indian recipe books, the success of television programmes about cooking Indian food, and the increasing sophistication of Indian restaurants, there is probably not a soul left without an array of whole spices in the kitchen cupboard and some recipe in their head for their personal garam masala. Remember, though, when 'curry' meant a jolly good pinch of Vencat and 'exotic' meant adding apples and sultanas and 'condiments' meant sliced bananas, grated coconut and Green Label Mango Chutney? Don't you sometimes long for those uncomplicated days?

This recipe will stir fond memories in anyone over a certain age –who knows, maybe curry is still made this way in schools and canteens – and is ideal for weekend entertaining as it improves upon being re-heated; in fact, it should be made one day and served the next. Serve with it a large bowl of Basmati rice (*see* VEGETARIANS) and little bowls filled with cashew nuts, sliced bananas sprinkled with lemon juice, Bombay duck heated through in the oven, mango chutney, lime pickle, wedges of tomato, cucumber cut into sticks, onions cut into rings and dressed with oil into which you have stirred some cayenne pepper, and poppadums bought in a packet and fried or grilled.

Serves 4–6

1 tablespoon flour
salt and pepper
1 large roasting chicken, cut into about
  10 pieces
2 tablespoons oil or 2 oz/60 g ghee
4 oz/125 g onions, peeled and thinly
  sliced
2 dessert apples, peeled and chopped

2 cloves garlic, peeled and crushed
2 tablespoons curry powder from a
  recently purchased tin
8 oz/250 g ripe tomatoes, skinned or 1
  small tin tomatoes
1 tablespoon redcurrant jelly or similar
juice of ½ lemon
2 oz/60 g Sharwood's creamed coconut

Season the flour and roll the chicken pieces in it. Heat the oil and brown the chicken pieces carefully; remove. Add the onions, apple and garlic and more oil if you need it and cook them gently until they begin to colour. Stir in the curry powder and cook for a few minutes, stirring constantly to remove the 'raw' taste. Next add the tomatoes, and enough water to make a thin sauce. Stir until smooth. Add the redcurrant jelly and lemon juice. Return the chicken pieces to the sauce and cook extremely gently for 45 minutes.

About 5 minutes before the end of the cooking time, add the creamed coconut broken into small pieces and shake the pan until it dissolves. Taste for seasoning and adjust as necessary. You might want to add more lemon juice or sweeten a little with a spoonful of mango chutney. Let it cool, then refrigerate. The next day, heat through gently, cooking for a further 15 minutes.

BREAD AND BUTTER PUDDING

Chef Anton Mosimann of the Dorchester Hotel can be credited with the fashionable revival of bread and butter pudding. His approach is not that of making a virtue out of left-overs, but creating a light and delectable dish in its own right.

It is very rich, so serve only small helpings.

Serves 6–8

8 fl oz/250 ml milk	*white bread, sliced*
8 fl oz/250 ml double cream	*1 oz/30 g butter, softened*
vanilla pod	*fine-shred marmalade*
¼ teaspoon salt	*½ oz/15 g sultanas, soaked in water or*
3 large eggs	*whisky (see recipe)*
4 oz/125 g sugar	*icing sugar*

Bring the milk, cream, vanilla pod and salt slowly to the boil. Beat together the eggs and sugar in a large bowl and add the milk mixture, combining well. Pour the liquid through a sieve into a bowl.

Butter the slices of bread and, here is a tip from Beth Coventry, who serves the pudding at Green's Champagne Bar, spread with the thinnest possible coating of marmalade. Butter a shallow ovenproof dish of a size that will hold the bread only just, and arrange the bread slices in the dish.

Scatter the sultanas around (soaking in whisky rather than water gives a more dynamic result). Pour in the custard and, if it suits your plans, leave for 1–2 hours.

Turn on the oven to 170°C/325°F, Gas 3.

Cook the pudding in a *bain-marie* in the pre-heated oven for 40 minutes. Remove it from the oven, crisp the surface under the grill, sieve on a small amount of icing sugar and serve.

TOFFEE SPONGE PUDDING

Serves 6

1 small stale loaf white bread	*8 level tablespoons golden syrup*
4 oz/125 g butter	*grated rind and juice of 1 lemon*
4 oz/125 g demerara sugar	*¼ pint/150 ml milk*

Cut the crusts off the bread and dice into 1-inch/2.5-cm cubes.

Put the butter in a non-stick frying pan and, when melted, add the sugar, lemon juice and rind and then golden syrup (warm the syrup tin in a saucepan of hot water to make it easy to measure). Boil this mixture until it is caramel-coloured. While it is boiling, dip the bread into the milk. Fry the milky bread in the sticky mixture, turning the pieces until they are clearly browned. Serve at once, preferably with some whipped cream.

This dish can be prepared up to the boiling mixture being ready, which you can then keep warm in a low oven or on a hot plate: the frying takes about 3 minutes. It is *not* a dish for the figure-conscious, but very popular indeed with children, men and all those nostalgic for good nursery food.

WINTER FRUIT SALAD

Serves 6

1 lb/500 g mixed dried fruit: apricots,   *grated rind and juice of 2 oranges*
   apples, pears, peaches, prunes and figs *grated rind of 1 lemon*
3 tablespoons dark brown sugar   *1 oz/30 g almonds, coarsely chopped*
2 tablespoons raisins   *2 oz/60 g walnuts, coarsely chopped*

Cover the fruit with water and soak for 1 hour. Then put the fruit and enough of the water you soaked it in to cover in a saucepan and stew fairly quickly until the fruit is soft, but not disintegrated (about 15 minutes, but this does depend a little on the quality of the fruit). Add the sugar the moment you take the pan from the heat and stir it in gently to dissolve. Then add the raisins and the grated rind. Leave to cool and finally add the orange juice and chopped nuts.

This dish can be eaten warm, but in our opinion it is better cold, but not chilled.

BROWN BREAD ICE-CREAM

Recipes for brown bread ice-cream have been around since the late nineteenth century. It may sound an odd notion; but have faith, the crunch of the crumbs contrasts well with the creamy ice and the whole has a surprising nutty flavour.

Serves 4–6

3 oz/90 g wholemeal breadcrumbs   *½ pint/300 ml single cream*
2 oz/60 g butter   *2 eggs, separated*
4 oz/125 g brown sugar   *1 tablespoon sherry or rum or brandy*
½ pint/300 ml double cream   *(all optional)*

Fry the breadcrumbs in the butter until crisp. Add 2 oz/60 g of the sugar and cook gently until it caramelises and coats the crumbs. Whisk the double cream until thick and then beat in the remaining sugar, the single cream, the egg yolks and sherry, rum or brandy if you are using it.

Whisk the egg whites in a clean bowl until stiff, and gently fold them and the crumbs into the ice-cream mixture. Freeze in a suitable container. It is a good idea to stir the mixture after it has been in the freezer for an hour and also remember to remove the ice-cream from the freezer at least 1 hour before you mean to eat it.

MARY COVENTRY'S COFFEE CAKE

This is a recipe from the mother of one of the authors. It is much enjoyed by her church discussion group when it is Mary's turn to provide the tea. Camp coffee essence is still available and is by far the best coffee flavouring for cakes, even if it does make a rather dubious hot drink.

8 oz/250 g Krona margarine (works
    better than butter)
8 oz/250 g caster sugar
4 eggs

8 oz/250 g self-raising flour
1 teaspoon baking powder
a pinch of salt
2 tablespoons Camp coffee essence

For the filling:

1 egg yolk
2 oz/60 g butter, softened
2 tablespoons icing sugar

2 oz/60 g plain chocolate
2 dessertspoons Camp coffee essence

Turn on the oven to 190°C/375°F, Gas 5.

Cream together the margarine and sugar with a wooden spoon (much better than using a food processor in this instance). Beat the eggs in a bowl. Sift together the flour, baking powder and salt, then alternately add the flour and eggs in small quantities to the creamed margarine. Half-way through, beat in 2 tablespoonsful warm water. When all the eggs and flour have been incorporated, stir in the Camp coffee essence. Divide the mixture between two sandwich tins which have been lightly greased and floured. Bake for 30 minutes.

To make the filling, beat the egg yolk with the softened butter. Add icing sugar to the desired sweetness. Over hot water, melt the chocolate and stir into the mixture, then stir in the Camp coffee essence. When the cake is cool, spread the bottom half with the filling and place the other cake on top. It needs no further icing.

PANSCONES

These are quick to make, practically foolproof and, served warm, are wonderful with butter and homemade jam. It is worth aiming to have left-overs as they can be fried in bacon fat at breakfast time – a very popular move.

Serves 6

8 oz/250 g plain flour	1 egg
1 teaspoon bicarbonate of soda	½ pint/300 ml milk
1 teaspoon cream of tartar	1 tablespoon sugar
a pinch of salt	½ oz/15 g butter, melted

Sieve together the dry ingredients, except for the sugar. Beat together the egg, milk and sugar, and then stir in the melted butter. Add the wet to the dry slowly as if making pancake batter, which you are doing, but aiming for a consistency that drops fairly reluctantly from a spoon. Leave to stand for about 15 minutes.

Heat a griddle or heavy-bottomed frying pan. Rub with butter or vegetable oil. Drop spoonsful of the mixture which should spread out to scones about 3 inches/7.5 cm in diameter. When bubbles appear on the surface, flip them over and cook the other side. Serving them hot in batches is preferable to keeping the panscones warm in the oven or wrapped in a napkin, as they quickly lose their perkiness.

MAKING YOGHURT

A large bowl of yoghurt on the breakfast table with, to add to it, some fresh fruit, good honey or just demerara sugar for crunch, satisfactorily symbolises health consciousness in what can often be a meal that is a riot of fats and carbohydrates if it is the egg and bacon, toast and marmalade variety. Do not be tempted to use more than a heaped teaspoon of commercial yoghurt as your starter, as using too much can give a sour, grainy result. The second batch of yoghurt is invariably better than the first.

1 quart/1 litre milk (whole, skimmed or reconstituted powdered milk)

1 heaped teaspoon commercially-made natural yoghurt, (preferably a 'live' yoghurt)

Bring the milk to the boil over a high heat. Watch it carefully and when it starts to rise in the pan, take it off the heat and allow to cool until you can keep your finger in while you count to ten. Should you have a thermometer, this is 43°–49°C/110°–120°F.

Put the starter yoghurt in a bowl and pour in the milk, mixing well. Put cling film over the bowl, wrap the bowl in a towel and put it in a warm place, such as an airing cupboard, or the back of a solid fuel stove for 6–8 hours or overnight.

Pour off any watery liquid and chill the yoghurt. A wide-necked thermos jar is a good container for making yoghurt, a glazed earthenware crock lends it a nice folksy feel.

MUESLI

8 oz/250 g All-Bran
8 oz/250 g crushed oats
8 oz/250 g bran flakes
4 oz/125 g almonds, chopped
4 oz/125 g hazelnuts, chopped

4 oz/125 g prunes, stoned and chopped
4 oz/125 g dried apricots
8 oz/250 g sultanas
4 oz/125 g sunflower seeds

Mix all the ingredients very thoroughly in a large bowl and then transfer to an airtight container. Stir up again before serving as the heavier items tend to sink to the bottom.

SHIPDHAM MARMALADE

Melanie and Justin de Blank run a most sympathetic 'restaurant with rooms' at Shipdham in Norfolk and the French style implicit in that is continued by the display case in the hall selling a few commodities to take home as mementos or presents. This wonderfully tangy marmalade is one, though when the recipe was tracked down it proved to be one called Colonel Gore's Marmalade from the *Constance Spry Cookery Book*. The colonel must have been the sort of chap who sees breakfast as a kick start to the day.

3 lb/1.5 kg Seville oranges (available usually in January)
½ lemon

4 lb/2 kg granulated sugar (see recipe)
1 handkerchief-size piece of muslin

Cut the oranges into four. Remove the pips and set them aside. Slice the oranges fairly thinly – depending on how chunky a marmalade you like – and weigh the slices. To every 1 lb/500 g of fruit, allow 3 pints/1.8 litres of water. Mix the fruit and water in a large bowl and leave to soak for 24 hours.

Rub your preserving pan with the half lemon. Simmer the fruit and its liquid (with the pips tied in a muslin bag; their pectin content helps set the jelly) until the skins are tender; this can take 2 hours or more. Remove from the heat, remove the pips and turn the fruit into a large basin. Leave until the next day.

Weigh your pulp – a messy business – and allow 1¼ lb/600 g sugar to every 1 lb/500 g pulp. Put both sugar and pulp back in the preserving pan, bring the mixture very slowly to the boil, making sure the sugar dissolves in the process. Then boil rapidly until the syrup jells, which means that a drip dropped onto a chilled plate will wrinkle when pushed with your finger. The translucent appearance of the fruit is another clue to the setting point. About 20 minutes' boiling is a rough guideline.

Cool the marmalade a little before potting as this helps stop the fruit swimming to the top of the jars. A thicker, more 'set' consistency continues to develop in the jars for about 2 weeks.

9 *Impressing People*

One of the things that makes impressing people difficult is that we don't often admit that this is what we want to do. Where meals are concerned, a lot of 'they must take me as they find me' goes on, while the owner of this rugged and unrealistic dictum wrestles with some covert pioneering – such as making their own hot water crust pastry for the first time, 'we just have a bit of pie and salad in the evenings'. Wanting to impress other people carries with it the notion that one is giving a false impression, trying to suck up, wanting to appear grander than one is – or cleverer, or more interesting; this is ignoring the fact that if one wants to *be* cleverer or more interesting, one has to practise. 'Pot luck' always reminds us of the witches in *Macbeth*, whose ingredients for a wicked brew seemed pretty haphazard rather than necessarily efficacious.

Possibly, some of the dishonesty about wanting to impress comes from the sad fact that we *do* sometimes want to impress people whom we don't much like or are afraid of – an uncomfortable feeling. People have been known to feel something of the sort about their in-laws, or their employer; of course, one doesn't have to stand in some formal relationship to somebody before disliking them, but it is the formal relationship that often pre-empts one cutting them out of one's life. We all find ourselves faced with having to cook for such people from time to time. Then there are the people who seem potentially powerful in our lives, whom we hardly know, or do not know at all. If faced with cooking for them, we call it 'wanting to make a good impression', by which we mean we want to impress them with cuisine and general hostmanship. One way and another, practically all of us fall into the trap.

It is worth beginning with two rules. The first is that if one is going to cook a rather splendid – even pretentious – meal, one might as well enjoy it. If that is agreed, the second rule is never to cook anything that you haven't cooked before: you can't enjoy an evening if you are anxious about the food. So we suggest that you select from the following menus and *practise*. You don't need to cook the whole dinner for one family meal: you can take each course separately for practising. The most expensive course is probably the sea bass: if you don't want to afford that for a rehearsal, buy a fresh haddock or a large trout – the principle is the same. Truffles are expensive, but what you need to learn is how to put things under the skin of a bird.

Finally, the best way of impressing people is to look as though you have tried – and succeeded. If you simply succeed without seeming to have tried at all, your efforts will be undervalued, or incur resentment – the one hand tied behind one's back syndrome is always irritating, except to another virtuoso.

Caviar Puffs
Broad Bean and Artichoke Salad
Filo Pastry Pies
Sea Bass Poached with Sauce Verte
Capon Stuffed under the Skin
Braised Chicory

Paillasson
Grilled Goats' Cheese with a
　　Prestigious Salad
Individual Cheese Soufflés
Raspberry Soufflé
Pistachio Parfait

CAVIAR PUFFS

Serves 4

8 oz/250 g frozen puff pastry (or make
your own, if you enjoy doing it)
3 eggs
dash of milk
½ pint/300 ml double cream

1 large Spanish onion
1 small bunch parsley
2 × 4-oz/125-g jars of Danish caviar
(or the same quantity of the red)

You can do all the preparations for this dish beforehand, but you have to put it together just before serving, as the point of it is that the pastry should be hot, and the whipped cream very cold.

Turn on the oven to 220°C/425°F, Gas 7.

Thaw the pastry and roll it out to a thickness of ¼ inch/0.6 cm. Cut out rounds about 3 inches/7.5 cm in diameter. Take a sharp knife, and gently score a rim ⅛ inch/0.3 cm deep and ¼ inch/0.6 cm in from the edge of each round.

Bake the pastry rounds in the oven for about 15 minutes, or until the pastry is a golden biscuit colour. Remove from the oven and put them on a rack.

Hard-boil the eggs and then put in cold water. When cool, peel and chop finely, adding a dash of milk to make the mixture creamy. Whip the cream until it is just stiff, and put in the fridge.

Chop the onion very finely, discarding any coarse leaves surrounding the bulb. Chop the parsley finely and set aside.

Ten minutes before serving, return the puffs to a moderate oven to heat through, and then spread them with a layer of egg, a layer of chopped onion, a layer of caviar and a dollop of whipped cream. Garnish with parsley, and serve at once.

BROAD BEAN AND ARTICHOKE SALAD

This is a starter, and can only be made when the vegetables are in season. The broad beans should be as small as possible; the artichokes can be small or large.

Serves 6

4 lb/2 kg broad beans in their pods
salt

6 globe artichokes if large or 9 small ones

Put a large pan of water on to boil. Cut off the artichoke stalks and when the water is boiling, add a good teaspoonful of salt and then the artichokes. They will take approximately 20 minutes to cook (longer for large ones), but you will have to test them, by pulling off an outer leaf and tasting it to see if the fleshy part is cooked. When they are cooked, drain them in a colander.

Meanwhile, pod the beans and steam them gently for about 6 minutes. They should be just *al dente*. While they are still warm, slough off the grey skins between your first finger and thumb.

Pull the leaves off the cooled artichokes (don't waste them, they are delicious to eat with vinaigrette), and cut out the choke with a sharp knife. Then slice the hearts thinly. Put the broad beans and sliced hearts in a dish and pour over them the following mixture:

Dressing:

2 tablespoons best olive oil	*1 teaspoon salt*
juice of 1½ lemons	*several good screws of freshly-ground*
1 teaspoon caster sugar	*black pepper*

Mix this dressing very thoroughly, making sure that the salt and sugar are dissolved. Toss the beans and artichokes gently until they are coated with dressing.

FILO PASTRY PIES

Filo pastry (paper thin leaves of dough available from Cypriot bakeries and some enterprising delicatessens and supermarkets; usually sold by the pound (in 500 g quantities), rolled up and sealed in cellophane) is one of your best weapons in the battle of impressing people. If your guests have never encountered it before, they will assume you have at your fingertips the talents of an Austrian strudel-maker and you, of course, will just cast your eyes down and let a little smile play round your lips.

Having mastered the technique of assembling a filo pastry pie (which basically means separating each sheet with melted butter and keeping the spare pastry under a damp tea-towel while you work to prevent it becoming brittle and crackly) you can invent your own fillings.

Spinach and cheese is a traditionally Greek one. We find that a mixture of ricotta and feta works with the spinach. The two ideas below make a delicious and quite sustaining first course which you could follow with something cold and luxurious, such as the Poached Sea Bass or the Cold Wild Duck which appear in the chapter DINER A DEUX.

Having prepared the filling, assemble the pie according to the instructions on page 116.

HARD-BOILED EGG AND MUSHROOM FILLING

2 oz/60 g butter
1½ oz/45 g flour
1 pint/625 ml skimmed milk
salt and freshly-ground black pepper
4 eggs, hard-boiled

8 rashers streaky bacon, crisply fried
12 oz/375 g mushrooms, wiped clean
    and sliced
1 dessertspoon vegetable oil
2 tablespoons chopped coriander or
    parsley (preferably coriander)

Melt 1½ oz/45 g butter in a heavy-bottomed pan, stir in the flour and cook gently for 5 minutes. Add the milk slowly, stirring until you have a smooth, thick sauce. You may need to adjust quantities of milk up or down. Season. Chop the eggs, crumble the bacon. Sauté the mushrooms in a mixture of oil and the remaining butter until they are softened. Strain carefully, leaving the mushroom juice in the pan unless you want to thin your sauce some more, but it will turn it a dull grey colour.

Add the mushrooms, eggs, bacon and coriander/parsley to the mixture and stir sensitively, but thoroughly. Let it cool. This preparation may be done in advance if you wish.

Turn on the oven to 190°C/375°F, Gas 5.

Decide whether you wish to separate your pastry leaves with melted butter or warm vegetable oil. Butter obviously has the better flavour, but you might be feeling health-conscious. Find a roasting tin or ovenproof dish about the size of one of the sheets of pastry. Melt 4 oz/125 g butter or heat up 4 fl oz/125 ml vegetable oil. Using a pastry brush, paint the base of the pan with butter or oil. Lay in a sheet of pastry. Brush this with your chosen fat and repeat with another four or five sheets. Spread your choice of filling on the pastry. Cover with another five sheets, separating each one with melted butter or oil. Brush the top sheet with oil or butter. Using a knife with a sharp point, score the pastry into diamond shapes, cutting down through quite a few layers. Think about the look of baklava.

Bake in the oven for 45 minutes by which time the pastry should look flaky and the top golden and crackling like autumn leaves. The pie can be served hot or warm.

FISH FILLING

Serves 6–8

1½ lb/750 g firm white fish such as
*   haddock or cod (this is not the moment*
*   to lash out on turbot or halibut)*
8 oz/250 g peeled prawns – the best you
*   can find*

1½ oz/45 g butter
1½ oz/45 g flour
1 heaped teaspoon ground turmeric
½ pint/300 ml skimmed milk
salt and pepper

For the court bouillon:

1 carrot, peeled
1 onion, peeled
1 bay leaf
a few sprigs of parsley

fennel leaves if you have them
6 black peppercorns
1 glass white wine

Poach the fish in a court bouillon which you do by covering it with water, adding the court bouillon ingredients and bringing it very slowly to the boil. Let the liquid only shudder until the fish is opaque right through – depending on your cut of fish, this could take 5–10 minutes. Remove the fish and let it cool. Continue to simmer the court bouillon to extract the maximum flavour from the vegetables.

Meanwhile, melt the butter in a heavy-bottomed pan. Stir in the flour and turmeric and cook over a low heat for a few minutes. Start your sauce by adding some milk and then more, and when you have a very thick, smooth mixture, use the fish stock to obtain a less thick texture, but with still enough body to act as a binder for the fish and prawns. Season to taste with salt and pepper.

Mix the flaked, cooked fish and the prawns gently into the sauce and let the mixture cool. This can be done hours in advance of dinner if you wish.

SEA BASS POACHED WITH SAUCE VERTE

This dish is delicious cold, and as a main course has many advantages. Ideally, you need a fish kettle, but if you don't have one, then substitute a very large pan in which the fish can lie curved. For 6 people, you need a 4 lb/2 kg fish, cleaned, but with the head left on.

First of all, make the court-bouillon.

Court-bouillon:

½ bottle white wine (preferably dry)	1 bay leaf
1 teacup/180 ml tarragon vinegar	12 peppercorns
2 onions, peeled and sliced	1 blade of mace (you can tie the
2 carrots, scrubbed and sliced	peppercorns and mace in a bit of
½ lemon, cut in slices	muslin if you like, but this is not
1 bouquet garni	essential)

Put all the ingredients into a large pan together with 3 quarts/3.5 litres water and simmer for 50 minutes. Strain and cool.

Put the fish into the kettle or pan, pour over the cool bouillon and bring gently to boiling point. Then, turn off the heat and leave the fish to cool in the bouillon. This method has the advantage that whatever size your fish, it will be cooked when the bouillon is cool. Lift it carefully out of the pan, put it on a board and remove the skin. Then put the fish on a serving dish; it can be garnished with lemon, parsley or any greenery that makes it look attractive.

Sauce Verte:

3 egg yolks	½ bunch watercress
1 pint/625 ml olive oil (see below)	6 good sprigs parsley with stalks removed
tarragon vinegar or lemon juice	a little fresh tarragon or fresh coriander if
salt and pepper	you can get either

Make a mayonnaise with the egg yolks and a light olive oil. Some people prefer to use sunflower seed oil for this; it makes a much lighter mayonnaise, but on the other hand it doesn't have the same taste. Season with tarragon vinegar or lemon juice, black pepper and salt.

Place the greenery in the liquidiser with a tablespoonful of water and whizz until you have a smooth green paste. Add this to the mayonnaise by degrees, until you have the colour that you like. Taste the sauce for final seasoning; a little sugar is often an improvement at this point.

Serve in a sauce boat with the fish.

CAPON STUFFED UNDER THE SKIN

Once you have learned to stuff a capon (or chicken or turkey) under the skin with butter, or fromage blanc, or a purée of vegetables, or truffle slices or whatever, you will probably never roast it straightforwardly again. There is every possible virtue in the process. The skin is separated from the flesh and so crisps more emphatically, the flavours go into the meat and not the baking dish, the bird is virtually self-basting though with none of the horrid overtones of injections with oil or stock that the phrase can have.

It is rare for the domestic cook to obtain black truffles that have retained worthwhile flavour. Should you do so, then thin slices of truffle slipped under the skin – a dish that rejoices in the name *poulet demi-deuil*, i.e. in semi-mourning – is perhaps the best flavouring. A chicken prepared this way and simmered wrapped up in a roasting bag to catch the juices would be very impressive.

However, we are not presuming upon your powers to obtain black truffles and suggest instead the mixture below:

Serves 6

1 capon or large free-range roasting chicken, weighing 5–6 lb/2.5–3 kg
1 tablespoon vegetable oil
4 oz/125 g fromage blanc or low-fat cream cheese

2 oz/60 g butter, softened
1 tablespoon fresh herbs – tarragon is best
1 clove garlic, peeled and crushed
salt and freshly-ground black pepper

Turn on the oven to 190°C/375°F, Gas 5.

Rub the chicken with the vegetable oil, giving it a little massage to loosen the skin and make it pliable. Mix together the cheese, butter and seasonings, using more garlic if you like an emphatically garlicky flavour.

Approaching the chicken from the back where there is a loose flap of skin, start to work your hand under the skin. Go gently and pull at the membranes holding the skin to the flesh. You will find there are one or two quite resilient ones, but once these are snapped it is plain sailing. Work your hand up to the tip of the breast bone and over the thighs. Holding a small fork with your fingers over the back and the tines pointing downwards, go in again under the skin and prick the capon flesh in a few places. The skin should now be quite malleable, and you should find it quite easy to spoon in the stuffing and pat it around evenly over the breast and thighs. Spoon any left-over stuffing into the cavity of the bird.

Season with salt and pepper and roast for 1½–2 hours depending on the size of the bird. Baste occasionally towards the end of the cooking time and if the breast is browning too deeply, cover with foil. Serve with the pan juices, which should be like a creamy sauce, and a large bunch of fresh watercress.

Note: To impress people when you are in a hurry, substitute a mashed-up Boursin cheese for the butter, cheese and herb mixture, or even a very mild blue cheese like Dolcelatte.

BRAISED CHICORY

Serves 4–6

2 lb/1 kg chicory (try and get the pieces   ½ pint/300 ml chicken stock
    roughly the same size)   juice of 2 lemons
2 oz/60 g butter

Turn on the oven to 150°C/300°F, Gas 2.

Wipe each piece of chicory with a damp cloth, and trim the ends. Lay the pieces in a shallow buttered baking dish, and pour in the stock and half the lemon juice. Cover the dish with a lid or aluminium foil.

Place the dish in the oven for 1 hour. Transfer to a clean, hot serving dish, with the remaining butter and lemon juice poured over. A little salt may be added at this stage if liked.

PAILLASSON

It is important to follow the instructions for this potato pancake to the letter, i.e. do not skip the rinsing and drying process. Should you do so, the result could be grey and gluey. It is also important to use a good variety of potato, not some hopeless mealy one suited only to mashing.

Serves 4

1½ lb/750 g potatoes, peeled   salt and freshly-ground black pepper
2½ oz/75 g butter

Grate the potatoes, either using a food processor or the medium blade of a mouli julienne. Rinse potatoes well in two changes of water. Drain them and spread out on a tea-towel. Roll the towel up tightly and squeeze the potatoes dry.

Melt 2 oz/60 g butter in an omelette pan, or a pan with a non-stick surface. Add the potatoes, pressing them down evenly. Cover and cook over a low heat for 20 minutes, when the potatoes should be golden and crisp on the bottom.

Turn out onto a large plate. Melt the rest of the butter and slip the potatoes back into the pan. Cook, uncovered, for another 20 minutes. Slip out onto a hot serving dish and cut as you would a cake, white side down.

GRILLED GOATS' CHEESE WITH A PRESTIGIOUS SALAD

This is both a more impressive cheese course than the assembly of a lot of different varieties, and a more economical one since there won't be little pieces and wedges left mocking you from the fridge or larder. If it is not possible to buy whole, small goats' cheeses, for example Chavignol, often sold from a jar of olive oil, use thick slices cut from a cylinder of chèvre.

1 goat's cheese or *1 slice of goats' cheese, per*
   person
1 slice rough country bread per person
a selection of interesting salad leaves, e.g.,
   lamb's lettuce (salade de mâche*), frisée,*
   oak leaf lettuce, raddiccio, watercress

vinaigrette dressing
black pepper

Toast the bread on one side. Put it in an ovenproof dish, untoasted-side up. Place the cheese on top, trim away the excess bread, and grind on some black pepper. Cook, either under the grill, or in a hot oven until the cheese is slightly browned, bubbling and melting, but not melted.

Arrange a heap of dressed salad leaves on each serving plate with the toasted cheese beside it.

INDIVIDUAL CHEESE SOUFFLES

Despite the fact that soufflés could almost feature in the chapter FOOLPROOF DINNER, they seem always to impress, individual ones even more so, as it looks as if the presumed skill and effort is all directed, channelled and funnelled at one person. What is less well-known about soufflés is that they can be monotonous in texture and, to avoid this, we suggest you bury a (nice) surprise in the centre of each small soufflé which you could be serving either as a first course, a cheese course or a savoury, depending on the structure of your meal.

Possible 'surprises' would be a sun-dried tomato taken with a teaspoon from a jar of sun-dried tomatoes put up in olive oil, an anchovy arranged in a coil, a prawn dusted with chilli pepper, a piece of smoked salmon or smoked haddock, some Parma ham cut into julienne strips and bundled together. Think carefully however about not springing an unwelcome ingredient on one of your guests. A confirmed oyster loather lulled into a sense of security by the sight of a cheese soufflé would be horrified – and unimpressed – to find the mollusc lurking inside.

Serves 4

1 oz/30 g butter
1 tablespoon flour
just under ½ pint/275 ml milk
1½ oz/45 g each Parmesan and *Gruyère cheese, freshly grated*

4 eggs, separated, and *1 extra white*
cayenne pepper
salt and freshly-ground black pepper
a little extra Parmesan cheese for dusting

Turn on the oven to 200°C/400°F, Gas 6.

Melt the butter, stir in the flour and cook very gently for a few minutes. Gradually add the milk, which will be incorporated more easily if you warm it first, and stir until you have a smooth mixture. On the lowest possible heat, or using an asbestos mat – or the eqivalent – let the sauce cook for about 10 minutes. Stir in the cheeses, then remove from the heat and, one by one, beat in the egg yolks. Season, remembering that the cheese is already quite salty, but also remembering that egg whites have a deadening effect on flavour. This part of the preparation can be done in advance, as well as deciding on your 'surprise' if you are going to have one.

Near the time of eating, butter individual soufflé dishes and dust them with Parmesan. Whisk the egg whites to firm, snowy peaks. Mix a quarter of the egg whites gently into the cheese mixture to lighten it, then fold in the rest of the egg whites, taking care not to squash the bounce out of them. Spoon into the prepared dishes, adding your surprise in the middle, i.e., spoon in some mixture, lay on the extra ingredient, fill to the top with more mixture. With a knife, cut a small circle about ½ inch/1.25 cm in from the circumference of the pot which will give a nice cottage-loaf-look result. Bake for 15–20 minutes until golden brown and risen. Serve immediately.

RASPBERRY SOUFFLE

Serves 6

1 lb/500 g raspberries
6 eggs
3 tablespoons caster sugar

juice of 1 orange
1 tablespoon gelatine
¾ pint/475 ml double cream

Reserve a dozen or so of the best raspberries for the garnish. Put the remainder in the liquidiser and pulp very thoroughly. Separate the whites of the eggs from the yolks. Put the yolks, slightly beaten, into a double saucepan with the sugar and the orange juice and whisk until the mixture thickens. Dissolve the gelatine in about 2 tablespoonsful of hot water in a small bowl in a saucepan of hot water. Add the raspberry purée to the egg and sugar mixture and put it in a large bowl to cool.

Meanwhile, beat the cream lightly, and the whites very stiffly. When the raspberry mixture is beginning to set a little, add the cream, and finally the whites, folded in gently but thoroughly so that there are no lumps of cream or egg white. Put into a serving dish and then quickly into the fridge.

Garnish with whole raspberries before serving.

PISTACHIO PARFAIT

Serves 6–8

3 oz/90 g pistachio nuts, chopped
3 oz/90 g almonds, chopped
1 pint/625 ml double cream
a few drops of green colouring

8 oz/250 g caster sugar
3 egg whites
1 tablespoon vanilla essence
1 teaspoon almond essence

Whip the cream fairly stiffly and add the green colouring, but only a few drops. Boil 2½ fl oz/75 ml water and the sugar together until the syrup threads when dropped from the tip of a spoon. While the sugar is dissolving and coming to the boil, beat the egg whites stiffly, so that you can turn the bowl upside down without the whites moving. We find that a hand electric beater is best for this.

Pour the sugar syrup slowly into the whites, beating hard all the time. Add the nuts and flavourings to the whipped cream, and then fold in the egg white mixture gently but thoroughly so that everything amalgamates. Spoon the mixture into a soufflé dish and put at once into the freezer, and remove 10 minutes before serving.

10 *Vegetarians*

Vegetarian cooking is on the up and up. It needed to be: for years we have watched vegetarians having to put up with anything from grated cheddar on a baked potato to hastily cooked pulses – murder on the digestion – or draught-excluding quiches made by hostesses who seemed to feel that it was pretty broad-minded of them even to produce that. For years, vegetarians have been covertly regarded as cranks and bores, social nuisances, out to make trouble for their hostess by their irritating whim of not eating as the majority do. Vegetarian food is still pretty awful in a good many places, but people are beginning to recognise that it is, and that is the first step towards it getting better.

Also, the number of vegetarians is increasing. There have always been people who do not eat fish or meat because of religious, or humane principles of one kind or another, but as factory farming has increased and has been exposed, more people are unprepared to eat meat at such a cost to the animal. So, far from being cranks, these people (of whom we are not two) should do nothing but inspire respect: many strict vegetarians still yearn for things like prawns or game.

But there is now a new reason for becoming vegetarian, and that is health. People are rightly starting to question what the food they eat contains, and unfortunately a great deal of meat is full of antibiotics, hormones and preservatives, so that much as the Victorians suffered widely from rickets and/or constipation due to a diet that for children of all classes consisted largely of carbohydrates, so children now are getting eczema, are hyperactive, insomniac and aggressive. New allergies are being discovered all the time and seem to be very much on the increase, but it remains to be seen how much and how precisely children – and adults – are being affected by additives to food of all kinds.

Vegetarians are more likely to occur in our social life, and as cooking for them can produce delicious results, you may simply broaden your repertoire by making a vegetarian menu.

First, it is important to know what kind of vegetarian you are cooking for. A surprising number of people who call themselves vegetarian do, in fact, eat fish, or even poultry, but the ones who don't, feel strongly about it. Never cheat – don't make a vegetable soup with a meat stock: they will almost certainly detect this and feel very uncomfortable about it. So, not only don't cheat, but tell them you haven't. Secondly, it is necessary to make the distinction between vegetarians and vegans. The former eat dairy products, as well as cereals, nuts, fruit and vegetables. Vegans are confined to cereals, nuts, fruit and vegetables: no cheese, eggs, milk or butter can be used for them. In the recipes below, we have indicated which would be suitable for vegans. Soya milk and miso – which can be used for stock among other things – have made vegan cooking easier.

Having a vegetarian guest does *not* simply mean providing those parts of a non-vegetarian meal that are acceptable; if everybody else is having roast turkey, you cannot get away with shoving chestnut stuffing and brussel sprouts onto your guest's plate and expect them to feel very welcome or cared for. It is better to provide a vegetarian meal for everyone.

In our experience, most vegetarians love puddings – generally because the main courses presented to them have been so stodgy or dull – so even if you are not ordinarily a pudding eater or maker, do take this part of the meal seriously. They are also too familiar with the omelette/ salad meal – often the only reasonable thing on the menu in non-vegetarian restaurants – just as vegans have to resort so often to pasta with a tomato sauce. The following recipes try to widen the field a bit. You will also find a number of vegetarian recipes elsewhere in this book.

Tomato, Avocado and Mozzarella
   Salad
Hot Onion Tart
Stir-fried Vegetables with Bean Curd
Piperade
Dal with Fried Onions and Crackling
   Eggs
Lentil Dal
Basmati Rice

Curried Spinach
Pasta Sauce No. 1 – For Vegans
Pasta Sauce No. 2 – For Vegetarians
Raspberry and Hazelnut Crumble
Pineapple and Orange Salad with
   Toasted Almonds
Baked Apricots with Yoghurt and
   Cream

TOMATO, AVOCADO AND MOZZARELLA SALAD
(Vegetarian)

A favourite in Italian restaurants, this assembly, though practically effortless, is excellent. The important part is buying the mozzarella. Truly ambitious shops should be able to supply mozzarella made from buffalo milk but, failing that, make sure you purchase the individually paper-wrapped mozzarella which should be sitting in a bowl of water. Do not bother making this salad with the plastic-wrapped Danish mozzarella which is fit only to become the glue on top of pizzas.

Serves 4

4 large tomatoes
1 Mozzarella cheese (see above)
1 ripe avocado
12 fresh basil leaves, roughly chopped (if available)

3 tablespoons olive oil
1 scant tablespoon wine vinegar or balsamic vinegar
sea salt and freshly-ground black pepper

If you can find the large Marmande or 'beef' tomatoes, a pretty way of presenting this dish is to slice the tomatoes through not quite to the bottom, fan them out and insert alternative slices of avocado and mozzarella cheese. Sprinkle with basil, or failing that, parsley, and trickle the vinaigrette, which you have made by mixing the oil, vinegar and seasonings over the whole.

Alternatively, slice all the ingredients to more or less the same thickness – about ¼ inch/0.6 cm. Arrange in one layer of overlapping slices and dress as above.

HOT ONION TART (Vegetarian)

Serves 4

For 8 oz/250 g shortcrust pastry:

3 oz/90 g butter
2 oz/60 g vegetable fat
8 oz/250 g plain flour

salt
1 egg yolk
1 teaspoon lemon juice

You can buy frozen pastry, of course, but it is also very easily made. One secret of light pastry is not to let the flour etc. get beyond your knuckles. Here is our way of making it.

Rub the fats into the flour in a large bowl and add a little salt. You may not need the whole yolk. Beat it in a cup with a little cold water and lemon juice, add to the bowl and mix with a wooden spoon to a stiff paste. Roll out the pastry quite thinly on a floured board and then place it into an oiled 8-inch/20-cm tart or flan tin. Put it into the refrigerator and leave for about 2 hours.

Filling:

1 tablespoon olive oil	*3 egg yolks*
2 oz/60 g butter	*6 fl oz/180 ml double cream*
1½ lb/750 g onions	*freshly grated nutmeg*
salt and pepper	

Heat the oil and butter in a pan. Peel and slice the onions finely, discarding any tough outer skins. Cook the onions gently until they are quite soft – don't fry them: they must not get brown or crisp. Season with salt and pepper.

Turn on the oven to 230°C/450°F, Gas 8. Beat the egg yolks with the cream and add grated nutmeg to taste. Put the onions into the tart case and pour the creamy mixture over them. Bake for about 30 minutes and serve hot.

STIR-FRIED VEGETABLES WITH BEAN CURD
(Vegan)

Serves 6

2 onions or *6 shallots*	*1 oz/30 g wholemeal flour*
1 lb/500 g mange-tout	*salt*
1 lb/500 g broccoli	*sunflower seed oil*
2 blocks of bean curd	*soya sauce (optional)*

This dish is most easily made in a wok, using a small frying pan for the bean curd, but if you don't have a wok, you can use a large frying pan or a large enamelled pan. You will use less oil with the wok.

Begin by preparing all your vegetables. It is important that you cut them all to the same thickness. Slice the onions and chop. Cut the mange-tout in diagonal strips. Remove the heavy part of the broccoli stalks and cut the florets into strips. Cut each piece of bean curd into nine pieces and roll in salted wholemeal flour. Heat 2 tablespoonsful of oil in a small pan. When the oil is really hot, put in the bean curd and turn down the heat a little. Turn the bean curd when it is has browned.

Meanwhile, put some oil in a large pan (about 1 tablespoonful for a wok, about 3 tablespoonsful for a pan), and heat until the oil is sizzling hot. Add the onions to the pan and stir-fry for 3 minutes, then add the mange-tout and continue stirring for 2 minutes. Finally, add the broccoli and stir for 2 more minutes.

This dish should be served at once in hot bowls with the bean curd on top and some soya sauce if liked.

PIPERADE (Vegetarian)

Serves 6–8

2 tablespoons sunflower seed oil or olive oil
1½ lb/750 g onions, chopped
1½ lb/750 g green peppers, de-seeded and chopped

2 cloves garlic (optional)
1½ lb/750 g tomatoes, chopped (or one 20-oz/600 g tin of same)
salt and pepper to taste
8 eggs

Heat the oil and add the onions. When they have begun to cook, add the peppers and garlic. Cook gently until the peppers begin to soften, then add the chopped tomatoes and season. Cook until you have a soft mélange of vegetables. Break the eggs into a bowl, and whisk until the yolks are well broken into the whites. Add this mixture to the vegetables and cook gently, stirring until the eggs are softly cooked.

This dish can be served on lightly buttered wholemeal slices of toast.

DAL WITH FRIED ONIONS AND CRACKLING EGGS
(Vegetarian)

The lentils to use for this dish are the small orange variety, sometimes called Egyptian lentils, that cook to a purée in about 15 minutes. In Indian shops they are called Masoor dal. A pool of plain yoghurt goes well with this dish.

Serves 4

12 oz/375 g lentils	*garam masala or your own blend of spices*
2 onions	*3 hard-boiled eggs*
vegetable oil	*salt and freshly ground black pepper*

Wash the lentils in a bowl of water to remove any dust or other aliens. Cover the drained lentils with fresh water to a depth of ½ inch/1.25 cm above the lentils, bring to the boil and simmer. Peel and slice the onions, cutting from root to tip to obtain crescents. When the dal has reached a sludgy consistency, start to fry the onions. Depending on the age of the lentils you find, you may need to add more water during the cooking or, conversely, simmer for longer to achieve the correct texture. Fry the onions to a deep golden brown, set aside and keep warm.

Clean the pan, heat up a little more oil and fry the spices. Slice the hard-boiled eggs thickly and cook the slices, turning them once or twice until a bubbly crust forms. Season the dal with salt and freshly ground black pepper. Serve with the eggs, any spicy oil remaining in the pan and the onions.

LENTIL DAL (Vegan)

This is a lentil dal from Madhur Jaffrey's excellent book, *An Invitation To Indian Cooking*.

Serves 4

1 lb/500 g green lentils	*¾ lemon*
1 cinnamon stick	*1½ teaspoons salt*
1 bay leaf	*⅛ teaspoon freshly-ground black pepper*
2 cloves garlic	*¼ teaspoon cayenne pepper (optional)*
2 slices freshly peeled root ginger about	*3 tablespoons vegetable oil or 1½ oz/45 g*
⅛-inch/0.3 cm thick	*ghee*
1 teaspoon ground turmeric	*a pinch of ground asafoetida*
	½ teaspoon whole cumin seeds

Wash the lentils well, picking out any stones you can see, then drain. Combine the lentils, 2½ pints/1.5 litres water, cinnamon stick, bay leaf, garlic, ginger and turmeric. Bring to the boil. Cover the pan, lower the heat and simmer gently until the lentils are tender, about 30–45 minutes.

Slice the lemon into 5 or 6 rounds, removing the pips. Add the lemon, salt, pepper and cayenne to the lentils. Stir and cover for another five minutes. Just before serving, heat the vegetable oil or ghee in a frying pan over a medium-high heat. When the oil is very hot, put in the asafoetida and cumin seeds. As soon as the asafoetida begins to sizzle and expand and the cumin seeds darken, pour the contents over the lentils and stir.

Note: Lentils take a varying amount of time to cook, depending upon their kind, and their age. Dal should be quite thick: as Madhur Jaffrey says, 'thinner than porridge, but not quite so thin as pea soup'.

BASMATI RICE (Vegan)

Serves 4

12 oz/375 g Basmati rice
1¼ teaspoons salt

1½ oz/45 g vegetable ghee (or butter if you are cooking for vegetarians)

Wash the rice well in cold water, then soak it in a bowl with 2 pints of water and ½ teaspoonful salt for at least half an hour. Then drain it thoroughly. Melt the butter or ghee in a heavy-bottomed pan. Pour in the drained rice and stir for 2 minutes until the rice is coated with fat. Add 18 fl oz/575 ml water and ¾ teaspoonful of salt. Bring to the boil, cover, lower heat to very low, and cook for about 20 minutes. Look at the rice occasionally, mix it gently and cook until the rice is tender and the liquid has evaporated.

Basmati rice cooked in this manner has a delicious flavour that goes excellently with many of the dishes in this chapter.

CURRIED SPINACH (Vegan)

Serves 4

3 lb/1.5 kg spinach
2 large onions, finely chopped
1 tablespoon sunflower seed oil
6 cloves garlic, sliced lengthways
a very small pinch of chilli powder

1 teaspoon ground cumin
1 teaspoon ground coriander
1 sprig of fennel, chopped
1 teaspoon chopped rosemary
salt

Wash the spinach well in a large bowl of water. Take it out and drop it into a large pan without extra water. Cook it, stirring from time to time for about 8 minutes, by which time all the water on the washed leaves will have evaporated. Strain the spinach and squeeze dry, then chop it roughly.

Fry the onions in the oil until they are transparent. Add the garlic, chilli powder, cumin and coriander and continue to fry for 3 minutes. Add the spinach to the pan together with the chopped fennel and rosemary and a good pinch of salt and cook for a further 3 minutes.

This dish is good with Basmati rice and a dal.

PASTA SAUCE NO. 1 (Vegan)

Serves 6

4 tablespoons olive oil
2 oz/60 g onion, peeled and finely
    chopped
2 oz/60 g celery, scrubbed and finely
    chopped
2 oz/60 g carrot, finely chopped
2 lb/1 kg fresh tomatoes or 1 20-oz/600 g
    can Italian plum tomatoes (see
    below)

salt
1 teaspoon dark brown sugar
12 oz/375 g mushrooms wiped clean and
    roughly chopped
1 teaspoon ground coriander or 1 oz/
    30 g fresh coriander chopped

This sauce can be made ahead of time and warmed up, in which case reserve the fresh coriander until the warming-up process. Most of the year, it is better to use tinned tomatoes: fresh tomatoes are seldom worth eating and have no flavour when cooked.

Put 2 tablespoons of the oil into a pan and add the onion, celery and carrot. Fry gently, stirring all the while, for 3 minutes. Add the tomatoes and their juice, salt and sugar and simmer for 30 minutes. Meanwhile, put 2 tablespoonsful of oil into a second pan and when it is hot, add the mushrooms and ground coriander. Sauté the mushrooms lightly until the oil is absorbed, then remove from the heat.

When the tomato mixture has finished simmering, put the mixture through a food processor, then return it to a clean pan, and simmer gently for a further 30 minutes. Add the mushrooms to the pan, stir and taste to see if you have added enough salt.

This sauce is good with most kinds of pasta. Buy fresh pasta if you possibly can: you will need about 1¼ lb/575 g for 4 people. Fresh pasta should be cooked in a large pan (or in two pans if you haven't got a really big one) three-quarters filled with water. When the water is boiling, add salt (which will further raise the temperature of the water) just before you put the pasta in the pan. Fresh pasta cooks very much faster than dried – a matter of minutes.

Note: The tomatoes will be greatly improved by the addition of a spoonful or two of sun-dried tomatoes. These come packed in oil in jars and can be obtained from good delicatessens.

PASTA SAUCE NO. 2 (Vegetarian)

This is a sauce from Delia Smith's book, *One Is Fun*; it is an excellent sauce for a vegetarian – but *not* for vegans.

Serves 6

1¼ lb/575 g green tagliatelle
6 oz/180 g Gorgonzola cheese
8 oz/250 g Ricotta or cottage cheese
4 small cloves garlic
12 fl oz/375 ml single cream
4 tablespoons olive oil

1 red or green pepper, very finely chopped
8 spring onions including green parts,
  finely chopped
salt and freshly ground black pepper
2 oz/60 g Parmesan cheese

Put the pasta in boiling salted water (with a few drops of oil to prevent it sticking) and when the water has returned to the boil, cook for exactly 8 minutes for dried pasta, and cook until *al dente* with fresh pasta. Meanwhile, put the Gorgonzola and Ricotta cheeses into the liquidiser with the garlic, cream and a tablespoonful of hot water. Season with pepper and blend until completely smooth.

When the tagliatelle is ready, drain it thoroughly in a colander, then return it immediately to its hot pan. Add the olive oil, chopped pepper and spring onions, season with salt and pepper, then toss well. Add the cheese mixture to the pasta, toss thoroughly, then serve straight onto hot plates. Sprinkle with the Parmesan.

RASPBERRY AND HAZELNUT CRUMBLE (Vegan)

Serves 4

1 lb/500 g raspberries
4 oz/125 g plain flour
2 oz/60 g sugar

2 oz/60 g margarine (or butter for
   vegetarians)
2 oz/60 g toasted chopped hazelnuts

Turn on the oven to 170°C/325°F, Gas 3.

Put the raspberries in a fairly shallow baking dish. (If you like your fruit very sweet, add a sprinkling of sugar – personally, we don't think this is needed.)

Mix the flour with the sugar and rub in the fat until the mixture is like crumbs. Add the hazelnuts and put the mixture on top of the raspberries. Bake in the oven until the top is golden brown. If you bake it too fast, the raspberry juice will bubble up and spoil the top.

PINEAPPLE AND ORANGE SALAD WITH TOASTED ALMONDS (Vegan)

Serves 4

1 pineapple
4 oranges

4 oz/125 g toasted almonds

You can tell if a pineapple is reasonably ripe by pulling a leaf from the top. If it doesn't come away from the fruit, don't buy it.

Peel the pineapple carefully, taking away all the husks. Slice thinly and then cut into small pieces. Peel the oranges, removing all the pith, then slice thinly with a very sharp knife on a plate, to catch the juice. Mix the fruit together and leave covered with a damp cloth.

Blanch the almonds and then toast them in the oven on a baking tray until they are a rich brown. Shake them from time to time in order to turn them. Split the browned almonds and chop coarsely. Add them to the fruit salad before serving.

BAKED APRICOTS WITH YOGHURT AND CREAM
(Vegetarian)

Serves 4

8 fl oz/250 ml double cream
8 fl oz/250 ml natural live yoghurt (see
page 108)
3 oz/90 g soft dark brown sugar

1½ lb/750 g fresh apricots
3 tablespoons caster sugar (if you have
any with a vanilla pod – good)
grated rind and juice of 1 lemon

This is a very simple but delicious pudding. It should be made the day before you eat it.

Mix the cream and yoghurt well together, and put into a shallow dish. Sprinkle the dark brown sugar thickly all over it and leave in the fridge for 24 hours.

Wipe the apricots with a damp cloth and score them with a knife down their crease. Pile them into a baking dish. Add 6 tablespoonsful of cold water and 3 tablespoonsful of caster sugar, plus the grated rind and juice of the lemon. Bake in a very slow oven until the fruit is soft. Serve cold with the yoghurt and cream.

11 *Jane Grigson to Dinner*

One of the drawbacks of being labelled a good cook is that when you entertain, other people are nervous about asking you back. If you go to a good deal of trouble to prepare a delectable meal, not in order to show off, but because that is what you enjoy doing and also because you hope that return matches will be arranged, you can well find yourself transformed into a social pariah. 'Oh, we can't ask you back,' guests have said to both of us confidently, 'our food wouldn't be good enough for you.'

If just a competent, practised and enthusiastic cook can run into this problem, imagine a situation in which you are synonymous with excellent food. Take Jane Grigson; imagine having her to dinner.

One of the authors was faced with the American version of this problem when Julia Child, doyenne of American cooking, was invited to celebrate the British publication of one of her books. A most curious meal resulted with influences impinging from all over the world – Oriental spices in one course, a French sauce in another, a steamed suet pudding as dessert just to wave the British culinary flag a little. Mrs Child looked puzzled and floundered for a moment but, being a statuesque woman with a hearty appetite, fell to and ate with the enthusiasm that is the sought-after response in a guest.

Professional cooks tend to fall into two groups where appetite is concerned: either it is birdlike and they are unsuitably and maddeningly thin or it is hearty and they are delightfully greedy, happy to find food they have not had to prepare themselves and ready to love everything you put in front of them, exclaiming over perfectly ordinary ingredients as if it had never occurred to them to cook them.

Professional restaurant chefs are another matter. On the whole, chefs pay lip-service quite literally to tradition and notions of classicism, and do not like the around-the-world-in-forty-mouthfuls sort of event.

However, most people for whom food occupies a central position in their life, whether they earn their living from it or not, appreciate simplicity.

Meals for dedicated and knowledgeable consumers are not the occasions when you experiment with copying that cutesy timbale of pheasant sitting on a puddle of sauce that you once ate in a restaurant in Nîmes. A well-bred chicken, perfectly roasted and served with the pan juices and a bunch of watercress, is a far more tempting dish.

We give a recipe for skate because it is illustrative of the sort of delicious foodstuff that frequently gets overlooked because it is not deemed chic or glamorous. Yet it is just what you hope to be fed after hearing that a nouvelle cuisine chef in Altrincham is flavouring his mid-meal sorbets with Chanel No 5. Skate, with nutty brown butter sharpened with reduced wine vinegar, is a perfect example of the homely dish too seldom found at home.

Given that your guest has a genuine love for food, there shouldn't be too much time spent drinking and chatting before getting down to the serious subject of what is for dinner, and the first course should be the one where artfulness resides. The Courgette Balls which follow have proved a great success on this kind of occasion and, since professionals tend to be more wary of spices than the home cook, it is a chance to demonstrate your insouciance. Chestnut Soup is worth every scrap of effort – and much is needed – of peeling the things. Good cheese, a simple salad and a proper pudding is what should conclude the meal so that satisfaction and even self-satisfaction reigns. Then you wait and hope that Jane Grigson invites you over to her place.

Confit of Chicken Livers
Chestnut Soup
Courgette Balls
Seafood Lettuce Wrap
Skate with Browned Butter
Perfect Roast Chicken
Quails with Supportive Rice

Sauté of Baby Vegetables
Potato, Brussels Sprout and Celeriac
  Cakes
The Cheese Course
Excellent Green Salad
Sussex Pond Pudding
Rice Pudding

CONFIT OF CHICKEN LIVERS

Confit refers to meat preserved in its own fat and if you can obtain chicken fat, it is the best medium for this recipe. Kosher butchers often sell chicken fat (schmaltz), or if you buy a boiling chicken from a Kosher butcher there is usually quantities of fat in the cavity of the bird which can be rendered down. Failing that, use duck fat or goose fat, both of these are usually in copious supply after roasting the duck or the goose.

As long as the livers remain covered by the fat, they are preserved, but after the pot is opened they should be eaten fairly quickly. Because this is a rich dish, put it into small jars.

Serves 4 as a first course

8 oz/250 g chicken livers
4 oz/125 g chicken fat or alternative such as duck fat (see above), or enough to cover the livers

1 large onion, peeled and thickly sliced
3 cloves peeled garlic (optional)
salt and freshly-ground black pepper

Pick over the chicken livers and discard any gristle or green bits which, on account of a taint from bile, will be bitter. Separate the livers into their natural portions, i.e. pieces about 1 inch/2.5 cm wide.

Find a glass kilner jar about the size to hold the livers or, failing that, seek out a clean jam jar. Pack in the livers interspersing the layers with salt and freshly-ground pepper. Top with onion slices. Melt the fat you are using and heat the cloves of garlic in it. Pour it on to the livers and, if necessary, add more until the livers are covered.

Turn on the oven to 180°C/350°F, Gas 4, and bring a kettle of water to the boil. Put the glass jar into a larger oven-proof dish. Add boiling water to come at least half way up the jar, then place them in the pre-heated oven for 1 hour.

Remove the jar from the *bain-marie*, cool and refrigerate. When you serve the *confit*, we advise mashing the liver and a little of its fat on some brown toast, making sure that it is garnished with some of the onion. It makes an ideal snack or something to serve with drinks.

CHESTNUT SOUP

This soup is quite a lot of trouble, but it is absolutely worth it.

Serves 4

2 carrots
2 leeks
1 large onion
1 small head of celery with leaves

a good sprig of parsley
1½ oz/45 g butter
1 lb/500 g sweet chestnuts
Salt and pepper

Chop the cleaned vegetables and put them in a pan with melted butter. When they begin to look transparent, add 2 pints/1.1 litres cold water and simmer gently. Meanwhile, score each chestnut on the rounded side with a sharp knife, drop them in boiling water and boil for about 10 minutes. Take the pan off the heat and, taking one chestnut at a time, peel them, removing both outer and inner skins.

Now take half the vegetable liquid and stew the peeled chestnuts in it until they are soft (about 45 minutes). Liquidise the vegetables with the remaining stock with the chestnuts and their liquid. Season when you heat up the soup before serving.

COURGETTE BALLS

Given that you are resigned to spending time over the preparation of food for what you are assuming will be a discerning guest, these spicy courgette dumplings – taken from a recipe by Madhur Jaffrey in her splendid *Eastern Vegetarian Cooking* – in our experience never fail to intrigue and impress. They are best followed by a simple main course. Gram flour can be bought in Oriental grocery shops.

Serves 6

4 medium-large courgettes (about 1½
   lbs/750 g)
salt
1 fresh hot green chilli, de-seeded and
   finely chopped
3 tablespoons finely chopped onion

1 tablespoon peeled and grated fresh root
   ginger
2 tablespoons finely chopped fresh
   coriander
1½ oz/45 g gram flour
vegetable oil for deep-frying

For the sauce:

5 tablespoons vegetable oil, taken from
   the deep-frying oil above
2 medium-sized onions, peeled and finely
   chopped
¼ teaspoon ground turmeric
a pinch of cayenne pepper
1 teaspoon ground cumin

1 teaspoon ground coriander
2 tomatoes, skinned, seeded and finely
   chopped
8 fl oz/250 ml single cream
½ teaspoon garam masala
salt
1 teaspoon cumin seeds

Wash, trim and grate the courgettes, using the small grating blade of a
food processor or a mouli-légumes. Put them into a bowl and sprinkle
lightly with a pinch of salt, then set aside for 30 minutes. Wrap the
courgettes in a clean tea-towel and wring them out, being sure to save
the green liquid that runs off.

Dry the bowl and return the courgettes to it. Add the chopped chilli,
onion, ginger and coriander. Sift the gram flour over the vegetable
mixture, mix well and form 16 neat balls with your hands. In a wok or
similar pan, heat 1½ inches/4 cm oil over a medium heat. When hot,
put in enough balls to make one layer. Fry for about 2 minutes until
the outside surface colours. If you are using a wok, you can tip and
wash the hot oil over the balls, thus ensuring they stay intact. Remove
them with a slotted spoon and drain them on kitchen paper. Fry all the
balls this way.

To make the sauce remove 5 tablespoons of the oil from the wok and
heat it in a separate frying or sauté pan. When hot, add the onions. Fry
for 7–8 minutes until they begin to brown at the edges. Take the pan
from the heat and add the turmeric, cayenne, cumin and coriander. Stir
around and return to the heat. Add the chopped tomatoes, discarding
any stray seeds. Stir and fry for 5 minutes. Measure the courgette juice,
and add water if necessary to make 8 fl oz/250 ml liquid. Add to the
mixture and bring to the boil, cover and simmer for 15 minutes. This
much of the recipe can be prepared several hours beforehand.

Nearer the time of serving, add the cream, garam masala and a good
pinch of salt. Roast the cumin seeds in a dry frying pan, crush them and
add to the sauce. Mix well and cook for a minute. Now put in the
courgette balls and heat through, spooning the sauce carefully over
them. They need gentle handling in order not to lose their shape. Cook
only long enough to ensure they are hot right through, then serve. A
home-made unleavened bread (such as chapatti) goes well but pitta
bread will stand in.

SEAFOOD LETTUCE WRAP

This recipe was inspired by a meal in a Chinese restaurant specialising in seafood. It is rather more sophisticated than the similar approach to pork which appears in the chapter DULL PEOPLE, but with enough guests, it is worth offering both fillings with perhaps two varieties of lettuce, say Cos and Webb's Wonder, to act as the packaging.

Serves 4

6 oz/180 g large peeled prawns
6 scallops
8 oz/250 g squid (if unobtainable, use more of the shellfish)
salt and pepper
5 tablespoons vegetable oil
1 cube of peeled fresh root ginger about 1-inch/2.5-cm square
1 medium-sized fresh green chilli
4 spring onions

2 cloves garlic
1 large carrot
4 oz/125 g cauliflower or broccoli
2 tablespoons fish or vegetable stock
1 tablespoon soya sauce
1½ tablespoons dry sherry mixed with 1 teaspoon cornflour
1 teaspoon sesame seed oil
1 Cos or Webb's Wonder lettuce, separated into leaves for serving

Chop the prawns and scallops into small dice. Clean the squid by pulling out everything inside and peeling off the flaps and purplish skin. Cut off the tentacles and reserve. Wash the 'bodies' and cut down one side giving you a roughly square-shaped white sheet of squid. With a sharp knife, cross-hatch the surface of the squid, making sure you don't cut right through; this tenderises the flesh. Now chop the squid into small squares. Add it to the tentacles, chopped if large. Mix the fish together and sprinkle with salt, pepper and a little vegetable oil.

Cut the ginger into threads and do the same with the chilli, discarding the seeds and membrane. Cut the cleaned spring onions (including the green part) into small rings, and chop the garlic finely. Peel the carrot and, using a vegetable peeler, take off thin strips which you then cut into ½-inch/1.00-cm pieces. Break up the cauliflower florets or broccoli head into tiny pieces and discard the stalk. Heat 3 tablespoonsful of oil in a wok or sauté pan and, when hot, stir-fry the fish for 1½ minutes. Remove and set aside. Add the rest of the vegetable oil, heat up and stir-fry the vegetables for about 30 seconds, pour off any excess oil and add the stock, soya sauce and the sherry-cornflour mixture, stirring the latter just before you tip it in. When the liquid comes to the boil, return the seafood to the pan. Mix well and cook for about 1 minute to ensure that all the ingredients are well heated through.

Pile onto a warmed serving dish, sprinkle with sesame oil and offer alongside the lettuce leaves. The guests put a spoonful of the mixture in a lettuce leaf, make a parcel, and eat.

SKATE WITH BROWNED BUTTER

There are certain foodstuffs and dishes that, good though they are, are rarely offered either in homes or restaurants. It is as if they are not sufficiently glamorous. A simple dish carefully and correctly cooked is sure to be received more enthusiastically by someone for whom food is their work and their life than an imitation of 'smart' food. Skate is an often overlooked pleasure and anyone truly keen on food will appreciate its faintly gelatinous quality. The butter needs last-minute attention but is simple to do.

Serves 4

4 medium-sized wings of skate	*1 dessertspoon capers*
4 oz/125 g butter	*2 tablespoons finely chopped parsley*
2 tablespoons red wine vinegar	

Court bouillon:

2 tablespoons white wine vinegar	*10 peppercorns*
1 onion, peeled and thickly sliced	*parsley stalks*
1 carrot, peeled and cut into chunks	*a pinch of sea salt*

In a large shallow pan, put just enough water to cover the skate and add the court bouillon ingredients. Put in the fish and bring it slowly to the boil. After one eruption of bubbles, lower the heat to achieve the barest simmering. Cook the fish for 10–15 minutes until the flesh is opaque beside the main bone. (The second part of this process can be done in the oven if you prefer, the oven being set at 180°C/350°F, Gas 4.)

Warm a serving dish and four plates quite thoroughly, and when the fish is cooked, drain it and arrange on the serving dish. Melt the butter in a frying pan and, watching like a hawk, cook it until it goes a deep brown. Pour it over the fish. To the hot frying pan, add the red wine vinegar, swirl it round and let it bubble a few seconds. Pour that over the fish. Scatter on the capers and sprinkle on the parsley.

Sauté potatoes go well with this dish, and they are a great treat in their own right.

PERFECT ROAST CHICKEN

We have noticed that the more involved with food you become, the more you gravitate towards simplicity. A well brought-up chicken, considerately cooked becomes a far more beguiling dish than any nouvelle cuisine flight of fancy, pushed and primped and served in pre-ordained portions, which obviate that pinnacle of eating enjoyment, second helpings.

Serves 4

1 lemon
1 large free-range, grain-fed chicken or
    failing that, the best chicken you can
    buy
1 tablespoon extra virgin olive oil

4 oz/125 g unsalted butter
a few leaves of tarragon (if possible)
sea salt and freshly-ground black pepper
a bunch of watercress, washed and
    trimmed

Turn on the oven to 180°C/350°F, Gas 4.

Rub the skin of the chicken with one half of the lemon, squeezing it the while. Squeeze a little lemon juice into the cavity as well. Then massage the chicken with olive oil until the skin is supple. Now work your hand under the skin of the chicken, starting at the back where there is a flap of skin; after you have tugged away one or two tough membranes, you will find it quite easy to get your hand between the flesh and the skin over the breast and the thighs. Stop where the skin is attached to the breast bone. If the butter is hard, chop 3 oz/90 g of it into small dice and insert it under the skin, distributing it fairly by pushing it around from above. If the butter is softened, the technique is similar but you may need to spoon it in. If you have tarragon leaves, dot them about under the skin also. Do not use more than about 6 leaves as tarragon can be overpowering and you want the flavour of the butter and chicken to predominate. Place the remaining 1 oz/30 g butter and the intact lemon half inside the bird. Sprinkle the chicken with sea salt and grind black pepper evenly over it.

Place the chicken in a roasting pan which you have lightly oiled with olive oil. Put it in the oven and cook for 60 minutes, beginning to baste occasionally after the first 30 minutes. The separation of the skin from the chicken flesh will render it extra crispy and the butter under the skin will act as a self-basting process, ensuring that the flesh is succulent.

Towards the end of the cooking time, heat a serving dish, a gravy boat and the plates. Remove the chicken to the serving dish. Pour off the accumulated buttery juices into the gravy boat. Arrange the watercress in two bunches on the serving dish, one at either end of the chicken. Carve and serve, and make sure that, as well as chicken, everyone gets some skin and also some watercress wilted by the cooking juices. Keep accompaniments simple; perhaps just some steamed new potatoes.

QUAILS WITH SUPPORTIVE RICE

This dish is inspired by a Greek method of serving the little birds. Spices have been added since quails, by law, are now all farmed and have none of the flavour benefits of an interesting and hazardous life. The amount of meat on a quail is limited to say the least, thus the sausage meat in the rice is a welcome addition. Serve 2 quails per person with a few extra for hearty appetites.

Serves 4

10 quails
½ lemon
1 teaspoon ground coriander
1 teaspoon ground cumin
1 teaspoon ground cardamon
½ teaspoon ground ginger
8 screws of the pepper mill

8 oz/250 g Basmati rice
a good pinch of salt
2 tablespoons vegetable oil
2 oz/60 g butter
6 oz/180 g sausage meat (you can skin high-quality sausages)
¼ pint/150 ml double cream
1 hothouse (Dutch) lettuce cut across into thin ribbons

Rub the quail with the lemon and then with a mixture of the ground spices including pepper; let them sit for as long as possible absorbing the flavours. Wash the rice in several changes of cold water, then drain and put into a heavy-bottomed wide pan (rice cooks more evenly when spread over a large surface, rather than piled up). Add water to come above the rice by a scant ½ inch/1 cm. Add a pinch of salt and put it on the heat. Bring to a simmer and cover.

Meanwhile, heat the oil and butter and sauté the quail in a large pan, turning them until evenly browned. Cook them carefully, turning often, for about 15 minutes. It should be possible to do this without the addition of liquid, but should they be catching, add a tablespoon or two of water. In a separate pan, fry the sausage meat in a little oil, breaking it up with a fork until it resembles browned crumbs.

Test the rice. When it is ready, all the liquid should have been absorbed. Mix the drained cooked sausage meat with the rice. Remove the quail from the pan and keep warm. Add the double cream to the spicy pan juices and stir while it bubbles, to produce a small amount of deep honey-gold sauce.

Arrange the sausage/rice mixture on a warm serving dish, and scatter the strips of lettuce on top. Pile the quail in the centre and dribble the sauce over them. It should cover each quail just a little, not swamp the dish. A salad of lettuce hearts follows this dish nicely.

SAUTE OF BABY VEGETABLES

Inevitably, this dish is better in the early summer when broad beans and peas can be obtained young and fresh. It is possible, however, to assemble it with carefully chosen frozen produce. Dill is an important flavouring and if you are unable to obtain it fresh, the freeze-dried variety works perfectly well.

Serves 4–6

3 lb/1½ kg fresh broad beans
2 lb/1 kg fresh peas
1 bunch spring onions, cleaned and
    chopped
1 tablespoon vegetable oil
1 oz/30 g butter
chicken stock

1 hothouse (Dutch) lettuce, trimmed and
    cut across into thin ribbons
salt and pepper
sugar
chopped dillweed
cream (optional)

Pod the broad beans and peas. Heat the oil and butter in a heavy-bottomed pan. Cook the onions gently for a few minutes, then add the broad beans and cook for a few minutes. Add the peas. Carefully stir them to glaze them with the buttery oil. (If the broad beans are tiny, they can be cooked with the peas.)

Add sufficient stock to come just level with the vegetables; add the lettuce, a pinch of salt and black pepper and the sugar. Cover and simmer gently until the vegetables are tender – for about 10–15 minutes.

Add the dillweed and the cream if you are using it. If you want a thicker sauce, mix 1 teaspoonful cornflour or potato flour in a little more stock. Add and shake the pan to blend.

POTATO, BRUSSELS SPROUT AND CELERIAC CAKES

Serves 4

8 oz/250 g cooked Brussels sprouts	*1 oz seasoned flour*
8 oz/250 g cooked mashed celeriac	*salt and black pepper*
8 oz/250 g cooked mashed potato	*3 tablespoons sunflower seed oil*
1 egg	

It is important to use fresh vegetables for these cakes, not left-overs.

Chop the Brussels sprouts and mash them with a fork. Then mix the celeriac, potatoes and Brussels sprouts well together, adding the egg, and salt and pepper. Make little cakes from this mixture with your hands and roll them in seasoned flour. Fry them in hot oil in a frying pan.

THE CHEESE COURSE

Your choice of cheese will be dictated to some extent by your sources of supply. These can range from the shelves of a late-night supermarket, apt to provide you with firmly sealed sweaty packs of generic cheeses much favoured by the wretched Milk Marketing Board; through local supplies of farmhouse and cottage industry cheeses, to a shop able to import cheeses from a master *fromagier*, such as Philippe Olivier in Boulogne, and keep them at the optimum temperature. Whatever your scope, remember that a few cheeses, as few as two, in prime condition are much more satisfying and appetising than lots of different cheeses that will get picked at and leave you with bits of some and triangles of others that are good for nothing but storing in the fridge until it is time to throw them away.

Aim for contrast – a hard cheese and a soft one, a cheese on the bland side and one that is pungent, a white cheese and a blue cheese. We like to theme the cheeses to some extent, making an effort to procure English country cheeses (but beware of the more arcane varieties which can some-times be quite horrid) if English is the style of the meal; Italian cheeses if, for example, you have decided to serve a Bollito Misto (*see* page 242).

If you know the tastes of your guests and you find that you can buy one cheese that they will like in its whole form without being wildly extravagant, do so as it looks marvellous and in an odd way it encourages people to eat more than if they were faced with a range of cheeses. Cheeses made with unpasteurised milk – *au lait cru* – are invariably superior, if you can find them. A home-made cheese – which can be as simple as mixing fresh herbs and sea salt into a fresh cream cheese, or dressing half a Ricotta with ground black pepper and virgin olive oil – always has appeal and will invariably be chosen in preference to anything else you provide.

We feel that bread is the best accompaniment to cheese, but offer biscuits as well and celery for those pretending to be on a diet. Cheese boards do not look better for the presence of a tomato or sprig of parsley. Large enough pieces of cheese are beautiful in their own right. Lastly, the cheese course is the moment to open a good bottle of red wine or, should you be serving Stilton, some port. It is now très snob to drink a sweet Sauternes or other dessert wine with Gruyère cheese. If you are planning to continue with a dessert wine after the cheese course anyway, why not try?

EXCELLENT GREEN SALAD

A salad that appears either with or after the cheese course should be notable for its simplicity. This is the moment to look for a selection of interesting leaves such as *salade de mâche* (also called lamb's lettuce or corn salad), *frisée*, oak leaf lettuce, baby spinach, *mesclun* (sometimes available in this country at specialist shops), watercress and so forth. It is not the time for adding cunning or surprising ingredients like chopped green peppers, or cooked peas.

The salad dressing that works best is one made at the moment of serving. Have your leaves and chopped fresh herbs washed, dried, and arranged in a salad bowl. When you want to serve the salad, pour on $2\frac{1}{2}$ tablespoonsful of the best olive oil you can buy and mix well. When all the leaves seem coated, add a scant tablespoonful of wine vinegar, or balsamic vinegar if you have some, and toss again. Lemon juice could be used in place of vinegar but it tends to do battle with the wine you are drinking. Sprinkle on some sea salt, grind on some black pepper, toss once more and serve. Save more complicated notions of dressings, such as those made with mustards and garlic, anchovies and so on, for first course salads or crudités.

A favourite mid-meal salad is just soft lettuce, finely chopped parsley and the dressing outlined above served in a glass bowl the way the French do.

SUSSEX POND PUDDING

If it were, indeed, Jane Grigson who was coming to dinner, we think she would be pleased to find this 'best of all English boiled suet puddings', which she revived alongside so many other worthwhile dishes which were becoming muddled and travestied until publication of her books on the subject of British cookery. As Mrs Grigson says in *English Food*: 'The genius of the pudding is the lemon. Its citrus bitter flavour is a subtlety which raises the pudding to the highest class. When you serve it, make sure that everyone has a piece of the lemon, which will be much softened by the cooking, but still vigorous.'

Actually, no one could fail to be impressed by this cornerstone of serious country house food. The name of the pudding refers to the sauce which runs out of it when it is turned onto a serving dish and provides it with a moat of brown buttery liquid.

Serves 4–6

8 oz/250 g self-raising flour	*slightly salted butter*
4 oz/125 g fresh beef suet, chopped	*soft light brown* or *caster sugar*
milk and water	*1 large lemon* or *2 limes*

Mix the flour and suet together in a bowl. Make into a dough with the milk and water, half and half; ¼ pint/150 ml should be plenty. The dough should be soft, but not too soft to roll out into a large circle. Cut a quarter out of this circle, to be used later as the lid of the pudding. Butter a pudding basin lavishly. It should hold about 2½ pints/1.5 litres. Drop the three-quarter-circle of pastry into it and press the cut sides together to make a perfect join. Put about 3½ oz/100 g butter, cut up, into the pastry, with the same amount of sugar. Prick the lemon (or limes) all over with a larding needle so that the juices will be able to escape, then put it onto the butter and sugar. Fill the rest of the cavity with equal weights of sugar and butter cut into pieces – at least another 3½ oz/100 g, possibly more.

Roll out the pastry which was set aside to make a lid. Lay it on top of the filling, and press the edges together so that the pudding is sealed in completely. Put a piece of foil right over the basin, with a pleat in the middle. Tie it in place with string and make a string handle over the top so that the pudding can be lifted out easily. Put a large pan of water on to boil, and lower the pudding into it; the water must be boiling, and it should come halfway, or a little further, up the basin. Cover and leave to boil for 3–4 hours. If the water gets low, replenish it with *boiling* water.

To serve, put a deep dish over the basin after removing the foil lid, and quickly turn the whole thing upside down: it is a good idea to ease the pudding from the sides of the basin with a knife first. Put on the table immediately.

RICE PUDDING

To restore delectability to a dish that has been desecrated and damaged by institutional, or simply negligent cooking, is a crafty tactic in the business of feeding a foodie. Rice pudding, sinned against by schools, hospitals, prisons, no doubt, and the nursery, is an ideal candidate. You might think, upon reading the recipe, that such a small amount of rice will not absorb the liquid but it does. Long, slow cooking is the key. The bottom oven of an Aga or other solid fuel stove or a crockpot are ideal.

Serves 4 with second helpings

generous 2 oz/60 g butter
3 heaped tablespoons caster sugar
4 oz/125 g pudding rice (it is vital to use pudding rice)

half a vanilla pod, split lengthways
1½ pints/900 ml creamy milk
½ pint/300 ml double cream
a pinch of salt

Turn on the oven to 150°C/300°F, Gas 2.

In a roomy shallow flameproof dish, melt the butter. Add the sugar and stir around while it froths together. Add the rice and keep stirring until every grain is glistening. Continue cooking for about 5 minutes. The rice should not colour but the sugar and butter will have a slight caramelising effect apparent in the finished dish. Add the vanilla pod, pressing it against the side or bottom of the pan so that it spills its seeds and its flavour. Add the milk and cream carefully, so as to avoid the spitting butter, and put in a pinch of salt. Bring almost to the boil and then put on the bottom shelf of the oven for at least 2 hours. If the top seems to be browning too deeply, turn the oven lower.

Serve the pudding warm rather than hot and don't hang back from also offering cold, loosely-whipped double cream on the side.

12 *Sunday Lunch*

However many conventional mealtimes go by the board as women embark on raw energy diets and men decide to work late at the office, or as men decide to go on raw energy diets and women work late at the office, and as children discover the joys of re-heating a boil-in-the-bag meal, Sunday lunch when friends and family gather tends to go on being prepared. The fact that Sunday lunch has a different image to other sorts of meals is borne out by the fact that restaurants, however chic or modernistic, will abandon their daily menu and put on one that features a joint and a luscious pudding.

One of the attractions of Sunday lunch, quite apart from the shopping which most probably has been done the day before – unless Sunday-opening delicatessens and supermarkets have eroded your efficiency – is that it will be the only meal needing to be prepared that day. Even sticklers for punctuality and conventional mealtimes, even hard and fast believers in breakfast, dinner, lunch and tea being at the very least what the human frame requires, will accept that Sunday lunch can be served at 2.00 pm or later and take you through the afternoon. A little cold collation of the leftovers at about 10.00 pm can satisfy the greedy or those who panic at the thought of a missed meal.

That said, you do not want to spend the entire morning cooking; there are papers to be read. For this reason, a joint of meat is apt since, along with probably being quite different to anything you have eaten during the week, it takes only minutes in preparation and afterwards more or less looks after itself. We have given a recipe for a slightly unusual way of going about roasting lamb as roasting beef is a matter of timing, instructions for which can be taken from any competent cookery book, and since it is necessary to roast a very large joint of beef to have real success with it, lamb seems more practical. The Chicken Pie can be assembled the day before and an advantage is its ease to serve, for unless a born carver numbers among your guests or your family, the dishing out of a roast, though comfortingly symbolic, can involve tedious waits and the food of the polite becoming tepid. Hot plates are essential if you are serving a roasted joint.

The suggestions in each course may seem rather few, but yet another plus of this weekend meal is that guests will not only not mind repetition, they may come to hanker after it. In this mutable world some fixed points, such as a pie with a well-considered lucky dip of ingredients or a dish of delicious potatoes, are important. Recipes with which you become so familiar in the making that you can knock them up without reference to a book or recourse to weighing and measuring can provide soothing occupational therapy, something that is frequently required at the close of an anxious week.

On the whole, the main course of Sunday lunch is recognisable by its substantiality and the pudding by its puddingy quality. Therefore, we feel a first course is inappropriate as well as being a bore to make. Some suggestions for little things on toast to precede the meal and eat with drinks are included. The very nicest drink for Sunday midday is champagne. You may balk at believing this, but it is also one of the cheaper alternatives these days since champagne prices have held pretty steady and some supermarket champagnes are far from negligible in quality. Opening a bottle (or two) of champagne makes guests feel special and saves the host fussing around preparing this, that and the other. If you wish to stretch it or embellish it, depending on your point of view, you could make a Bellini with peach juice, a Kir Royale with cassis, a Paradis with raspberry juice, a rather fashionable mix with the juice of blood oranges, or whatever you will. Establish your own house cocktail.

A further consideration with Sunday lunch is the mix of age groups it usually attracts. Whilst we view the meal as a time to educate the young palates, it should also be a pleasure for children and obviate whining noises about how they don't like salsify and, in the case of separated parents, how Mummy/Daddy never makes them eat polenta. The very old can be similarly difficult and share with children a dislike of strange things sprung on them and can misconstrue a nouvelle cuisine purée as a thinly veiled insult. However, the Purée of Leeks we have suggested with the lamb is so delicious that is worth risking the implicit irony.

All the puddings, bar the Jam Roll, can be prepared ahead of time and the Jam Roll will provide you with the virtuous glow that attaches from 'using the oven'.

Anchovy Surprise

Honeycomb Mould

Smoked Salmon Pâté

Chocolate Mousse

Chicken Liver Pâté

Treacle Tart

Chicken and Mushroom Pie

Baked Jam Roll

Lamb Boulangère

Apple Charlotte

Purée of Leeks

ANCHOVY SURPRISE

Serves 4

4 thin slices wholemeal or granary bread
1 tin anchovy fillets
¼ pint/150 ml double cream or clotted
   cream or soured cream

vegetable oil
chives or fresh parsley, chopped (optional)

With a small biscuit cutter, stamp out rounds of bread; you want a size that constitutes one mouthful. Wash the anchovies quickly in warm water to remove excess salt (or don't if you like saltiness), and pat dry. Cut each fillet into three. If you are using double cream, whip it until quite stiff and put it back into the fridge. Leave the soured cream or clotted cream in the fridge until the last minute. Fry the rounds of bread in hot vegetable oil, then drain on kitchen paper. Place 3 pieces of anchovy on each round and cover with a spoonful of cold cream. If you like, sprinkle with chopped parsley or chives. Serve immediately.

The contrasts in this are delectable; hot and cold, crisp and soft, salty and bland.

SMOKED SALMON PATE

It is usually possible to find smoked salmon bits wherever smoked salmon, the whole fish, is sold. They tend to be very good value and used in a pâté, their bitty appearance is not a problem. To forego the monotony factor in pâtés, this one has three layers, which is less time consuming than it sounds if you have a food processor.

Serves 4–6

8 oz/250 g smoked salmon bits
7 oz/200 g curd cheese
lemon juice

freshly-ground black pepper
1 tablespoon chopped fresh parsley

In a food processor fitted with a steel blade, or in a liquidiser, chop the salmon into small pieces. Remove about a quarter of the salmon and set aside. Add the cheese to the mixing bowl and run the motor until you have a smooth mixture. Flavour with lemon juice to taste and freshly-ground black pepper. Switch on the motor for one more second. Remove half this mixture to another bowl and stir in the parsley.

Lightly oil the base and sides of a small straight sided dish, e.g., a small soufflé dish. Into the base evenly press the mixture of smoked salmon and cheese. Arrange on top the smoked salmon pieces and then smooth on the salmon/cheese mixture flavoured with parsley. Chill in the fridge for a few hours or overnight.

To serve, run a knife around the pâté and unmould. Arrange thin slices of hot brown toast in a napkin on a plate and serve with drinks.

CHICKEN LIVER PATE

Serves 8

1 lb/500 g chicken livers	*1 large clove garlic*
4 oz/125 g butter	*½ teaspoon dried thyme*
2 tablespoons brandy	*salt and freshly-ground black pepper*
2 tablespoons medium-dry sherry	

Clean the livers, removing any green parts with a sharp knife. Melt half the butter in a frying pan and cook the livers gently for a few minutes: they should be pink inside, but not raw. Remove the livers and put them in a liquidiser. Put the brandy into the pan with the cooking butter, let it bubble and then add the sherry. Add to the livers in the liquidiser the chopped garlic, thyme, the rest of the butter, the salt and pepper, and the liquid from pan, then whizz until you have a smooth paste. Decant into a bowl or pot. You can, if you wish, melt a further ounce of butter to seal your pâté in its container, in which case it will keep for a week or two in the refrigerator. In any case, the pâté is better if you keep it for a few days before eating it. Serve with hot toast.

CHICKEN AND MUSHROOM PIE

This recipe, evolved by Beth Coventry, the sister of one of the authors, is influenced by her many stays in Greece. The addition of cheese is a very Hellenic touch; it adds a surprising richness to what is essentially a homely dish.

Serves 6–8

1 chicken, preferably free-range
2½ oz/75 g butter
1½ oz/45 g flour
1 heaped teaspoon mustard powder
1 glass dry white wine
4 oz/125 g Cheddar cheese, grated
salt and pepper
2 tablespoons finely chopped parsley

1 tablespoon vegetable oil
1 large onion, peeled and finely chopped
forcemeat balls made from 8 oz/250 g top
*   quality sausage meat (optional)*
8 oz/250 g mushrooms, wiped and
*   chopped*
1 8 oz/250 g packet frozen puff pastry,
*   thawed*
1 egg, beaten

Vegetables for stock:

1 onion
1 large carrot
1 stalk celery

3 sprigs parsley
1 bay leaf
8 peppercorns

Turn on the oven to 220°C/425°F, Gas 7, 20 minutes before the pie goes in.

Put the chicken in a pan with water just to cover and add the vegetables and seasonings for the stock. Poach until tender, which will be no more than 1 hour for a large roasting chicken but up to 3 hours for a tough old hen.

Melt 1½ oz/45 g butter in a heavy-bottomed pan, stir in the flour, and mustard powder and cook gently until you have a smooth roux. Add up to 1 pint/625 ml of the chicken stock, or more if necessary to achieve a silky sauce of the consistency of single cream. Stir in the white wine and the cheese and cook gently. Taste for seasoning and add salt, pepper and the finely chopped parsley.

Heat the oil and remaining butter, and fry the onion until softened. Add the mushrooms and stir until they, too, are cooked. Remove the flesh from the chicken in fairly large chunks. Mix the chicken, onion and mushrooms into the sauce. (If you are including forcemeat balls, buy the best quality pork sausages you can find, skin them, and roll it into small balls which you should dust with flour and fry until crisp.) Pour the chicken mixture into a pie dish and add the forcemeat balls which have been drained on kitchen paper. Cover with the puff pastry and decorate the pie with any left-over pastry. Glaze with a beaten egg and cook for 30 minutes, or until the pastry has risen and is golden. If you want to make the filling in advance, re-heat it before covering with pastry and cooking in the oven.

LAMB BOULANGERE

The purpose of this recipe is to place the meat straight on one of the racks of the oven and let its juices 'weep' onto a tin of sliced potatoes sitting below. This produces delicious potatoes and crisply cooked meat.

We like to use masses of garlic but you could reduce the quantities if it is not to your taste. If you slash the lamb radically as described below, it will open out during cooking and appear quite different from the usual leg of lamb.

Serves 6

3½ lb/1.75 kg leg of English lamb
6–8 cloves garlic, peeled and chopped
herbs, such as rosemary and mint
salt and pepper

olive oil
3 lb/1.5 kg good quality potatoes, peeled
*   and thinly sliced*
butter

Turn on the oven to 200°C/400°F, Gas 6.

Make deep diagonal slashes in the lamb, rather as if you were criss-crossing on a baked ham. Push three-quarters of the chopped garlic into the cuts and sprinkle with herbs. Season with salt and pepper and dribble olive oil over the whole leg.

Layer the potatoes in a roasting tin, interspersing the layers with salt, pepper, dots of butter and the remaining garlic. Set the tin on the bottom rack in the pre-heated oven and the meat on a rack above. Roast for about 1½ hours if you like the meat pink, or for another half an hour if you like the meat well done.

Slice the meat and serve on the juice-impregnated potatoes. Letting the lamb 'rest' in a warm place for 15 minutes is always a good idea. During that time, you can brown and crisp the potatoes on a high rack in the oven.

PUREE OF LEEKS

Serves 4–6

3 lb/1.5 kg leeks
2 oz/60 g butter

freshly grated nutmeg
salt and freshly-ground black pepper

Trim and wash the leeks thoroughly. As you are going to chop them up, you can be quite ruthless in the cleaning, pulling them apart to see that no sand or mud is lurking. Chop them into 1-inch/2.5-cm slices using some of the dark green part. Cover the leeks with cold water and bring to the boil. Simmer them for about 15 minutes, or until they are quite tender; this is not a moment to aim for *al dente* veg. Strain the leeks rather carelessly so that some water clings, then empty them into the bowl of a food processor. Add the butter cut in pieces and whizz to a purée: depending on the size of your machine, you may have to do this in two batches. Put the purée back into the cleaned pan, or into the top of a double saucepan if you wish to keep it warm for quite a long period. Season with salt, pepper and a little freshly grated nutmeg.

At the time of serving, dribble some of the meat juices onto the purée.

HONEYCOMB MOULD

This nursery pudding appeals to children and grown-ups alike. The fresh lemons lend a clear singing flavour appropriate after a heavy main course. If you have a fancy jelly mould, this is the moment to use it. The pudding splits into layers providing a summit of lemon jelly and two bands of creamy mousse.

Serves 6–8

3 large eggs
rind and juice of 2 lemons
1 tablespoon gelatine
3 oz/90 g caster sugar

6 tablespoons/90 ml single or *double*
*   cream*
¾ pint/475 ml creamy milk

Separate the eggs. Whisk the yolks in a basin and add the lemon rind, gelatine, sugar and cream. Heat the milk to scalding point and whisk it into the eggs. Don't fret if it looks grainy – it will smooth out.

Put the basin over simmering water and cook, stirring, until you have a mixture as thick as double cream that coats the back of a spoon. Mix in the lemon juice. Taste to see if you want more sugar, but try to resist. Beat the whites into stiff peaks and strain the lemony custard onto them, folding it carefully and with a light hand, using a metal spoon. Pour into a 2-pint/1.25-litre jelly mould and chill until set. To unmould, slip a knife round the edge, put a plate on top and turn over. It should plop out pretty as a picture.

CHOCOLATE MOUSSE

The simpler a chocolate mousse the better. What you need is 1 oz/30 g dark bitter chocolate and one egg per person. Melting the chocolate in strong coffee or adding a little grated orange rind are the only flourishes allowed. Forget from here on recipes that include milk, cream, gelatine, alcohol, etc.

Serves 8

8 oz/250 g plain chocolate (Menier is a
   good choice or Terry's bitter)

8 eggs
2 tablespoons instant coffee

Either in a bowl that fits over a saucepan without touching its base, or in a double saucepan, place the squares of chocolate with 3 tablespoons of strong hot coffee that you have made by pouring not too much boiling water onto the instant coffee. Let it melt very gently, preferably in one layer so that you don't have to disturb it. The water in the lower saucepan should just shudder or, if you want to be sure not to overheat the chocolate, which makes it grainy, bring the water to the boil and then turn off the heat. The chocolate will eventually melt. Remove the pan from the heat and stir to blend.

Separate the eggs. Beat the yolks one by one into the chocolate. In a clean bowl, whisk the egg whites until they stand in stiff, dry peaks. Add a quarter of the volume of the beaten whites to the chocolate mixture and fold in with a light hand. Pour this onto the egg whites still in the bowl and fold again, blending carefully so that there are no white 'islands' but not hammering the air out of the mousse. Pour into small ramekins or pretty cups.

Chill in the fridge for a few hours. The chocolate hardening will set the mousse to just the right consistency. If you must serve cream, use single cream.

TREACLE TART

Serves 6

8 oz/250 g self-raising flour
a pinch of salt
3 oz/90 g butter
4 oz/125 g lard (Trex is very good)

2 tablespoons golden syrup
1½ tablespoons black treacle
4 oz/125 g fresh white breadcrumbs
grated rind and half the juice of 1 lemon

Turn on the oven to 200°C/400°F, Gas 6.

Rub the fats lightly into the flour to which you have added the salt. The fats should be cold and cut into nut-sized nobs before you start rubbing. When you have a gravelly texture, add a little cold water and bind the mixture with your hands or a wooden spoon. Roll out to ¼ inch/0.6 cm thick and put into a greased tart tin, then put it into the fridge for half an hour.

Put the syrup and treacle tins with their lids off into saucepans of hot water to melt the contents. This makes it easier to measure the quantities you require.

Put the breadcrumbs into the tart tin, and pour over the treacle and syrup. Sprinkle with the lemon rind and add the lemon juice. Bake in the oven for about 35 minutes.

BAKED JAM ROLL

Serves 4
½–¾ lb/225–375 g blackcurrant or
raspberry jam

Suet crust:
6 oz/180 g self-raising flour   *2 oz/60 g fresh white breadcrumbs*
pinch of salt   *4 oz/125 g finely-chopped suet*

Put the jar of jam into a saucepan of very hot water to soften it. Turn on the oven to 180°C/350°F, Gas 4.

Sift the flour, salt and breadcrumbs together. Add the suet and rub it in lightly for a minute – use only the ends of your fingers. Add cold water by small degrees until you have a light spongy dough; use a wooden spoon for this. You should end up with a non-sticky ball of pastry.

Roll out on a floured board to a rectangular shape about 8 inches/20 cm wide and ¼ inch/0.6 cm thick. Spread with jam to within 1 inch/2.5 cm of the edge of the pastry. Roll up the pastry, seal the ends and flap together with your fingers. Put the roll on a baking tin and bake for 40 minutes.

APPLE CHARLOTTE

Serves 4

1 small white loaf
6 oz/180 g butter
rind and juice of 2 lemons

2 lb/1 kg cooking apples
4 oz/125 g Demerara sugar
3 oz/90 g sultanas

This dish is best made in a fairly shallow baking dish – about 4 inches/ 10 cm deep. Turn on the oven to 180°C/350°F, Gas 4.

Slice and butter the bread generously. Finely chop the rind of the 2 lemons and squeeze out the juice. Peel, quarter and slice the apples, put them on a damp tea towel and keep covered to prevent discoloration.

Line the bottom of the dish with the bread, butter-side downwards. Put in a layer of apple, a scattering of sugar, sultanas, lemon rind and a little lemon juice on top. Then put in another layer of bread. Continue like this until the dish is full, ending with bread and butter with the butter-side facing upwards. Scatter the remains of the sugar and rind on top and bake in the oven for about 45 minutes. The top should be brown and crisp.

This dish can be eaten either hot or cold, and many people like whipped cream with it.

13 *Shopping After 7 pm*

There was a time when, unless you shopped during the day, which often meant a mad scramble around during an office lunch hour, you were consigned to an evening spent eating in a restaurant, munching take-away food or picking at a meal composed from the dry goods and tins in your store cupboard. Late night supermarkets, Asian grocers – usually one and the same thing – and ambitious delicatessens, have changed all that.

Butchers and fishmongers, however, resolutely believe that the day should wind down around tea-time, so meals shopped for after 7.00 pm still have certain constraints. Implicit in shopping at this hour is the need to make a meal in a hurry or anyway the wish to assemble food rather than laboriously prepare it. It is here that delicatessens can help out, though we feel they must be viewed circumspectly as so often the prepared salads and pâtés are astonishingly nasty. For example, it would be wiser to buy a tin of white haricot beans, a tin of tuna fish and some onions and quickly put together your own Italian salad rather than buy the mixture that has been sitting in the cabinet throughout the day and is feeling, and looking, weary. It will also work out considerably cheaper. A tin of sauerkraut might be a more interesting solution – particularly if you enhance it with some white wine and additional spices when you warm it up – than a carton of cole slaw which invariably seems to be made with malt vinegar and inadmissable amounts of sugar.

Certain items do not exactly benefit from being canned, but adopt a quite distinct personality which can turn out to be pleasing, rather the way the dullest looking person at a gathering can sometimes eventually prove the most diverting. Tinned *petits pois* come to mind in this category and, in a sense, tinned salmon is so unlike its fresh counterpart that it can be considered a whole new fish. Tinned salmon sits perfectly well in fish cakes.

We are not of the school that believes it takes only a spoonful of cream and a dash of sherry to turn a tinned soup into a gastronomic event. The one variety of soup that can provide a useful base are the fish soups put up in France. Often they have an intensity of flavour quite hard to achieve in the domestic kitchen. Such a soup embellished with prawns and perhaps even some smoked trout, could be served with croûtons, grated cheese and a fiery Sauce Rouille and not be an ignoble thing.

Continental sausages are usually well represented in late night shops. Varieties such as Bratwurst have a high meat content and usually a less harmful fat content than an English breakfast variety. Served with a warm potato salad and a choice of mustards, they make an excellent quick supper. Superior English pork sausages, with a minimum of rusk and some emphatic herbs, could be the springboard for Toad In The Hole, a dish for which most people will reveal an atavistic fondness.

The availability of boxed fresh pasta has been a great boon for the instant cook and this chapter includes two good and slightly unusual sauces. Bought fresh pasta will never quite match pasta made at home, but it is nevertheless delicate and should not be swamped by the more conventional sauces, like Bolognese and certainly not by tinned Bolognese. An invaluable item to store in the least chilly part of your refrigerator is a lump of Parmesan cheese well wrapped in layers of foil. Freshly-grated Parmesan perks up many a dish, and just butter and Parmesan is a fine dressing for pasta. Packet spaghetti, for which we are developing renewed liking and respect (it seems to have moral fibre), is equally delicious just served with garlic and a good brand of olive oil. Eggs are, of course, the eternal stand-by and the omelette recipe is one thought up at a time of true deprivation when the cupboard resembled Mother Hubbard's, for there are times when, even though shops are open, it is late and you simply don't want to go out at all.

Sardine and Yoghurt Pâté

Omelette with Spring Onions and Croûtons

Tinned Salmon Fish Cakes with Tomato Sauce

Ham with a Piquant Sauce

Toad in the Hole

Bratwurst with Warm Potato Salad

Fresh Pasta with Mushroom Sauce

Fresh Pasta with Smoked Trout and Fish Eggs

Chick Peas with Spinach and Fried Breadcrumbs

Sauce Rouille

Lemon Syllabub

Black Cherries with Soured Cream

SARDINE AND YOGHURT PATE

Serves 4–6

2 tins sardines
¼ pint/150 ml natural yoghurt

juice of 1 lemon
a pinch of cayenne pepper

Drain the sardines of their oil; if you have a cat, it will be delighted with the oil, and it is good for its coat.

Put the sardines and yoghurt in the food processor and whizz. Add the lemon juice and cayenne pepper to taste.

This pâté is better if it is left in the fridge for a couple of hours before you eat it.

OMELETTE WITH SPRING ONIONS AND CROUTONS

This dish was invented in a Mother Hubbard situation but turned out to be good enough to suggest even were you to have some mushrooms, bacon, or other conventional omelette fillings to hand. The crunch of the croûtons provides relief from the softness of the egg and if you use wholemeal bread it also lends a nice nuttiness.

Serves 2

4 eggs
salt and freshly-ground black pepper
a few sprigs parsley, chopped
1 small bundle chives, finely chopped
2 slices brown bread
vegetable oil

1 fat clove garlic, peeled and chopped
1 oz/30 g Parmesan cheese, grated
1 bunch spring onions, trimmed, peeled
   and finely chopped
1½ oz/45 g butter

We like to cook omelettes one at a time. If you are of this persuasion, break 2 eggs into a bowl and add 1 teaspoonful cold water. Season with salt and pepper and add half the herbs. Beat lightly.

Leaving the crusts on, chop the bread into cubes. Heat some vegetable oil in a small frying pan with the garlic and fry the bread, turning until you have croûtons, crisp on all sides. Roll them in Parmesan, then keep warm. In the same oil, quickly fry the spring onions. Drain on kitchen paper and keep warm.

Heat half the butter in an omelette pan. When it is foaming, add the beaten eggs. Push them and lift them, as you do with an omelette, and when it is set on the bottom and tacky on the surface, scatter on half the croûtons and onions. Fold over, tip out and serve with a little butter rubbed on top of the omelette to give it gloss.

Repeat the procedure with the other 2 eggs.

TINNED SALMON FISH CAKES WITH TOMATO SAUCE

Tinned salmon is now often more expensive than the fresh variety, but you might be feeling like having fish cakes and find the fishmonger closed. You could use pilchards if you draw the line at paying a lot for tinned fish; they lend themselves to a perfectly good, if different, fish cake. Tinned tomatoes are often considerably better in flavour than the fresh ones on sale nowadays.

Serves 4

1 lb/500 g potatoes, peeled
butter
2 tins (8 oz/250 g) salmon or pilchards
1 egg
1 teaspoon dried dillweed (optional)
a squeeze of lemon juice

a splash of anchovy essence or
*   Worcestershire sauce*
1 dessertspoon chopped fresh parsley
salt and pepper
1 egg for coating
home-made breadcrumbs
vegetable oil for frying

For the sauce:

1 tablespoon olive oil
1 clove garlic
1 14 oz/420 g tin peeled tomatoes
1 glass red wine

a pinch of cayenne pepper or chilli
*   powder*
1 teaspoon sugar
salt and freshly-ground black pepper

Boil the potatoes until they are cooked through and practically falling apart. Drain them not all that assiduously and mash with a knob of butter, but no milk as you want a stiff mixture. Drain the fish of oil or brine, break up and mix into the potatoes. Add an egg, stir well, and season with dillweed if you have it, lemon juice, anchovy essence or Worcestershire sauce, parsley, salt and pepper.

Form the mixture into cakes. Chill to firm them while you make the tomato sauce.

In the olive oil, gently heat the finely-chopped garlic; don't let it brown or burn as bitterness results. Tip in the tin of tomatoes, and break them up as best you can with a wooden spoon. Add the wine and seasonings including the sugar and let simmer and thicken while you fry the fish cakes.

Beat the egg in a soup plate. Cover the base of another soup plate with breadcrumbs; try not to resort to the packet variety that is bright orange. You can buy more respectable crumbs these days or easily make them in a food processor. Coat the fish cakes in egg, then breadcrumbs. Fry slowly in about ¼ inch/0.6 cm hot vegetable oil until they are heated through and the coating is crisp. Serve with the sauce.

HAM WITH A PIQUANT SAUCE

This recipe is a simplified version of one given in Elizabeth David's *French Provincial Cooking*. It is considerably finer than Ham in White Sauce and a good alternative to the sort of meal you *meant* to shop for at the butcher's but when you arrived, found that the butcher had shut up shop.

Serves 4

4 shallots or *1 onion*
3 juniper berries
4 tablespoons wine vinegar
2 oz/60 g butter
2 tablespoons flour
8 fl oz stock/250 ml or *½ stock cube*

a splash of white wine (optional)
¼ pint/150 ml double cream
salt and pepper
4 thick slices ham (from a whole ham,
    not out of a packet)

Turn on the oven to 180°C/350°F, Gas 4.

Peel and chop the shallots finely or, failing shallots, an onion. Put the shallots, the juniper berries and the wine vinegar into a small saucepan. Bring to the boil and reduce until there is practically no vinegar left.

In a larger saucepan, melt the butter, stir in the flour and continue stirring watchfully until the mixture is smooth and a pale coffee colour. Dissolve the stock cube in 8 fl oz/250 ml of water, or heat the same amount of stock should you have some. Add the stock to the flour and butter mixture gradually, stirring until the mixture thickens. Add a splash of white wine if it is around, and then the shallot mixture. Cook gently until there is no taste of flour, about 20 minutes.

Stir in the cream, taste for seasoning and thin if necessary; you want a fairly liquid sauce. Arrange the ham in a single layer in a shallow oven-proof dish. Strain the sauce over the ham and heat through in the oven.

TOAD IN THE HOLE

Serves 4

1 lb/500 g best pork sausages you can
  buy

12 oz/375 g streaky bacon, cut finely
1 tablespoon sunflower seed oil

For the batter:

8 oz/250 g plain flour
a large pinch of salt
1 egg

½ pint/300 ml skimmed milk or half
  water and half ordinary milk

Make the batter by mixing the flour and salt together in a bowl, then make a hole in the centre and drop the egg into it with one-third of the milk. Beat well, gradually adding the rest of the milk. Beat until perfectly smooth. Leave to stand for at least half an hour in the fridge.

Turn on the oven to 180°C/350°F, Gas 4.

Wrap each sausage in the bacon. Put them in a baking dish and bake for 20 minutes. Take the sausages out of the dish, pour off the fat, then pour in the oil and return the dish to the oven. When the oil is really hot, lay the sausages, brown-side down, along the centre of the dish. Take the batter, beat it briskly for 1 minute, and then pour over the sausages. Return the dish to the oven and bake for 50 minutes; when ready, the batter should be crisp and light brown.

BRATWURST WITH WARM POTATO SALAD

This assembly, typical of a meal you might find in a brasserie, makes a most satisfactory supper. Serve it with a selection of mustards, including a grainy one, a German one and English mustard powder made up according to your preference with water, milk or wine vinegar, about 10 minutes before you are going to eat. A really good chilled lager is the appropriate drink.

Serves 4

2 lb/1 kg potatoes – new ones or a waxy
   variety
8 Bratwurst sausages
6 tablespoons olive oil or 3 tablespoons
   olive oil and 3 tablespoons vegetable oil

2 tablespoons wine vinegar
salt and freshly-ground black pepper
4 shallots or 1 bunch of spring onions,
   peeled and chopped
1 tablespoon chopped parsley (optional)

Peel the potatoes and cut them in half if large. Boil them in salted water until just tender. While they are boiling, grill the Bratwurst, starting gently so they remain intact, but increasing the heat to finish with a nice browned surface. Mix together the oil, vinegar, and salt and pepper with the back of metal spoon – you want an amalgamation but not an emulsion. Drain the potatoes, slice immediately and while still hot turn in the dressing with the shallots or spring onions. Sprinkle with parsley and serve warm.

If you like an oily dish as they do, for instance, in Alsace, dress with a little more oil.

FRESH PASTA WITH MUSHROOM SAUCE

Serves 6–8

2 packets dried wild mushrooms
12 oz/375 g fresh mushrooms
1 large sweet onion
2 tablespoons light olive oil
2 cloves garlic
⅓ bunch fresh coriander, roughly
   chopped, or 10 coriander seeds,
   pounded in a mortar or 1 teaspoon
   ground coriander

1 teaspoon tomato purée
1½ lb/750 g fresh pasta – tagliolini is
   best, but you may not have a choice
½ pint/300 ml double cream
2 tablespoons chopped fresh parsley
salt and freshly-ground black pepper
3 oz/90 g Parmesan cheese, freshly
   grated

Soak the dried mushrooms in ¼ pint/150 ml of water just off the boil. They should soak for at least half an hour, so it should be the first thing that you do when you get back with the shopping.

Peel – or wipe clean – the fresh mushrooms and slice. Peel and chop the onion finely, then heat the oil in a pan and sauté the onions until they are transparent. Add the fresh mushrooms, pressed garlic and coriander and cook gently, stirring often. A little salt may be added at this stage to help the mushrooms sweat.

Add the dried mushrooms, roughly chopped and drained of their juice (but keep it). Stir well, and then add the juice by degrees. Add the tomato purée and leave to simmer for 15 minutes. (You can at this point turn off the heat and leave the sauce until you are boiling water for the pasta.)

While the pasta is cooking, stir the double cream into the sauce, cooking gently as you do so. Just before serving, add the chopped parsley and black pepper. The Parmesan should be in a bowl on the table for people to use as they like.

FRESH PASTA WITH SMOKED TROUT AND FISH EGGS

Boxed fresh pasta is now easily available, but should you need to buy the packet kind, choose a narrow width, i.e. tagliolini rather than tagliatelle. If you choose green pasta, try to find the red lump fish roe as the colours are pretty together. This idea, as with most ideas about food, came from another cook; in this case Alice Waters who owns Chez Panisse restaurant in Berkeley, California.

Serves 4

4 oz/125 g smoked trout
6 fl oz/180 g double cream
1 lb/500 g fresh pasta

4 tablespoons fish eggs, i.e., caviar,
* lumpfish roe (known as Danish caviar)*
* or salmon eggs*
freshly-ground pepper

Skin and bone the smoked trout and carefully flake the flesh; set aside. While a large pot of water is boiling for the pasta, reduce the cream slightly in a small pan over a medium heat. Cook the pasta until it is *al dente* – if it is fresh to begin with, this should be a matter of a minute or two, otherwise consult the packet, but test the pasta some time before the suggested limit.

Add the smoked trout to the hot cream and then mix carefully with the drained pasta. Put the pasta onto warmed plates and crown each heap with a tablespoonful of fish eggs. A pepper mill should be at the ready.

CHICK PEAS WITH SPINACH AND FRIED BREADCRUMBS

This is a satisfying dish, and though the ingredients can be assembled by a quick dash around the supermarket, this is not reflected in the taste.

Serves 2

1 onion
olive oil
1 lb/500 g frozen leaf spinach
1 tin (14 oz/435 g) chick peas

1 dried red chilli
salt and pepper
1 slice bread
1 large clove garlic

Peel the onion and slice it from tip to base in thin crescents. Fry until golden in 1 tablespoonful olive oil. Add the leaf spinach and cook according to the instructions on the packet until softened; drain off any excess water.

Drain the chick peas and stir them into the spinach with a dribble more of olive oil and the crumbled chilli pepper. Season with salt and pepper, cover the saucepan and allow the mixture to simmer. Meanwhile, fry a slice of bread in olive oil into which you have put a finely chopped or crushed large clove of garlic. When the bread is golden brown, drain and crumble it roughly onto the spinach and chick peas. Put into a serving dish. You could now fry another slice of bread and cut into triangles to serve alongside. Put the dish on the table before the breadcrumbs have lost their crunch.

SAUCE ROUILLE

This sauce will glamourise tinned or bottled fish soup, both of them often surprisingly good. If you also serve croûtons made of slices of French bread fried in olive oil and some grated cheese, you have a real meal on your hands. Try not to resort to bottled mayonnaise as a base. However fancy the label on the jar, it is never much like the real thing. Oddly, mayonnaise in tubes is better.

There are alternative methods to follow:

First method:

2–3 cloves garlic, peeled
2 small dried red chillies
1 slice white bread, crusts removed

3 tablespoons olive oil
1 dessertspoon of the soup
salt and pepper

Pound together the garlic and chillies in a mortar or a small pudding basin. Squeeze out the bread in water and stir into the garlic mixture thoroughly. Gradually add the olive oil as if making mayonnaise and moisten with the soup. Season to taste with salt and pepper.

Second method:

2–3 cloves garlic
2 small dried red chillies
2 egg yolks
1 teaspoon Dijon mustard

3 tablespoons olive oil
3 tablespoons vegetable oil
salt and pepper
a squeeze of lemon

Pound the garlic and chillies as above. Beat in the egg yolks and mustard. Gradually add first the olive oil and then the vegetable oil; as if making mayonnaise. Stop when you have a thick, viscous mixture. Season with salt and pepper and perhaps a squeeze of lemon juice.

Float a piece of fried bread on each serving of soup. Add a dessertspoonful of rouille and sprinkle with grated cheese. Serve the remaining rouille in a bowl on the table.

LEMON SYLLABUB

Serves 6

1 pint/625 ml double cream
2 oz/60 g caster sugar
grated rind and juice of 1 lemon

¼ pint/150 ml dry sherry
¼ pint/150 ml brandy

Put all the ingredients together into a bowl and, with a hand-held electric beater, whisk until very thick; this will take about 20 minutes. Pour into small glasses and put in the fridge until serving.

BLACK CHERRIES WITH SOURED CREAM

Serves 4

1 tin (14 oz/435 g) black cherries
2 oranges
1 lemon

½ pint soured cream (if you cannot get soured cream, buy fresh double cream and sour it with a small squeeze of lemon juice)

Drain the cherries and reserve the juice. Grate the orange and lemon rinds and squeeze the fruit.

Put a small amount of cherry juice into a small pan with the orange rind and simmer for a few minutes. Put the cherries into a serving bowl with the rest of the cherry juice, add the orange and lemon juice, then the contents of the pan. Finally, add the grated lemon rind. Serve with dollops of cream.

14 *Invalid Cooking*

Cooking for invalids conjures up depressing memories of over-steamed fish, milk puddings and stewed fruit. All these things can, of course, be good in their way, but the people in charge who make the rules and carry out the results feel it is so good of them to make a special effort that the gastronomic result is often beside the point. Invalid food, in many people's minds, should be bland and tasteless – in return for being digestible. We believe that invalid food should taste delicious, nourish the eater and set him or her on the road to recovery. But it *is* a key point that the meal should be easy to digest.

If you are faced with cooking a meal for your family and friends *plus* an invalid, the first rule is not to cook two separate meals: it is curiously demoralising to sit in front of a milk pudding or a steamed plaice while everybody else is tucking into roast lamb. It is perfectly possible to make a delicious meal that will suit everybody. The second rule is that whatever kind of invalid you are dealing with, a minimum of butter, cream, egg yolk or alcohol in the meal (and preferably none) is the kindest course. Alcohol and fats are hardest on the liver, and if you avoid them entirely, almost any invalid will benefit. Naturally, if you are faced with an invalid who announces beforehand that their doctor has told them to eat nothing but bananas, that is what you must provide – in which case you won't need to read this. Do, however, ask whether any particular food is taboo – apart from illness, there are such things as allergies.

The third rule is not ever to pile the invalid's plate: even if you feel that it would do them all the good in the world to eat more, you won't achieve it by this method. Give them a small helping, and after a decent interval, offer them a second. Invalids often start by thinking that they hardly want to eat, but usually, if sufficiently tempted, they can surprise themselves and you. Finally, we think a two-course meal is desirable: if you fill the invalid up with a starter, they may find it hard to keep going, and generally the main dish is what you want them to eat.

The following menus are almost without fat. The Orange Jelly contains a very little sherry, but provided your invalid is not recovering from hepatitis this should be allowable.

Supposing, however, that your invalid is not actually visiting but a resident, and entirely, or largely, in bed to boot? Many invalids have the tiresome habit of not wanting the meals you provide and then being overcome with hunger for a snack – a little something – an hour later. Hot and cold drinks are an essential part of an invalid diet. Almost all patients are better for as much liquid as you can get into them, and it is useful if some of the drinks are nourishing as well as enjoyable. For this reason, properly made Beef Tea is a first consideration. It seems expensive, and it takes time, but you can make a lot of it at once and if necessary, freeze some and then heat as required. We also think that fresh Lemonade and Barley Water are a great boon, and so have included recipes for them. For a hot snack (or supper), poached Soft Roes on Toast could be a winner as could a couple of steamed scallops. But all too often, the need for a snack comes at an awkward moment and a sandwich is what is wanted. So we have suggested a few Sandwich Fillings that are quick and easy to prepare. If sweet things are required, it is sensible to make a cake that will keep well, so a good Cherry Cake has been included.

Eggs as a hot snack have to be considered: if you can get a really fresh free-range egg, boiling or coddling it is unbeatable. (Samuel Butler used to range about the Home Counties telling farmers frightful lies about how he needed absolutely fresh eggs for an invalid friend. He then returned to London and triumphantly boiled them for himself.) If you can't buy an egg with real personality, then you will have to get good at omelettes, or scrambling.

Apart from the Carrot Soup in this chapter, soups that are nourishing and easy to make are Watercress (see page 64), Spinach and Celery (*see* page 226). Small salads are also acceptable. A tomato and mozzarella could be one: cress, watercress and avocado would be another good combination.

Carrot Soup   Orange Jelly
Stuffed Fresh Haddock   Cherry Cake
Poached Chicken   Beef Tea
Soft Roes on Toast   Lemonade
Sandwich Fillings   Barley Water
Baked Apples

CARROT SOUP

Serves 4

1½ lb/750 g carrots
1 onion, peeled and chopped
1 dessertspoon sunflower seed oil

1½ pints/.63 litres chicken stock
salt and pepper
sugar

Scrub and chop the carrots; if you have a food processor, you can grate them. Sauté the onion in the oil with a little salt to make it sweat. Add the carrots when the onion becomes transparent; stir until the carrots are well coated with oil and onion. Add the stock and simmer until the carrots are soft.

Liquidise everything or preferably use a French mouli which gives a far more interesting texture. Season with pepper and sugar if liked.

STUFFED FRESH HADDOCK

You may need two fish depending upon their size and how many people you are feeding: it is safe to say that a 4 lb/2 kg fish will do 6 people. Whether you buy fresh haddock, cod, or hake depends upon what looks best at your fishmonger that day. The stuffing calls for sorrel, but it can be quite difficult to buy. Sorrel is very easy to grow and we strongly recommend that anybody with room for one or two roots does so. It is invaluable for cooking and has a long picking season. However, if you cannot procure sorrel, use spinach.

Serves 6

4 lb/2 kg fish (see above)

For the stuffing:

12 oz/375 g fresh breadcrumbs
2 oz/60 g parsley, chopped
2 oz/60 g sorrel, chopped
a handful of chopped chives or 1 small
onion, chopped finely

grated rind of 2 lemons
salt and pepper
4 oz/125 g butter
1 egg yolk
vegetable oil

Put the first six stuffing ingredients in your food processor and add the butter straight from the fridge. When this is well-mixed, add the egg yolk.

Turn on the oven to 180°C/350°F, Gas 4. Stuff the fish. You can fasten the flaps with small wooden toothpicks, or you can sew the fish with a needle and fine twine. Paint the fish with oil and wrap in aluminium foil and bake in the oven. The cooking time will depend upon the size of the fish: test after 30 minutes by pricking the fish near its spine to see if the flesh is opaque.

Serve a purée of potato, and a steamed green vegetable, such as broccoli, spinach or french beans, with this dish.

POACHED CHICKEN

Chicken is best poached in a previously-prepared stock. If you go to a really good butcher who does a big trade, you may be able to get or buy a raw carcass of chicken as well as the one you are going to poach. In any case, you can use the giblets: be sure to cut off all the fat from the heart, etc.

Serves 4–6

3½-lb/1.75-kg roasting chicken
  (free-range if possible)

For the stock:

3 large carrots, scrubbed and sliced	*herbs – including a sprig of rosemary*
1 onion, peeled and roughly chopped	*3–4 cloves*
2 stalks celery, chopped	*6 peppercorns*
	a little sea salt

Simmer the vegetables and seasonings in 2 pints/1.1 litres cold water very slowly for 1½ hours and then strain.

Put the chicken into a deep pan, and pour over the strained stock. If the breast is above the stock, cover it with buttered paper. Simmer gently for half an hour and then add:

1 lb/500 g carrots, scrubbed and cut so that their size is uniform	*1 parsnip, peeled and sliced*
	1 turnip, peeled and sliced
1 lb/500 g onions, peeled and cut into quarters	*2 oz/60 g rice*

Simmer everything together until the chicken is cooked and the vegetables tender – this will take about an hour. This dish may be served with a parsley sauce, and it is also good with the vegetables mentioned in the previous recipe.

SOFT ROES ON TOAST

Serves 1

½ teaspoon mustard powder
salt
1 oz/30 g butter

4–6 oz/125–180 g soft roes
1 slice wholemeal bread

Put the mustard and a little salt into a bowl with the butter and work it all into a paste with a fork. Melt the paste in a double saucepan to avoid browning the butter, then put the roes into a non-stick pan and pour the melted butter over them. Cook gently for 8–10 minutes while you are toasting the bread. When the roes are cooked, arrange them on the toast.

SANDWICH FILLINGS

Sandwiches can be very useful – not only as snacks for convalescent adults, but for children who are off their food. We have provided a small collection here: obviously you must choose what is suitable for the age and state of your patient. Do use the best wholemeal bread for your sandwiches, as this will provide much-needed fibre for your patient.

HONEY AND OATMEAL

Put a handful of oatmeal in a baking dish and bake it in a moderate oven until it is pale brown.

Butter thin slices of bread, and spread with honey. Do get good honey: read the label carefully. Also, it is easier and less messy for your recipient if you use the stiff honey rather than the kind that drips and oozes. Sprinkle toasted oatmeal on top of honey and add a second piece of buttered bread.

EGG AND WATERCRESS

Hard-boil 2 eggs. As most people hard-boil eggs until they are like cannon balls, it may be worth remarking that the best results are obtained by putting eggs into cold water, bringing them slowly to the boil and then boiling for exactly five minutes. Take out the eggs and plunge them into cold running water until cool. This way, the yolk will be a little soft, or at least yielding.

Mash up the eggs with a little top of the milk. Add salt and pepper to taste. Chop watercress (washed and dried, of course) fairly finely. Combine the mixtures.

CHEESE AND SULTANA

Butter the bread. Grate mild Cheddar cheese coarsely, and put on the bread with a scattering of sultanas. These sandwiches, that became famous in the last war when they were served at the National Gallery in London at lunchtime concerts, are popular with children and very nourishing.

CREAM CHEESE AND TOMATO

Blanch and skin tomatoes – tomato skin is utterly indigestible. Put cream cheese – Petit Suisse is good, or a double cream cheese bought from the delicatessen – onto unbuttered bread, then put thinly sliced tomato on top. The tomato may be garnished with chopped chives or finely-chopped parsley but this is a matter of taste. A very light sprinkling of salt, and a touch of sugar will help the flavour of the tomatoes. Add a second slice of bread spread with cream cheese.

CREAM CHEESE AND BLACKCURRANT JAM

Spread cream cheese as above. Use only home-made blackcurrant jam, or a superior brand such as Tiptree.

BANANA AND BROWN SUGAR

Slice bananas thinly and put them on buttered bread. Scatter with demerara sugar and add a squeeze of lemon juice.

BAKED APPLES

Turn on the oven to 180°C/350°F Gas 4.

Large Bramley apples are the best to use: one per person. Wipe the skin with a hot wet cloth and then, using an apple corer, be sure to remove all the core. This will make a slightly large hole in the middle of the apple, but you will need it for the stuffing.

Put the apples on a clean baking tray and stuff each cavity with butter, dark brown sugar and sultanas in that order until the hole is full; pour a little lemon juice into the top. Bake in the oven for about 45 minutes.

Baked apples are delicious with thick cream, but your invalid may also enjoy one without.

ORANGE JELLY

Most people think of jelly as being boring, but this is because it is made from packets. Home-made jellies are easy to make, and are refreshing and delicious.

Serves 6

4 oranges
2½ fl oz/75 ml sherry
⅔ packet of gelatine

4 oz/125 g white sugar
1 lemon

Wash the oranges and dry them. Buy good dessert oranges rather than oranges you would use for juice. Peel 2 of the oranges very thinly (a potato peeler is easiest) and steep the rind in sherry for 1 hour.

Soak the gelatine in 2½ fl oz/75 ml water, stir over a gentle heat until dissolved, then strain onto the sugar and add another 2½ fl oz/75 ml hot water. When the sugar has melted, stir in the strained juice of the oranges and the lemon. Strain the sherry from the rind; add the sherry and discard the rind.

We put these jellies into small individual pots, but you can, of course, put the liquid into a wetted jelly mould.

CHERRY CAKE

4 oz/125 g butter
4 oz/125 g caster sugar
3 eggs, separated
4 fl oz/125 ml milk

8 oz/250 g plain flour
1 teaspoon cream of tartar
12 oz/375 g glacé cherries
1 teaspoon bicarbonate of soda

Beat the butter and sugar to a white cream. Add by degrees the yolks of the eggs, and then add the milk little by little – beating all the while.

Turn on the oven to 200°C/400°F, Gas 6.

Take the flour, add the cream of tartar to it, and use a little to coat in the cherries. Add the flour to the creamed mixture, beating all the time. Fold in the cherries. Whisk the egg whites to a stiff froth and add bit by bit. Then add the bicarbonate of soda mixed in a little milk. Pour into a greased 7-in/17.5 cm tin and bake in the oven for 20 minutes until the cake has risen; then lower the temperature to 180°C/350°F, Gas 4.

The cake should take about an hour to cook, but you can test whether it is done by inserting a fine skewer or knitting needle. If the cake is done, the skewer will come out clean. Take out of the oven: leave to cool a little, and then turn out gently onto a cake rack.

BEEF TEA

1 lb/500 g lean beef – shin is good   *1 small onion*
1 oz/30 g butter   *salt*
1 clove

Cut the beef into small dice, and put into a saucepan with the butter, clove, onion and a little salt. Stir the meat over the heat until it produces a thin gravy: then add 1 quart/1.1 litres water and simmer for 1 hour, skimming off every particle of fat.

After cooking, strain the liquid through a sieve and keep cool until required.

As the beef tea is needed for the patient, heat it through in a double saucepan. These quantities make about 1 pint/625 ml of good beef tea and heating in a double saucepan means that you don't lose any of it by reduction.

LEMONADE

Put 6 ice cubes, 1 whole lemon, 1 tablespoonful caster sugar and 1 pint/625 ml water into the liquidiser. Switch on to full for a slow count of 10. Strain. This makes excellent lemonade and is very little trouble to make.

BARLEY WATER

2 oz/60 g pearl barley

Wash the barley in cold water, put it into a saucepan with 1 pint/625 ml cold water and when it has boiled for about 15 minutes, strain off the water and add 2 quarts/2.3 litres of freshly boiling water. Boil until the liquid is reduced to half, strain it and it is ready – if plain barley water is required. You can flavour it with a little lemon rind and sugar, or you can mix it with the Lemonade described in the previous recipe. Barley water is very good for the kidneys.

15 *Greedy People*

The French make a distinction between those who insist upon very small quantities of delicious food (gourmet), and those who want everything to be frightfully good, but above all want a great deal of it (gourmand). Our experience in this country leads us to conclude that gourmands are thicker on the ground. The English do not, on the whole, pick at their food. In 1693, the Duke of Hamilton was spending over £1,000 a week on provisions: admittedly this covered the state banquets at Holyrood, but it did not include meat, butter and vegetables that were brought from his own estates – and £1,000 in the seventeenth century would be approximately £150,000 today. We must infer that apart from the excellence of the fare, people ate a very great deal of it. The habits of the Prince Regent were certainly gourmand, and Edward VII was no mean trencherman. One of many affectionate memories of James Robertson Justice is of his looking pensively at the carcass of a wild goose and remarking to his fellow diner, 'Tiresome bird: too much for one, and not enough for two.'

Greed is regarded as bad – is indeed famous for being sinful. We feel that as with so much else, it is a matter of degree. People who are utterly indifferent about what they eat are missing a basic, and often simple pleasure. On the other hand, people totally preoccupied with their bellies are dull – and usually unattractive to be with. We find it rewarding to cook for moderately greedy people, but we also recognise that, from time to time, the immoderates occur in life. Someone you are very fond of is married to one, for instance, and marriage usually implies a social package deal.

The menu we suggest is comprised of dishes that any moderately greedy person might appreciate: for the immoderates, you simply double the quantities. In much the same way that heavy drinkers are disquieted by the absence of spare bottles of wine on the table, or a least in view, so heavy eaters will get nervy if they have to count the roast potatoes, or worse, won't count but will simply scoff an unfair share. They are also very keen on second helpings, however large the first one was. They expect a minimum of three courses; they don't like being fobbed off with cheese and fresh fruit instead of a pudding – although they will almost certainly want cheese as well. How much you pander to them is up to you.

Oeuf Froid Câreme
Sizzling Prawns
Fried Sole with Iced Fennel Butter
Cold Poached Salmon
Cucumber Salad
Filet de Boeuf en Croûte
Saddle of Venison

Excellent Roast Potatoes
Potato Pie
Cornbread
Duke of Cumberland's Pudding
Stuffed Peaches
Iles Flottantes

OEUF FROID CAREME

This is a Roux brothers' recipe that has always been, and still is, served at their 3-star Michelin restaurant, Le Gavroche in Brook Street, London. The recipe details are taken from *New Classic Cuisine*, the Roux brothers' first cookery book, packed with delights for greedy people.

Serves 4

4 globe artichokes, preferably Breton
juice of ½ lemon
6 tablespoons white wine vinegar
4 eggs
4 medium-sized slices of smoked salmon
   weighing altogether about 6 oz/180 g
1 small truffle, about 1 oz/30 g

mayonnaise made with 1 egg yolk and ⅓
   pint/200 ml oil (see page 117)
1 tablespoon tomato ketchup
1 teaspoon Cognac
chervil (optional)
salt and pepper

Snap the stalks off the artichokes and, using a sharp knife, trim off the leaves until only the neatly shaped hearts are left. Squeeze a little lemon juice over them. Cook the artichoke hearts in a saucepan of boiling, salted water with 3 tablespoonsful wine vinegar, or in a white court bouillon (1 tablespoonful flour, 3 tablespoonsful wine vinegar and salted water). They will need 25–30 minutes, depending on their size. Use the point of a knife to test whether the artichoke hearts are done, then leave them to cool in their cooking liquid.

Next bring a shallow pan of water to the boil, add 3 tablespoonsful vinegar and poach the eggs. Lift them out with a slotted spoon and place them in a bowl of very cold water; then remove to a tea towel and trim any ragged edges from the white.

Use a plain 3½-inch/9-cm pastry cutter to cut a neat circle from each slice of smoked salmon. Decorate prettily with some of the truffle and place in the refrigerator. Cut the smoked salmon trimmings into small dice and keep them in a bowl. Roughly chop the remaining truffle and add it to the diced salmon. Stir in the mayonnaise, add the ketchup and Cognac and season to taste with salt and pepper. Keep at room temperature.

To serve, remove the chokes from the artichoke hearts and pat dry with a cloth. Divide the mayonnaise mixture between the 4 artichoke bottoms. Place an egg on each one and top with a round of smoked salmon. You could add a sprig of chervil for colour (and in place of the truffle) if you wish.

SIZZLING PRAWNS

Prawns – either the large ones you have to peel or the tiny brown ones (shrimps) that you can eat whole, whiskers and all – are delicious when fried in lots of oil spiked with garlic and chilli which provides a wonderful sauce for mopping with bread – an activity much enjoyed by the greedy.

Serves 4

2 pints/1.1 litres shrimps or 3
   pints/1.75 litres larger prawns
6 tablespoons olive oil or vegetable oil,
   depending on preference
3 cloves garlic, peeled and finely sliced

2 teaspoons cayenne pepper
1 teaspoon ground ginger or 2 teaspoons
   grated fresh root ginger
1 teaspoon salt
French bread for mopping

In a sauté pan which you can bring to the table, heat the oil. Add the garlic, cayenne, ginger and salt. Sizzle for a moment but do not let the garlic brown. Add the prawns, turn up the heat and fry them fast and furiously, turning with a wooden fork or spoon until the shells are well coated with oil and seasonings. Take the pan to the table with the oil still bubbling.

FRIED SOLE WITH ICED FENNEL BUTTER

Greedy people like a whole large sole each, no messing about. The crisp breadcrumb coating adds substance and deliciousness and the hot fish with cold butter is another appeal to the senses.

Serves 4

1 small head fennel
6 oz/180 g salted butter at room
   temperature
freshly-ground black pepper
4 × 12 oz/375 g Dover soles

seasoned flour
2 eggs, beaten
6 oz/180 g dry white breadcrumbs
vegetable oil for frying

Trim the fennel, quarter it and steam until soft; then purée it in a food processor or liquidiser. Strain off the excess liquid, add the butter and whizz together. Season with pepper and whizz again. Pack into a small dish and freeze.

Skin and trim the soles, leaving the heads on or ask the fishmonger to do this when you buy them. With a small sharp knife, make a cut, one side only, down the centre of the backbone. Raise the side fillets, loosening them with a knife, so that you can snip the bone just below the head and above the tail. Later you will remove the whole backbone, so work the fillets away from the bones, but leave them attached at each end and along the outer edge of the fish: you are working from the centre out. Rinse the fish and pat dry.

Dip each fish into seasoned flour, then into beaten egg and then press the fish into the breadcrumbs. Also egg and crumb the underside of the raised fillets. Heat the oil and fry the fish until golden brown, turning once. Drain on kitchen paper. Leave for a minute or two and then carefully pull out the backbone, taking care not to disturb too much of the breadcrumb coating.

Remove the fennel butter from the freezer, and cut into slices. Tuck the slices into the cavity of the soles. Serve with wedges of lemon.

COLD POACHED SALMON

You should allow ½ lb/250 g of salmon per person, with a bit over. Wild Scotch salmon is the best; it is also the most expensive. If you are buying a piece, try to get the middle cut of a large salmon, but you may find a smaller whole one that is the right weight for your party. For a whole salmon, you really need a fish kettle, otherwise you will have to cook it curved in a large pan: if you have no kettle, a piece may be the best answer.

Salmon (see above)
Court bouillon for poaching:

½ bottle dry white wine	*1 bay leaf*
¼ pint/150 ml tarragon vinegar	*1 blade mace*
1 lemon, cut in slices	*2 sprigs fresh thyme or 1 heaped*
2 onions, sliced	*teaspoon dried thyme*
2 carrots, chopped	*2 sprigs parsley*
12 peppercorns	

Put all the court bouillon ingredients into a pan with 3 quarts/3.5 litres water and simmer for 45 minutes. Allow to cool, then strain.

Put the court bouillon into a pan suitable for poaching the salmon, lay the fish in it and bring it very slowly to the boil. The moment that it reaches this point, turn down the heat, allow it to simmer for 1 minute and then turn off heat. Leave the salmon to cool in the liquid.

This method ensures that your salmon is not overcooked, but is juicy and *à point*. It should be served with a cucumber salad (*see* following recipe) and a mayonnaise; we suggest a *mayonnaise verte* (*see* page 117).

CUCUMBER SALAD

If possible, use rice vinegar rather than tarragon vinegar for the dressing. It is a sweeter vinegar and is particularly suitable for this salad. You can buy it at an oriental grocery shop.

Serves 4

1 large cucumber
1 tablespoon olive oil
1 tablespoon tarragon vinegar or *rice vinegar*

1 teaspoon sugar (if you are using tarragon vinegar)
½ teaspoon salt and black pepper
small bunch chives

Wipe the cucumber with a clean damp cloth. Leaving the skin on, slice it as finely as possible. Put it in a pudding basin and make a dressing of the oil, vinegar, sugar – if tarragon vinegar is being used – salt and pepper. Pour this over the cucumber and leave – turning it from time to time, so that all the slices get impregnated. Before serving, transfer it to a shallow dish and sprinkle with chopped chives.

FILET DE BOEUF EN CROUTE

Serves 4–6

a piece of fillet steak weighing not less than 2 lb/1 kg
garlic
3 oz/90 g butter

8 oz/250 g button mushrooms, sliced
a wine glass of port or *dark sherry*
salt and freshly-ground black pepper

For the pastry:
12 oz/375 g plain flour

9 oz/275 g pure beef dripping

Rub the dripping into the flour (use dripping from the fridge so that it's not too soft), and mix with a little water until you have a soft dough. Put the pastry in the fridge to rest.

Turn on the oven to 190°C/375°F, Gas 5.

Spike the beef with a few slivers of garlic, rub it lightly with salt and freshly ground black pepper, then brown it lightly in a pan with the butter. Remove the beef and sauté the mushrooms in the pan with the meat juice and butter. Take mushrooms from the pan and add a wine glass of port or sherry. Let it bubble until thick.

Roll out the pastry to ¼-inch/0.6 cm thickness, put the beef on one side of the pastry with enough left to cover the top, put the mushrooms on top of the meat and then add the sauce from pan. Fasten the pastry flap down firmly by using a little cold water and your fingers – so long as the pastry is properly closed along the front side and ends, no juice can escape. Bake in an oiled tin for 40–45 minutes.

We think this dish is best served with freshly made English mustard. It can be eaten hot or cold.

SADDLE OF VENISON

A saddle of venison weighing at least 3½–4 lb/1.75–2 kg would be ideal for 6 greedy people.

2 cloves garlic
1 oz/30 g bacon fat

8 oz/250 g fat streaky bacon
1 tablespoon olive oil

For the marinade:
½ pint/300 ml red wine
3 tablespoons olive oil
2 oz/60 g carrots, chopped small
2 oz/60 g onions, chopped small

2 bay leaves
10 juniper berries, crushed
8 peppercorns, crushed
½ teaspoon salt

For the sauce:
2 tablespoons redcurrant jelly
1 port glass of port or dark sherry

1 dessertspoon arrowroot
salt

Put all the marinade ingredients into a pan, bring slowly to the boil, remove from the heat and leave to cool. When it is cold, pour it over the venison which you have laid in a narrow deep container – preferably one that will just hold it. Leave the venison in this marinade for 2 days in a cool place, turning it twice a day.

Turn on the oven to 200°C/400°F, Gas 6.

Take out the venison and wipe it dry with a cloth; retain the marinade for the sauce. With a sharp knife, remove the blue, muscley membrane from the top of the back. Do this gently, in layers if need be, but try to leave the flesh intact. Insert strips of garlic into the saddle's back. Melt the bacon fat in a frying pan large enough to hold the saddle, and when the fat is hot, brown the saddle. Put streaky bacon all over the top of the saddle, tucking it into the sides. Put the saddle into an ovenproof container – into which you have put 1 tablespoonful olive oil; a baking tin will do, but we have got the best results from using a deeper earthenware dish. Cover the top with aluminium foil and roast for 1½ hours. Meanwhile, you can prepare the sauce.

Strain the vegetables etc from the marinade, put the liquid in a saucepan and boil briskly to reduce the mixture by about a half. Add the redcurrant jelly and the port or sherry. Slake the arrowroot in half a cupful of this liquid and add to the saucepan, stirring briskly until the mixture is smooth and thickens slightly. Taste the sauce, and correct the seasoning – it may want more salt, or jelly, or port according to your taste. You can then transfer the sauce to a double boiler where you can keep it hot until needed.

To test the venison, gently stick a sharp knife halfway between the backbone and side flaps. It should be tender without a lot of blood coming out. The time for cooking a saddle does depend upon the age of the deer, but greedy people will wait until it is ready. It will not take *less* than an hour and a half.

EXCELLENT ROAST POTATOES

As greedy people often like a lot of whatever they like, you should allow at least two medium-sized potatoes per person.

Serves 8

16 potatoes   *8 oz/250 g Trex or Cookeen*
salt

Turn on the oven to 200°C/400°F, Gas 6.

Peel the potatoes and then boil them in salted water for 15 minutes. Drain, and cut them in half horizontally. Lay them on a board and score the exposed part of the potato deeply with a fork, the ploughed field effect. Heat the lard in a large baking tin (two tins if you cannot get all the potatoes into one, in which case you may need more lard), and when it is very hot, put in the potatoes. Baste with a spoon and roast for 1 hour, basting twice. The potatoes should be covered with crispy ridges.

POTATO PIE

Serves 6

1 lb/500 g new potatoes
1 lb/500 g puff pastry
2 good cloves garlic, finely chopped
2 oz/60 g butter

salt and black pepper
¼ teaspoon grated nutmeg
1 egg
2 tablespoons single cream

Turn on the oven to 220°C/425°F, Gas 7. Grease a round 10-inch/25-cm flan or tart tin.

Scrape the potatoes and cut them into thin slices. Put them in boiling salted water and cook until just tender – about 4–5 minutes. Drain them, rinse them under the cold tap and drain again.

Divide the pastry into 2 pieces, one slightly larger than the other. Roll out the smaller half and line the tin. Arrange the potatoes on the pastry in layers, leaving a ½-inch/1.25-cm border round the edge. Dot each layer with the garlic and butter, and sprinkle with salt, pepper and nutmeg. Beat the egg with the cream and brush the border. Roll out the second piece of pastry to about an 11-inch/27.5-cm circle and lay it over the potatoes; press the edges together to seal. Brush all over the top with the egg and cream mixture and bake for 25 minutes until golden brown. If it starts to get too brown too soon, put a piece of aluminium foil loosely over the top.

Just reading this, you can see that this pie will not improve the figure, but greedy people are so responsive to cream, butter and carbohydrates that they won't mind at all.

CORNBREAD

It is easy to make a greedy person out of anybody with freshly baked hot bread onto which butter so deliciously melts. The slightly sweet taste of cornbread makes it extra sinful and irresistable. Cornmeal is often sold under the name polenta or maize flour. Originally an American recipe, the quantities have been translated from their maddening addiction to cups. Because of that and because cornmeal comes in varying fineness and roughness, use your judgement over the consistency.

Serves 4–6

2½ oz/75 g plain flour
7 oz/200 g cornmeal
1 teaspoon salt
1 teaspoon sugar
2 teaspoons baking powder

2 eggs, well beaten
8 fl oz/250 ml milk
2 fl oz/60 ml cream
2½ tablespoons melted butter (approx. 1¼ oz/35 g)

Turn on the oven to 200°C/400°F, Gas 6.

Sift the dry ingredients together into a mixing bowl. Add the eggs and milk and beat with a wooden spoon. Beat in the cream and lastly the melted butter. Pour into an 8½ × 11 inch/22 × 27.5 cm buttered cake tin. Cook for 15–20 minutes.

Cut the cornbread into squares while it is still hot and wrap in a cloth napkin.

Should, by some extraordinary chance, there be cornbread left over, it makes a splendid stuffing for a bird when it is mixed with sautéed onions, crumbled fried sausage meat, perhaps the bird's liver chopped and fried, and seasoning.

DUKE OF CUMBERLAND'S PUDDING

Serves 4–6

1 lb/500 g jar brandied cherries
2 oz/60 g caster sugar plus extra for rolling cherries
1½ pints/900 ml double cream

½ pint/300 ml single cream
4 egg yolks
3 oz/90 g toasted almonds, crushed

Turn on the oven to 170°C/325°F, Gas 3.

Drain the cherries from their liquor, which you should reserve, and roll them in caster sugar. Then place them to cover the bottom of a lightly-buttered soufflé dish. Put 1 pint/600 ml double cream, all the single cream and 2 oz/60 g sugar into the top of a double saucepan, bring to the scalding point and gradually add the beaten egg yolks, stirring all the time. Strain this mixture onto the cherries in the soufflé dish, then put in a baking tin half full of water and into the oven for 45 minutes–1 hour, or until the custard is just set. Remove from both the oven and the baking tin and leave to cool.

Whip the remaining ½ pint/300 ml of double cream fairly stiffly, season with the retained liquor from the cherry jar, and put on top of the cold custard. Strew the top with the toasted almonds and keep in the fridge until serving.

STUFFED PEACHES

This recipe is from Josceline Dimbleby's *Book of Puddings*. She says, 'When my husband tried this pudding he said, "This is the kind of food which soldiers at the front dreamed about!"'

Serves 6

2 tablespoons redcurrant jelly
grated rind and juice of 1 lemon
6 ripe peaches
4 oz/125 g cream cheese
2 oz/60 g caster sugar

¼ pint/150 ml double or whipping cream
1 oz/30 g hazelnuts or almonds or walnuts, chopped (we recommend the walnuts)
1 tablespoon Demerara sugar

Put the redcurrant jelly into a pan and melt gently. Add all but 1 tablespoonful of the lemon juice and stir until smooth, then pour the redcurrant sauce onto a flat serving dish. Put the peaches in a bowl and pour boiling water over them, leave for 30 seconds, then remove the peaches and peel off the skins. Cut them in half and remove the stones and arrange the halves on the plate of redcurrant sauce, hollow side uppermost.

Beat the cream cheese with the caster sugar until soft and fluffy, then beat in the reserved tablespoonful of lemon juice. Whisk the cream until thick and stir it into the cream cheese mixture. Stir in the grated lemon rind and the chopped nuts. Pile this mixture on to the peach halves and sprinkle demerara sugar on top. Chill until ready to serve.

ILES FLOTTANTES

We have known someone sink his face into the dish containing the custard for this pudding after everyone had been served, so blissful did he find it. The spun sugar is important for looks and also the contrast of texture.

Serves 6

6 egg yolks
7 oz/200 g caster sugar
salt
½ pint/300 ml single cream
6 fl oz/180 ml creamy (gold top) milk

1 vanilla pod
3 egg whites
1 pint/625 ml ordinary milk
4 oz/125 g sugar (for the caramel)

Combine the yolks, scant 4 oz/110 g sugar and a pinch of salt in the top of a double saucepan. Heat the cream, creamy milk and vanilla pod in the base saucepan of the double saucepan until it steams. Pour it slowly onto the yolks, whisking all the while. Rinse the base pan, fill with hot water and set on the stove with the yolk mixture above. Cook over simmering water, stirring constantly, until the mixture coats the back of a metal spoon (it thickens also upon cooling). Strain the custard through a sieve or *chinois* into a shallow dish in which you will serve the floating islands. Set in the fridge.

Near the time of dinner, whisk the 3 egg whites with a pinch of salt to soft peaks. Add the remaining 3 oz/90 g sugar a tablespoonful at a time, whisking until the peaks are stiff and glistening. Heat the ordinary milk and enough water to fill a grill pan to the depth of ½-inch/1.25 cm. When it is near boiling, pour it into the grill pan. Float spoonsful of the meringue on the milk and grill under a low to medium heat until they are set and just tinged with brown – a matter of minutes. Lift them out with a slotted spoon and keep them on a large plate, tilted, or in a large colander – they tend to exude liquid.

When it comes to dessert time, pile the meringues prettily onto the custard. Put the 4 oz/125 g sugar for the caramel into a small heavy-bottomed saucepan. Add enough water to wet it thoroughly. Bring it slowly to the boil and, when the sugar is dissolved, boil quickly until the syrup begins to look golden and will spin a thread if dripped from the tines of a fork. Test that you have reached the right point by letting a drop of syrup fall into a cup of cold water. It should set hard. Turn off the heat. Working quickly and using two forks, weave threads of the caramel and drop splodges of it onto the îles flottantes. Try to spin a shining nest on top but don't worry if all you get is brittle droplets – they will give the requisite crunch. Take to the table. You cannot do the sugar work much before dessert time as it quickly softens and loses the point.

16 New Year's Eve

The good thing about New Year's Eve – unlike Christmas – is that you don't *have* to ask people because you are sorry for them or because they are related to you or even because you are sorry that they are related to you; you can ask your friends, people you love and like and want to entertain. It is important to ask them early, however, or you'll find that they are going somewhere else. It is also an occasion for careful planning of food, since everybody will have been sated with straightforward Christmas fare and you should aim to avoid things like being clever with the remains of turkey, or of bombarding people with yet more mince pies.

Some New Year's Eve parties have no food at all; others fall back on quiches like savoury underfelt, plus bowls of nuts and seaweed biscuits. We think all good parties should include food: hosts should say that they are going to and then do it. Ideally, people should be able to sit to eat: we are not herbivores and few people are much good at dealing with a plateful of food and a glass (and a handbag if they carry one) while standing – which, if you are Occidental, entails being bumped into – *and* carrying on a conversation with someone in like plight which is no fun for either of you. This could be known as the bad method of entertaining. So, don't have more people than you can seat – even if you can't provide tables for all of them.

The following menu provides ample food for 24 people: quantities could be adjusted either way depending upon the room and geography of your home. This menu will do equally well for a sitting-at-table dinner or a buffet where guests help themselves. It is a simple meal to prepare, but none the worse for that. It is important when you are cooking for this quantity to clear your fridge of all inessentials to make room for party dishes.

If you prepare a shopping list carefully and make sure that you have everything, you should be able to cook the whole thing if you start after lunch. We always make puddings first in order that there will be no danger of onion or any other obtrusive tastes. We would do the fish terrines next and put the potatoes in the oven as soon as they are done. Meanwhile, lentils can be cooked, the other salad can be made and dressings and sauces prepared.

Finally, don't start the party too early. It is the one party that is going to go on until well after midnight, which means food around 9.30 and most people seem to need feeding after about an hour of drink.

Fish Terrines
Cooked Ham
Avocado Sauce
Walnut and Horseradish Sauce
Baked Potatoes

Lentil Salad
Apple, Beetroot and Celery Salad
Cold Lemon Soufflé
Port Wine Jelly

FISH TERRINES

You will need two of these, and as most food processors will only cope with one at a time, we are giving quantities for one. You simply make it twice. Fresh haddock is the best white fish to use; the contrasting fish is to add to the flavour and also to make the terrine look pretty when you cut it; smoked haddock, smoked salmon pieces, fresh shrimps or prawns are all good.

1 lb/500 g white fish (see above)
2 egg whites
½ pint/300 ml whipping cream

juice of 1 lemon
salt and pepper
12 oz/375 g contrasting fish (see above)

Turn on the oven to 180°C/350°F, Gas 4. Chill all ingredients including the food processor bowl. The actual making should be done fast while everything is still as cold as possible.

Dice the white fish and put into the food processor with the egg whites. Whizz until the mixture is smooth and add the cream. Season, and add lemon juice – taste to see whether you need the juice of the whole lemon or not.

Butter the terrine dish and add the white fish mixture in layers with strips of contrasting fish. Cover with aluminium foil and put the terrine into a baking dish half-filled with boiling water. Put in the oven. Test after 25 minutes with a skewer which will come out clean when the terrine is cooked. Leave it to cool in the baking dish and then put it in the fridge.

Remove the terrine from the fridge about half an hour before you eat it, and turn it out. It can then be garnished with shrimps, parsley, pieces of lemon etc.

COOKED HAM

Two things are important about a cooked ham. You need to know that your supplier does produce good hams. Go to your local delicatessen or grocer and buy 4 oz/125 g of whatever ham he recommends that will also be available in the piece. If you don't like it, try again. The second point is that the ham should be properly carved. This means a really sharp ham knife – i.e. a long, slender knife that is flexible or whippy. If you are no good at carving, find a friend who is coming to the party who is. People who are good at it (like anything else) enjoy carving and it makes all the difference.

The two sauces which follow are delicious with ham.

AVOCADO SAUCE

Scoop out the flesh from two avocados. Put it in the food processor with some black pepper, salt and lemon juice. When puréed, turn it into a small bowl and cover with a damp cloth to prevent it going brown and put it in the fridge. This should be made as late as you can manage.

WALNUT AND HORSERADISH SAUCE

6 fl oz/180 ml natural yoghurt *sugar*
1 tablespoon horseradish sauce *2 oz/60 g walnuts*
salt

Mix in a pudding basin the yoghurt with the horseradish sauce. Add a pinch of salt and a little sugar. Put the walnuts into a liquidiser and mix for 3 seconds; you can chop them finely if you prefer a more gritty texture. Add these to the horseradish mixture. Taste it, and see whether you have enough of the two main ingredients for your liking.

BAKED POTATOES

18 potatoes will be enough for 24 people.

These are only acceptable if they are prepared beforehand. Nobody enjoys opening them, scalding their fingers and trundling butter into them with a fork. Bake them during the afternoon of the party. When cooked, cut them in half and scoop out the insides. Mix the potato in a big bowl with a fork, adding melted butter, milk, pepper and salt. When you have got the mixture right (by which we mean *you* like the taste of it), put it back into the skins and set the potato halves on baking trays ready to be warmed up in the oven. In our experience *everybody* eats them if they are presented in this way – particularly if you paint the skins with oil before the first baking to get them crisp.

LENTIL SALAD

1½ lb/750 g brown lentils
4 tablespoons olive oil
2 tablespoons wine vinegar

salt and pepper
2 sweet onions, finely chopped
4 tablespoons coarsely chopped parsley

Soak the lentils for about an hour. Cook in boiling water with some salt until they are just cooked, 45 minutes to an hour, *al dente* as the Italians say, before they go into a mush. Drain, and while they are still warm, add a mixture of the olive oil, the wine vinegar and a little salt and pepper. Mix thoroughly. When cool, add finely chopped onion and coarsely chopped parsley.

APPLE, BEETROOT AND CELERY SALAD

3 lb/1.5 kg cooked beetroot
3 lb/1.5 kg Cox's apples

2 large heads of celery

For the dressing:
6 tablespoons olive oil
2 tablespoons vinegar
2 teaspoons mustard powder

4 teaspoons sugar
2 teaspoons salt
black pepper – a generous screwing

Peel and dice the beetroot and set aside. Peel, core and dice the apples and mix with the beetroot in the bottom of a salad bowl. Wash and chop the celery and add to the bowl. (It is best to put this bowl in a cool place covered by a damp cloth). Make the dressing by mixing the ingredients thoroughly; leave it in the kitchen, not in the fridge.

Dress and mix the salad just before you eat.

COLD LEMON SOUFFLE

These ingredients make enough for about 10 people. If you want to have enough for 24, you should make it twice as processor bowls and liquidisers will not cope with a greater quantity than this. However, if you are also making port wine jelly, you will probably find that this quantity of soufflé seems enough.

6 lemons   ½ oz/15 g gelatine
6 eggs   ½ pint/300 ml double cream
6 tablespoons caster sugar

Grate the rind from three of the lemons and squeeze all six. Separate
the yolks from the whites of the eggs. Put the egg yolks, lemon juice and
sugar in a double saucepan, whisk over hot water until the sugar is
dissolved and the mixture thickens, and pour into a basin. Thoroughly
dissolve the gelatine in two tablespoons of hot water in a small bowl over
a saucepan of hot water, and add to the lemon mixture. Add the grated
lemon rind and stir in well. Put the bowl in a basin of cold water to help
it cool. Meanwhile, whip the cream lightly. It should be thick, but
without peaking. When the lemon mixture is almost cold and near
setting, whisk the egg whites stiffly – so that the bowl will turn upside
down without the mixture falling out. Add the cream to the lemon
mixture and then add the egg whites, folding them in lightly but
thoroughly.

Put the combined mixture into a 3-pint/1.75 litre soufflé dish, or
individual pots if you have them. This should be done as quickly as
possible so that the whites don't start to dissolve. Put the pudding into
the fridge.

PORT WINE JELLY

This is best made in small pots or glasses. It is quite rich and the
quantity given here will fill 10 of the small white pots in which the
French put chocolate mousse or cold creams or soufflés, but custard
glasses or any small and pretty containers would do.

¾ pint/450 ml port   1-inch cinnamon stick
½ oz/15 g gelatine   grated rind of 1 lemon
4 oz/125 g lump sugar   a good pinch of freshly-grated nutmeg

Put all the ingredients, except half the port, into a double saucepan and
heat until it is well blended. Strain through muslin. Add the rest of the
port. Pour into pots or glasses and chill.

---

17 *House-Moving Supper*

Nowadays, everybody moves house far more often in their lives than they used to do. The combination of people being moved because of their work and the terrifying inflation of house prices has meant that everybody has had to start by buying any place, anywhere, that they could afford, but luck, age, affluence and attachments – not to mention progeny – make further moves inevitable. However, excluding the professionals, like Foreign Office staff or Service families, most people don't move often enough to get really good at it.

This means that after a day of seemingly endless excitement and fatigue they may find themselves at eight in the evening feverishly unpacking tea chests full of kitchen equipment in a vain attempt to find their tin opener, the electric kettle and the bread knife. Of course, it isn't always as awful as that, but you may have done quite a lot of planning and made a nourishing stew only to find that the previous owners decided to take the cooker after all, or the Gas Board has declined to connect yours as arranged – and when it comes to eating cold stew, your family won't feel that it was the thought that counted.

Even if you know perfectly well how to organise and make the first meal in your new house, the nesting instinct (very noticeable – particularly in women – when confronting new territory) dictates that you should be arranging saucepans on shelves rather than cooking in them, and hanging up your clothes or making at least one room feel like your home before you fall into bed. If only a meal would simply *appear* – a picnic or a feast, preferably a bit of both, anything, or almost anything that you have not had to think about! This is where real friends come in, and where *you* could come in for your friends.

The following recipes are all designed to be easy to transport and not too complicated to serve: we do suggest, however, that you should assume that the china and cutlery won't have been unpacked, so take the bare necessities. The soup can be transported in thermos flasks and drunk or spooned out of mugs; all the other dishes can be eaten with a fork or with the fingers. This might be an occasion for paper plates although, personally, we don't care for them. In addition to a mug, glass, fork and plate for each person, you should take serving spoons, drink, sugar, salt and pepper and a couple of tea towels – and don't forget the corkscrew. If the recipients have a telephone, you can ask them if they have a kettle for tea or coffee. If you want to be really munificent, add a loaf of bread, ½ lb/250 g of butter, a jar of marmalade – preferably made by you – and two pints of milk for breakfast.

Spring Minestrone
Stuffed Anchovy Eggs
Tomato and Mustard Quiche
Pissaladière
Lasagne with Meat Sauce

Mixed Meat Salad
Fromage à la Crème
Lemon Meringue Tarts
Brownies

SPRING MINESTRONE

The important thing about this soup is to keep the vegetables in the same colour range and avoid the dolly mixture look of commercial minestrone. A plus about this recipe is that it actually improves on being served lukewarm, as the flavour of the vegetables comes through more positively – a fact understood in Mediterranean countries. The better the olive oil you use, the better the soup will be.

Serves 4–6

1½ lb/750 g fresh broad beans in their pods
1 lb/500 g fresh peas in their pods
1 oz/30 g butter
4 tablespoons virgin olive oil
8 oz/250 g asparagus
8 oz/250 g broccoli

¼ cauliflower
1 bunch spring onions, trimmed and peeled
2 cloves garlic, peeled and chopped
8 oz/250 g French green beans
salt and freshly-ground black pepper
3 oz/90 g Parmesan cheese, freshly grated

Prepare the vegetables, shelling the broad beans and peas, cleaning and chopping quite small the rest. Heat the butter and two tablespoonsful of the olive oil in a large heavy-bottomed sauté pan. Add the asparagus stalks (saving the tips for later), the broccoli, cauliflower, spring onions, garlic and green beans. Toss them in the fat until they are glistening and beginning to soften. Add the peas and beans. Add just enough water to cover and season with salt and pepper. When the vegetables are tender, but still crunchy, turn off the heat. Remove half the vegetables and whizz in a food processor or liquidiser until you have a none too smooth purée.

Pour the mixture into a clean pan and bring to a simmer, adding more water if you want a thinner consistency. Add the remaining vegetables plus the asparagus tips. Stir and heat through. Taste for seasoning and for texture.

If you are serving this soup in the context of a picnic, take some olive oil along separately and trickle a little into each plate or cup and also hand round some grated Parmesan cheese.

STUFFED ANCHOVY EGGS

Serves 4–6

6 anchovy fillets
6 eggs
2 tablespoons mayonnaise

2 tablespoons single cream
salt and black pepper (optional)
paprika or parsley to garnish

Hard-boil the eggs, cool and peel. Cut the eggs in half, scoop out the yolks and put them into a small bowl. Trim the bottoms of the whites so that each half is stable. Chop the anchovy fillets as finely as possible and add to the yolks with the mayonnaise.

Mix and mash the contents very thoroughly with a fork, adding cream by degrees until the consistency is creamy, but not sloppy. Test for seasoning. Pile the mixture into the egg whites and garnish with a pinch of paprika and/or parsley.

Note: you could transport these in egg boxes quite safely.

TOMATO AND MUSTARD QUICHE

The sort of quiche to avoid is the sort that the owners of the new house might feel would come in handy for lagging the attic. In this recipe, the tomatoes add a nice moistness. Blandness is side-stepped by the unexpected sting of mustard.

Serves 4–6

1 shortcrust pastry case, baked blind for
    10 minutes (see page 203)
2 tablespoons Dijon mustard (or
    whatever mustard you favour)
1 lb/500 g ripe tomatoes

4 eggs
½ pint/300 ml double cream
1 tablespoon finely chopped parsley
sea salt and freshly-ground black pepper
3 oz/90 g Gruyère cheese, grated

Turn on the oven to 170°C/325°F, Gas 3.

Spread the mustard on the base of the partially cooked pastry case. Skin the tomatoes by plunging them briefly into boiling water. De-seed them and chop roughly. In a large pudding basin, beat the eggs and add the cream, parsley, salt and pepper. Stir in the tomatoes and two-thirds of the cheese. Pour into the pastry case and sprinkle the remaining cheese over the top. Bake for 35–40 minutes until golden and endeavour to transport and consume the quiche while it is still warm.

PISSALADIERE

This Niçoise version of a pizza should be made with a bread base but we think it works just as well with pastry which, if crisp, provides a nice contrast to the softness of the onions. If you are truly in a hurry, you could use thick slices of bread cut lengthways from a loaf and then fried on one side in olive oil. However, the key to the success of this dish is long, slow cooking of the onions – allow at least 40 minutes for the process – so during that time you might just as well knock up some shortcrust pastry.

Serves 4–6

¼ pint/150 ml olive oil
2½ lb/1.25 kg onions, peeled and quite thinly sliced

2 cloves garlic, peeled and crushed or chopped
8 anchovy fillets
8 black olives

For the pastry:

6 oz/180 g plain flour
2 generous teaspoons mustard powder
2 oz/60 g butter

1 oz/30 g lard
pinch of salt
cold water

Make up the shortcrust pastry using the quantities above, or your own recipe, but taking on board the inclusion of mustard which goes well with the onions. Roll out thinly and line a large pie dish. Bake for 15 minutes in an oven set at 190°C/375°F, Gas 5 with foil over the base of the pastry and some dried beans dotted about on top: 'baking blind' gives a crisper result.

In 4 fl oz/125 ml oil, cook the sliced onions gently, stirring occasionally. After about 20 minutes, add the garlic. At the end of the cooking time, the onions should almost be a purée.

Spread the onion mixture on the pastry. Arrange the anchovy fillets in a lattice pattern and place olives in some of the diamond-shaped spaces. Dribble on the remaining oil and bake in the oven (temperature as before), for 30 minutes. This pie is at its best neither hot nor cold, but lukewarm.

LASAGNE WITH MEAT SAUCE

This recipe for meat sauce comes from Marcella Hazan's *Classic Italian Cookbook* because it is quite simply the best we know. When we make the sauce, we always make treble quantities and freeze some. It is an invaluable standby for a quick and delicious meal.

Serves 6

For the sauce:

2 tablespoons chopped Spanish onion
3 tablespoons olive oil
1½ oz/45 g butter
2 tablespoons chopped celery
2 tablespoons chopped carrots
12 oz/375 g best beef mince

salt
8 fl oz/250 ml dry white wine
4 fl oz/125 ml milk
⅛ teaspoon freshly-grated nutmeg
14-oz/435 g can of Italian tomatoes,
   roughly chopped with their juice

An earthenware pot should be your first choice for making the *ragù*. If you don't have one available, use a heavy, enamelled cast-iron casserole, the deepest one you have (to keep the *ragù* from reducing too quickly). Put in the chopped onion with all the oil and butter, and sauté briefly over a medium heat until just translucent. Add the celery and carrots and cook gently for 2 minutes.

Add the mince, crumbling it in the pot with a fork. Add 1 teaspoon salt, stir, and cook only until the meat has lost its raw, red colour. Add the wine, turn the heat up to medium-high, and cook, stirring occasionally, until all the wine has evaporated.

Turn the heat down to medium, add the milk and the nutmeg, and cook until the milk has evaporated. Stir frequently. When the milk has evaporated, add the tomatoes and stir thoroughly. When the mixture has started to bubble, turn the heat down until the sauce cooks at the laziest simmer, just an occasional bubble. Cook uncovered, for a minimum of 3½–4 hours, stirring occasionally. Taste and correct for salt. (If you cannot watch the sauce for such a long stretch, you can turn off the heat and resume cooking later. But do finish cooking in one day.)

This sounds a trouble to make, but it works very well if you are cooking other things, and if you treble the quantities, you won't find you have wasted your time: it is delicious.

You can now buy fresh lasagne in many delicatessens or supermarkets. Don't buy the dried lasagne; it is far too thick and is stodgy.

1 lb/500 g fresh lasagne
1½ pints/900 ml béchamel sauce (the
   consistency of cream)

6 oz/180 g Parmesan cheese
2 oz/60 g butter

Turn on the oven to 190°C/375°F, Gas 5.

This dish is better put together after the *ragù* has cooled. Use a 14 inch/35 cm dish deep enough to contain 6 layers of meat and pasta. Smear the bottom of the dish with the fat that will have risen to the top of the meat sauce, and then place a single layer of pasta in the dish, overlapping strips but no more than ¼ inch/0.6 cm. Spread a thin layer of meat sauce, then a thin layer of béchamel over the sauce. Sprinkle with cheese. Then add another layer of pasta, and so on. Finish with a pasta layer, cover that with béchamel, sprinkle with cheese and dot with butter.

Bake at the top of the oven for 10–15 minutes until a light golden crust forms on top. If after 10 minutes, the crust is not forming, turn up the oven for the last 5 minutes. Do not cook longer, or it will become dry.

MIXED MEAT SALAD

This salad can be made with various selections of meat: we are suggesting beef, tongue and chicken. It is an excellent way of using up the remains of a roast chicken or a tongue that you have served hot. We suggest that you cook a piece of beef and use the other meats if they are easily available: the salad is very good simply with beef.

Serves 8–10

To cook the beef:

4 large carrots
2 large onions
1 stalk celery with leaves
4 leeks
1 turnip
3 lb/1.5 kg (approx.) beef – topside or
silverside

3 sprigs parsley
2 sprigs thyme or *1 teaspoon dried thyme*
3 bay leaves
1 dessertspoon sea salt

Chop all the vegetables and put them, the beef and the other ingredients into a pan that will just accommodate the beef, and cover with cold water. Bring very slowly to simmering point. Skim off the scum that accumulates during the next 15 minutes and then allow to simmer for about 2½ hours, or until the beef feels tender with a sharp knife. Turn off the heat and allow the beef to cool in its liquid.

For the salad:

2 lb/1 kg potatoes	2 hard-boiled eggs
1 bunch spring onions or ½ lb/250 g shallots	4 large dill cucumbers
	2 oz/60 g capers
1 bunch radishes	2 oz/60 g fresh parsley

For the dressing:

1 tablespoon tarragon vinegar	1 teaspoon sugar
3 tablespoons olive oil	1 teaspoon salt
1 teaspoon made mustard	generous screws of black pepper

New potatoes are infinitely preferable, but the salad can be made with old ones. Boil the potatoes gently until they are just cooked. When cool, slice them. Chop the spring onions or shallots finely.

Slice the cold beef thinly and arrange in layers with the potatoes, soaking each layer with the prepared dressing. If you need a larger quantity of dressing, be sure to stay with the proportions above.

Garnish with radishes and hard-boiled eggs, sliced cucumbers, capers, chopped spring onions and parsley.

FROMAGE A LA CREME

This is a dish designed to eat with fresh fruit – raspberries are the best, but any of the berries are good with it.

Serves 8

1 lb/500 g fresh double cream cheese	5 egg whites
4 tablespoons caster sugar	½ pint/300 ml double cream

Beat the cream cheese in a large bowl until it is perfectly smooth – a hand whisk is best for this – and then add the sugar. Whisk the egg whites until they are stiff and then mix them in thoroughly with the cheese. Put the cheese mixture into a piece of muslin or a large old handkerchief (the old-fashioned nappie called a Harrington Square is ideal), and then you can either place the muslin in a colander, or more simply tie the corners of the muslin together and hang it over a basin to drip in a cool place. It should be left for at least 4 hours.

Turn the cheese out of the muslin. Whip the double cream very slightly and pour over the cheese; this can be done just before you serve the dish.

LEMON MERINGUE TARTS

Serves 6

For the pastry:
8 oz/250 g self-raising flour   *2 oz/60 g Trex*
2 oz/60 g butter   *juice of ½ lemon*

Rub the fats into the flour until you have fine crumbs. Make a hole in the centre of the mixture, and pour in a little of the lemon juice which has been diluted with an equal quantity of cold water, and mix with a wooden spoon. Add just enough of the lemon water to make the pastry into a soft dough so that sides of bowl are clean. Put the pastry in the fridge while you make the curd.

For the lemon curd:
4 eggs   *6 oz/180 g caster sugar*
2 lemons   *3½ oz/100 g caster sugar (for meringue)*
2 oz/60 g butter

Separate the egg yolks from the whites (the whites will be used for the meringue). Grate the rind of both lemons and then squeeze the juice. Put the butter, sugar and lemon juice into a double saucepan and stir until everything has dissolved. Then add the beaten egg yolks in a thin stream, stirring vigorously all the time. Continue stirring the mixture until it thickens slightly; it will stiffen more when cold. Add the grated lemon rind and put the mixture in a bowl to cool.

Turn on the oven to 180°C/350°F, Gas 4.

Roll out the pastry as thinly as you can, and cut out rounds for tartlet tins. We use non-stick pans but if you don't have them, you must of course butter the pan. If you haven't got a pastry cutter, you can use a cup or a glass, but it must be of a size that allows the pastry to reach the top of the sides of the tart tin hollows. Put the tins in the oven and bake until they are a pale biscuit colour. Allow to cool.

Whip the egg whites stiffly, and then fold in the caster sugar. Put a rounded teaspoonful of lemon curd in each tartlet and cover with a generous helping of meringue. Bake in a very cool oven (70°C/150°F, Gas ¼), until the meringue is the colour of milky coffee.

These tarts should be eaten the same day, or the meringue may become sticky. If you don't have tart pans, you can make a pie, but the tarts can be eaten with the fingers which is useful for a possibly crockery-free new household.

BROWNIES

Serves 6

2 oz/60 g bitter chocolate
4 oz/125 g butter
8 oz/250 g brown sugar
2 eggs
½ teaspoon salt

½ teaspoon baking powder
2 oz/60 g plain flour
8 oz/250 g walnuts, coarsely chopped
1 teaspoon vanilla essence

Turn on the oven to 180°C/350°F, Gas 4.

Melt the chocolate and let it cool slightly. Cream the butter and sugar, add the eggs and then the cooled chocolate, and mix well. Add the salt and baking powder to the flour, mix, and then add to the chocolate mixture. Beat well, and then add the chopped nuts and vanilla essence.

Put the mixture into a shallow buttered baking tin (8 inches/20 cm square is about right), and bake for 30–35 minutes, until the testing skewer comes out clean. Allow to cool for ten minutes before cutting it into small squares.

18 *Picnics*

Our earliest memories of picnics turned out to be identical: sitting on a beach, in a gale, aubergine-coloured from a short battle with the sea, crunching our way through sandwiches that for years one of us thought were called that because of the high proportion of beach they contained. Some people don't mind this sort of thing, they expect conditions to be rough: if not a gale, then being bitten by gnats or stung by wasps, or drenched to the skin. They seem to feel that a picnic is a sort of organised *emergency* – that dry sandwiches and half a cup of fairly warm tea with that mercifully unique taste associated with an ill-kept thermos flask is what to expect or provide.

There are those who have so little faith in the weather or their enjoyment that they like to picnic on the doubtful verge of some highway, comfortingly near their own car and with any suggestions of rural solitude enlivened by the traffic. But some people think of picnics as a *fête champêtre* – an outdoor feast with elaborate and elegant food that happens not to be consumed in the dining-room. We agree with this, with the proviso that as much food as possible should be able to be eaten with the fingers or, failing that, in some cases with either a spoon *or* a fork. Cutting things up with a knife and fork is no fun with a plate on your lap.

We have divided our suggestions into those best suited to summer and those desirable in winter, although in some cases the food is suitable for any time of the year. The first thing to take into account when catering for a picnic is that everybody is mysteriously hungrier out of doors. This would not be surprising if it were a shooting picnic, or one where the participants were engaged in a lot of healthy exercise, but it is equally true of people going to Glyndebourne, for instance, or simply driving somewhere in order to eat. So although we don't suggest that you make everything on either the summer or winter menus, we do advise your making more of whatever you choose than you would for an indoor meal.

Then there is the question of picnic equipment. The elderly find sitting on the ground difficult and uncomfortable, and a surprising number of men behave like frightfully old deck chairs whose hinges will not adjust to outdoor sitting conditions. If you are catering for either of these categories, a couple of those small and very light folding canvas and metal chairs would be popular. You should also provide a large American cloth or plastic sheet on which to lay out the food: a large plate apiece, a glass and a cup, spoons, forks, and bowls if you are serving fruit salad, and an extra cup apiece if you are serving soup. Paper plates – and cups – can save a lot of trouble. China is also heavy to carry, and if you are not a verge picnicker, you should take this into consideration. You also need ladles for soup and fruit salad, large sharp knives for cutting up pie or cake and plenty of paper napkins, a corkscrew for wine, and containers of salt, sugar and pepper, and finally, of course, thermos flasks of soup, coffee or tea (bring milk separately and the tea will taste better) and whatever refrigerating bags are needed to keep cold drinks cold.

Finally, we are assuming yours will be a lunch or supper picnic: if you are doing a tea, some of the things on these menus will be suitable and there are other cakes and sandwiches elsewhere in this book that could be used.

Summer
Scotch Quail's Eggs
Kuku
Greek Loaf
Cold Lamb Cutlets
Lettuce-wrapped Duck
Tomato and Cucumber Salad

Brown Bread, Walnut and Crème
   d'Isigny Sandwiches
Individual Summer Puddings
Geranium Cream
Peaches in Orange and Lemon Juice

Winter
Giblet Soup
Cold Rabbit and Gammon Pie
Pheasant Croquettes

Home-made Sausage Roll
Mary's Fruit Cake
Coffee Eclairs

SUMMER

SCOTCH QUAIL'S EGGS

Bought Scotch eggs can be a dire thing and if you make them at home using hen's eggs and sausage meat they can be too much of a mouthful even for the great outdoors. Quail's eggs give a more delicate result and there is something rather sweet about them, particularly if they are arranged in a nest of lettuce leaves. Take along a jar of good chutney or some home-made tomato sauce as an accompaniment. Do not emulate the supermarket by using those bright orange packet breadcrumbs. For the sausage meat, use high quality sausages and remove the meat from the skins by cutting a slit in the skin and holding the sausage under the cold tap.

Serves 4

8 quail's eggs
1 lb/500 g sausage meat
flour seasoned with salt and
  freshly-ground black pepper

2 small eggs, lightly beaten
4 oz/125 g fine breadcrumbs
vegetable oil for frying

Boil the quail's eggs for three minutes, immerse in cold water and shell carefully. Divide the sausage meat into 8 balls and pat each one out thin and flat. Roll the eggs in seasoned flour, then in the sausage meat; roll each in the beaten egg and finally in the crumbs. It is less messy if you perform the first two processes with all the eggs before applying the crumbs which will stick to your eggy fingers.

Heat enough oil to come half-way up the eggs. Cook, turning in two stages; once at a medium-hot heat to cook the sausage meat, the second time at a higher heat to crisp and brown the crumbs. Drain on kitchen paper.

KUKU

This Iranian omelette – the idea comes from Claudia Roden's *A Book of Middle Eastern Food* – is ideal picnic food, easy to slice, faintly exotic, and not heavy on the stomach. Take along a spot of natural yoghurt, preferably the creamy Greek variety, as an accompaniment.

Serves 4–6

1 large onion, peeled and finely chopped
2 tablespoons vegetable oil
1 large leek, peeled, washed and finely
*   sliced or 4 spring onions, cleaned and*
*   chopped*
1 lb/500 g minced beef

4 oz/125 g chopped spinach (frozen will
*   suffice)*
salt and freshly-ground black pepper
1 teaspoon ground cinnamon
6 eggs

Fry the onion in half the vegetable oil with the leek or spring onions until they are soft. Add the minced beef and cook it until it has changed colour and completely lost its rawness. Add the spinach, salt, pepper and cinnamon and cook gently.

In a large mixing bowl, beat the eggs lightly. Add the meat mixture, which shouldn't be too hot or it will start to cook the eggs. Clean the frying pan. Heat up the other tablespoonful of vegetable oil and pour in the mixture. Cook over a gentle heat for about 15 minutes, until the eggs have set on the bottom and, indeed, most of the way through.

Turn on the grill, slip the pan under and cook until the top of the omelette is golden. Serve lukewarm or cool. If you have used a heavy- bottomed frying pan, the kuku should be easy to cut into wedges for it will have shrunk slightly from the sides in the cooking and cooling process.

GREEK LOAF

This recipe was devised by artist Dickie Chopping on a holiday in Greece when each day saw a more elaborate picnic being prepared to be taken by boat to a remote and primitive beach. The contents were dictated by what was available in a relatively small village but the principle can successfully be applied to more sophisticated fillings.

Serves 8

1 large rectangular loaf: the one used in
*   the original was white but brown*
*   would work*
5 tablespoons (approx) olive oil
2 large onions, peeled and sliced

2 large green peppers, cored, de-seeded,
*   trimmed of membranes and sliced*
6 rashers streaky bacon, crisply fried
4–5 eggs
a handful of stoned black olives

For the tomato sauce:

1½–2 lbs/750 g–1 kg fresh tomatoes,   *1 small glass red wine*
    peeled and sliced or 1 14-oz/400 g tin   *salt and freshly-ground black pepper*
    peeled tomatoes   *a good pinch of sugar*
1 heaped tablespoon tomato purée   *2 teaspoons oregano* or *chopped basil*
2 cloves garlic, peeled and chopped

Turn on the oven to 180°C/350°F, Gas 4.

With a small sharp knife, cut around the loaf about ¼ inch/0.6 cm in from the edge and without hitting the bottom. The idea is to create a container and a lid. Carefully ease the knife under one of the short ends of the 'lid' and cut off. Pull out the crumbs from the loaf and from the lid until you have a box with a base and walls about ¼-inch/0.6 cm thick, and a thin lid. Do not make the container too thin or it will collapse in the carrying. Using about 3 tablespoonsful olive oil (or you may need more), paint the inside of the box and lid and set in the oven to crisp – 15–20 minutes.

Meanwhile, in 2 tablespoonsful olive oil, sauté the onions and peppers until they are softened and just beginning to brown. Take them from the pan and set aside.

Make the tomato sauce by simmering together the tomatoes, tomato purée, the garlic and wine. Season with salt, pepper, sugar, oregano or basil. Cook for about 20–30 minutes, or until the sauce has thickened. Taste for seasoning and adjust.

In the bottom of the loaf, spread the onions and peppers, well-drained of any oil that has accumulated. Lay on the bacon slices. Pour on the tomato sauce, which shouldn't be too liquid or it will sog the loaf. Break the eggs along the surface of the sauce. Dot with black olives. Return the loaf to the oven and bake until the eggs are set – about 10 minutes. Place the lid on the loaf and slice at the picnic site.

COLD LAMB CUTLETS

This is a very simple dish, but how good it is depends on obtaining first-class lamb and a butcher who understands what a cutlet is, i.e. not a chop, and not a cutlet off the best end of some middle-aged lamb or sheep. It should be from the best end of a young lamb, and the butcher should trim the fat from the cutlet for you.

Heat the grill very hot, paint the cutlets with sunflower seed oil and a sprinkle of salt and grill them for about 5 minutes on the first side, and about 3 minutes on the reverse. Cool them on a rack, so that any excess fat may drip away. They should be just pink inside when done. They look pretty with white paper cutlet frills round their stems.

LETTUCE-WRAPPED DUCK

This method for cooking the duck is similar to that employed for Peking Duck, but with the option of speeding the process by using a hairdryer trained on the bird rather than letting it hang in an airy place overnight. If you have the time, however, the latter process can give a crisper result.

Serves 6

1 large fresh duck
1 large Cos lettuce or *Webb's Wonder (or similarly crisp variety)*
2 tablespoons honey

Plum sauce or *Hoisin sauce (available in supermarkets)*
½ cucumber
1 bunch spring onions

Wash the duck and place it in a large sieve or colander. Bring a kettle full of water to the boil and, when boiling, pour it over the duck, turning the bird once or twice so that it is well and truly scalded. Pat dry and place in a large bowl.

Melt the honey in a jug with ½ pint/300 ml hot water. Pour it over the duck, then drain it off back into the jug and repeat. Turn the duck over and repeat again. Contrive some way of hanging up the duck (e.g. with a butcher's hook or sturdy wire coat hanger) and train a warm (not hot) hairdryer on it until it is dry. You can, of course, just leave it in an airy place overnight.

Heat the oven to 200°C/400°F, Gas 6. Without any fat, roast the duck on a wire grid, breast side up, for 20 minutes. Turn over (being careful not to puncture the skin) and roast for a further 25 minutes. Turn over again and roast for 20 minutes more. The skin should now be golden and crisp. Remove from the oven, let cool and then carve, prising every morsel of flesh from the bones.

The lettuce leaves should be separated, and washed and dried if necessary; the cucumber should be cut into matchsticks, but leave on the skin; and the spring onions should be trimmed, cleaned and sliced lengthways. Bite-sized pieces of skin and meat are taken to the picnic in one container, with the prepared lettuce, cucumber and spring onions packed in another. The Hoisin or Chinese plum sauce can be carried in its jar.

A teaspoonful or so of sauce is spread onto the lettuce leaf, meat and crispy skin is added, then strips of cucumber and spring onion, and the whole made into a delectable parcel.

TOMATO AND CUCUMBER SALAD

This is a very simple salad, but it is crunchy and refreshing and can be easily eaten with just a fork.

Serves 6–8

2 lb/1 kg tomatoes
2 medium-sized cucumbers
¼ pint/150 ml natural yoghurt

1 clove garlic
salt and pepper and sugar to taste

Cut the tomatoes into quarters, then in half. Cut the cucumber into ½-inch/1.25 cm cubes. Put both in a container. Mix the yoghurt, crushed garlic, salt, pepper and sugar and return the dressing to the yoghurt carton. Dress the salad just before serving for the picnic.

BROWN BREAD, WALNUT AND CREME D'ISIGNY SANDWICHES

4 Crème d'Isigny cheeses or 4 oz/125 g
*   double cream cheese*

3 oz/90 g walnuts, finely chopped
1 small brown wholemeal loaf

Mix the cheese and the chopped walnuts well together and spread on thin slices of unbuttered bread. Be generous with the filling and cover with a second slice of bread. Cut off the crusts.

INDIVIDUAL SUMMER PUDDINGS

Serves 6

6 × 4-inch/10-cm diameter pudding
    basins
1½ lb/750 g raspberries
12 oz/375 g redcurrants

3 oz/90 g caster sugar
1 stale white loaf
arrowroot
½ pint/300 ml double cream

Note: Other soft fruit is good for this pudding: blackberries (with a small amount of apple), loganberries, black and white currants, mulberries and stoned black cherries when in season.

Put the fruit and sugar into a stainless steel pan with ½ pint/300 ml water and cook very gently to draw the juice from the fruit. Cut the bread very thinly and line the bottoms and the sides of the basins. Strain the fruit from its juice: at this point, taste it to see if there is enough sugar for your liking. Measure the juice in a pint/.5 litre jug – it will vary with the fruit that you use. To each ½ pint/300 ml of juice, use one heaped teaspoonful of arrowroot, which you should slake in a little of the juice in a separate bowl. Return the juice to the pan and pour in the slaked arrowroot mixture. Bring to the boil and cook until it has the consistency of thin cream. Leave to cool.

Now add the fruit to the pudding basins until they are half full. Pour in a little of the juice. Then add a layer of bread; then the rest of the fruit. Cover the fruit with a final layer of bread and pour over the rest of the juice. Put a coffee saucer on top of each pudding basin and use paperweights or kitchen weights wrapped completely in aluminium foil to weight down the saucers. Leave overnight. There should be no trace of white bread in these puddings.

They can be transported to the picnic in their basins and turned out onto soup plates. Serve with slightly whipped double cream.

GERANIUM CREAM

This recipe comes from Elizabeth David's *Summer Cooking*.

Serves 6

½ pint/300 ml double cream
3 tablespoons caster sugar
6 sweet scented geranium leaves

6 small fresh cream cheeses – Crème
    d'Isigny or Chambourcy

Put the cream in a double saucepan, and add the sugar and geranium leaves. Heat gently to let the mixture get thoroughly hot without boiling. Leave it to cool with the leaves still in the cream. When cool, gently beat in the cream cheeses with a spoon – a fork will break up the geranium leaves, which you take out before serving.

We put this cream into little pots and garnish them with geranium petals. It should be served very cold.

***

PEACHES IN ORANGE AND LEMON JUICE

Resist the temptation to add alcohol to this mixture – it is in the clarity of the flavours where lies the appeal. You could always carry a flask of peach brandy in the basket. A swig is champion should the weather get nippy.

Serves 6

6 ripe peaches *juice of 2 lemons*
juice of 2 oranges *caster sugar – optional*

Put the peaches in a large bowl and pour on boiling water to cover. Strain them immediately into a sieve or colander. This brief immersion should make the skins slide off with ease. Slice the peaches into segments about ½ inch/1.25 cm thick. If the fruit is ripe, the flesh should pull away easily from the stone. Place the peaches in a bowl. Pour on the orange and lemon juice, then leave in the fridge for a few hours. Taste and only add sugar if you feel it is really necessary.

Transport the peaches in a chilled, wide-mouthed thermos.

***

WINTER

GIBLET SOUP

The subtle stroke of this soup is the use of the cucumbers, fresh and pickled. Although it is the same vegetable, it is almost like two different ingredients. If you want to emphasise the difference, take the fresh cucumber strips to the picnic separately and add them at the moment of serving the hot soup.

Serves 6

carcass of a turkey or *game birds, the feet, neck and giblets of the same*
1 onion
1 large carrot
1 stalk celery
1 tablespoon vegetable oil
2 oz/60 g bacon or *salt pork* or *ham in a piece (optional)*
1 clove garlic
1 teaspoon peppercorns

2 dried mushrooms, if you have some
5 juniper berries (optional)
1 pickled cucumber, cut into matchsticks
1 tablespoon port or *a heaped teaspoon redcurrant jelly*
a squeeze of lemon juice
salt
½ small fresh cucumber, cut into matchsticks

Chop up the carcass, leaving on any meat, raw or cooked that is attached. Separate the liver from the giblets, cut away any greenish parts and set aside. Cut along the outside wall of the gizzard where there is a natural seam and peel it away from the inner bag of grit; throw away the grit and wash the gizzard. Peel the onion and scrape the carrot clean; cut them and the washed celery stalk into large dice.

Heat the oil in a large pan. Dice the bacon, salt pork or ham and heat it in the oil until the fat begins to run. Add the vegetables and the carcasses and cook carefully until the vegetables begin to brown and the meat on the bones begins to darken. Don't let them char or burn, but the browning is an important step that guarantees an appetising colour of soup. Add about 4 pints/2 litres water, the feet and neck (if you have them), the heart, the gizzard and kidney. Add the peeled clove of garlic, the peppercorns, and the dried mushrooms and juniper berries if you have them. Simmer over a low heat until the stock is considerably reduced and of a good flavour.

Strain the stock into a clean pan and then pick out the kidneys, heart and gizzard, bacon and any meat; chop into small cubes. Sauté the liver in a little butter in a small pan and chop. Return the giblets, meat and bacon to the stock, add the liver, the pickled cucumber and the port or redcurrant jelly. Simmer for a few minutes. Taste and see if you think a little lemon juice would be good; sometimes the tart taste of pickled cucumber is enough. Taste again for salt and add it if necessary.

Pour the soup into a thermos jar which you have rinsed out with extremely hot water. Serve in fairly small quantities garnished with the fresh cucumber.

COLD RABBIT AND GAMMON PIE

Serves 6

1 large rabbit or 2 small ones
1 lb/500 g lean gammon
2 pig's trotters
1 large glass white wine
½ lemon, sliced
1 bay leaf
1 onion, peeled and sliced

3 carrots, scrubbed and sliced lengthways
2 stalks celery
8 peppercorns
1 blade mace
1 sprig thyme or flat teaspoon dried thyme
6 coriander seeds, crushed

For the crust:
1 lb/500 g plain flour mixed with a good pinch of salt   *4 oz/125 g lard*

Put the rabbit and gammon together with all the other ingredients into a large pot. Cover with water and bring gently to the boil. Lower the heat and simmer until the gammon feels tender and the rabbit comes away from the bones when you probe it: this will take approximately 1½ hours, but depends upon the age of the rabbit. Remove the rabbit and gammon from the pot, but continue simmering the rest. Bone the rabbit carefully and cut it into largish chunks. Cut the gammon into cubes.

Turn on oven to 180°C/350°F, Gas 4.

Now make the crust as follows. If you don't have a pie mould, you will need a round cake tin 7 inches/17.5 cm in diameter.

Put the seasoned flour into a large bowl. Bring the lard and 7½ fl oz/235 ml water to boiling point; pour immediately onto the flour. Mix to a dough. You must do this very quickly because the paste must be moulded into shape before the lard has time to set; done too slowly and the paste would become brittle. Use your hands to mould the paste.

Put one-third of the paste in a cloth and keep warm (the linen cupboard is a good place); put the rest of the paste into the cake tin and press it down over the bottom and then up the sides with your fingers. Now take the rabbit and gammon and fill the tin but don't press the meat down. Take the remaining third of pastry and press it lightly with the palm of your hand into a round for the lid. Place this on top of the pie and pinch it round the edges to seal. You can use the left-over trimmings to decorate the pie with diamond-shaped pieces etc. Make a hole in the centre of the pie with your little finger. Bake in the oven for about 1½ hours. The pastry should be golden brown.

Meanwhile, remove the stock from the heat and strain.

When the pie is cold and the stock has become a jelly, take some of it (about ½–¾ pint/300–450 ml) and warm it in a pan until it is just dissolved. Pour this liquid gently through the centre hole of the pie. Do this in little spurts; you will find that if you wait a moment between each pouring, the pie will absorb a surprising amount of liquid. Leave pie to set. There will be stock left in the pan, but you can freeze this for future use.

PHEASANT CROQUETTES

These patties would not be appetising stone cold, so although you can, and should, prepare them well ahead of time, fry them just before setting out and insulate them well to keep them warm and the coating crunchy. Green peppercorns can be bought in tins or jars and can be used whole. They are included to contribute a bit of zest, but if you cannot obtain them, add instead a splash of Worcestershire sauce or some other savoury condiment.

Serves 4

1½ oz/45 g butter
1 onion, peeled and finely chopped
2 tablespoons flour
1 teaspoon mustard powder
12 fl oz/375 ml milk
8 oz/250 g cold cooked pheasant, chopped
2 oz/60 g Prosciutto or San Daniele ham, chopped

1 level dessertspoon green peppercorns
1 tablespoon chopped parsley
salt and pepper
seasoned flour
1 egg, beaten
fresh breadcrumbs for the coating
vegetable oil for frying

Ideally start the recipe the day before the picnic. Melt the butter in a heavy-bottomed pan and gently cook the onion until softened; don't let the butter burn. Stir in the flour and mustard powder and cook for a minute or two. Add the milk in stages and cook as for a thick béchamel sauce. Stir in the pheasant, ham, peppercorns, parsley and salt and pepper to taste. Tip into a shallow dish and chill overnight. If you cannot start the recipe this far ahead, chill the mixture in the freezer.

When it is solid enough to handle, form the mixture into small patties. Dust them with seasoned flour, coat with beaten egg and then the breadcrumbs. Fry in hot oil in two batches, turning them a few times to make sure the mixture is well heated through and the coating crisp. Pack surrounded by kitchen paper to absorb any excess oil.

A spicy tomato sauce or some chutney goes well with these.

HOME-MADE SAUSAGE ROLL

Serves 8

1 tablespoon vegetable oil
1 large onion, peeled and finely chopped
2 lb/1 kg belly of pork, rind removed
1 egg
4 oz/125 g fresh breadcrumbs, white or wholemeal
grainy French mustard
soya sauce

thyme
sea salt
black pepper
1 lb/500 g puff pastry (frozen bought puff pastry, defrosted, is fine)
1 egg + 1 tablespoon milk for pastry wash

Turn on the oven to 180°C/350°F, Gas 4

In the vegetable oil, sauté the chopped onion until softened. Mince the belly of pork or chop it in a food processor; turn it into a large bowl. Add the egg, the cooked onion, the breadcrumbs and the seasonings. Seasoning should be a matter of taste but a guideline is 2 teaspoons mustard, 1 tablespoon soya sauce, 1 flat teaspoon dried thyme, a hefty pinch of salt and 12 screws of black pepper. Form the mixture into a large sausage shape and bake for 15 minutes.

Turn up the oven to 220°C/425°F, Gas 7.

Roll out the pastry into a rectangle about ½ inch/1.25 cm thick. Place the sausage down one long side, leaving an inch (2.5 cm) clear at the edge. Bring the pastry flap over the sausage and seal at the three ends using cold water and your fingers. Beat together the egg and milk and brush over the pastry. Bake in the oven for 25–30 minutes until the pastry is puffed and golden. This is good eaten cold.

MARY'S FRUIT CAKE

This cake, made from a recipe of Mary Coventry', mother of one of the authors, was taken on many a chilly seaside picnic at Westward Ho! in Devon. Its richness is just what is needed to uncurl fingers and toes numb from Atlantic waves. If you happen to have a cake tin with a central funnel, i.e. an angel cake tin, this helps to bake the cake evenly by providing a heat source in the centre. Otherwise, use a 10-inch/25-cm cake tin.

8 oz/250 g glacé cherries
8 oz/250 g currants
8 oz/250 g sultanas
6 oz/180 g raisins
2 oz/60 g muscatel raisins (optional)
4 oz/125 g mixed peel
3 tablespoons brandy

12 oz/375 g butter
12 oz/375 g caster sugar
4 eggs
12 oz/375 g plain flour
1 teaspoon baking powder
1 teaspoon ground cinnamon

Pre-heat the oven to 140°C/275°F, Gas 1.

Cut half the glacé cherries in two, keeping the others whole for decoration. Mix together the halved cherries with the rest of the dried fruit, pour on the brandy and leave to steep a while.

Cream the butter and sugar, then beat the eggs. Add alternately, and in stages, the flour, sifted with the baking powder and cinnamon, the fruit and the eggs.

Line the cake tin with greaseproof paper. Pour in the mixture and smooth the surface, and dot with the whole cherries. Wrap brown paper around the outside of the tin and tie with string. Bake the cake for 3 hours at the given temperature, then at 130°C/250°F, Gas ½ for a further half-hour. Cool the cake on a rack, then store in a tin with a tight-fitting lid.

COFFEE ECLAIRS

These should be made the day they are eaten.

Serves 4

3¾ oz/110 g plain flour
3 oz/90 g butter

3 eggs
½ pint/300 ml double cream

For the icing:
8 oz/250 g icing sugar, sieved
2 egg whites

1 tablespoonful incredibly strong instant coffee

Turn on the oven to 220°C/425°F, Gas 7. Have ready the non-stick baking sheets, or greased sheets if you don't have non-stick.

Sift the flour and put it onto a piece of paper so that you can shoot it into the boiling liquid all at once. Put the butter and 7½ fl oz/235 ml water into a pan and boil together. When bubbling, draw the pan aside and shoot in the flour. Beat the mixture until it is smooth, and at the moment that the paste will leave the sides of the pan, set it aside to cool. Do not overbeat the mixture or it will become heavy and won't rise properly.

Whisk the eggs lightly, and then add to the cooled mixture by degrees. At this point, you should beat the mixture very thoroughly, and if your eggs are large, you may not need all of them. When finished, the paste should be smooth and shiny.

Put spoonsful of paste on the baking sheets – round or long, whichever shape you prefer for éclairs – and bake until the paste is quite firm to the touch. If you take the pastry out too soon, it will sink when taken from the oven. Put the éclairs onto a cake rack to cool.

Whip the cream stiffly, split the éclairs when cool and fill.

Next make the icing: add the sugar by degrees to the egg whites, beating all the time. Add the coffee. The proportions of sugar to egg white will vary depending upon the size of the egg. The icing should be fairly stiff to prevent it running down the sides of the éclairs. The longer you beat, the shinier your icing will be. Smooth the icing onto the tops of the éclairs with a knife dipped in hot water.

19 *Funeral Tea*

Most of us, at some time or another, are presented with this sad, and often difficult occasion. Even if you are not the person most intimately bereaved, it may fall to your lot to be the organiser of what is to happen after the funeral. Why tea, you may ask? Well, if it is a country funeral, it usually happens early in the afternoon, in order to give people time to make the journey to wherever it may be. But, in fact, the following menu could as well be a lunch if that is what is required.

You may think that people coming away from a funeral, whatever their feelings, will not want to eat very much – or anything at all. This is not so. The North Country wakes were encrusted with food: it was a sign of respect to the departed to provide a heavy, rich and varied repast and this, in turn, was because no serious friends or relatives would contemplate leaving the widow, say, immediately after the funeral to go home alone. The ritual of mourning – too much neglected until very recently when it is beginning to be recognised as a psychological necessity to those most affected – is all about accepting that death is an occasion. It needs marking and serious acknowledgement, and is no small matter; it is, after all, the last great adventure for the person concerned and therefore a send off; a farewell party is due to them.

Another aspect of funerals is that, apart from relations who may not ordinarily keep in touch with one another, they invariably contain a disparate collection of friends of the bereaved, who have nothing but the occasion in common. Food helps to break down some of the awkwardness that can arise.

The party, or tea, or gathering after the funeral is also often of some comfort to those who most feel their loss. If you know someone in this situation who is feeling too stunned to cope with the domestic side of the funeral, it can be a kindness to offer to do that part of it for them.

When planning the food, it is well to remember that funeral

gatherings may have people of all ages, and that many of them may not have had time or opportunity for much lunch, on top of which they may have a long journey home. Simple, but substantial food is the best solution, but also food that people can eat standing, or which they can have as little or as much of as they please. Also, if you are making the food for someone else, it is necessary to have food that you can largely prepare at home and transport fairly easily. Finally, we cannot give quantities here, as the numbers may vary from a dozen to sixty or seventy. Ask how many people are expected and then cater for ten more to be on the safe side. Be responsible for any extra china, glass or cutlery that may be needed.

Suggested beverages to go with this menu – apart from strong Indian and weak China tea – are hot chocolate (very popular with children) lemonade, (see page 178), sloe gin, (if you have been provident enough to make any) and, if the weather is icy, a mulled wine.

Celery Soup

Chicken Sandwiches

Ham Sandwiches

Cucumber Sandwiches

Mona's Fruit Cake

Lemon Curd Sponge Cake

Damp Gingerbread

Flapjacks

Mulled Wine

Summer Punch

CELERY SOUP

If this meal is not to be a tea, but a midday affair, we suggest that you make a soup. The following is good and can be drunk from a cup which is easier than having to deal with a spoon and bowl for those who are standing.

Serves 8

1 large head of celery
1 oz/30 g butter
1 dessertspoon sunflower seed oil
1 large onion, chopped

salt and pepper
2 pints/1.1 litres chicken stock
Single cream (optional)

Clean and chop the celery into pieces about ¼ inch/0.6 cm wide. Melt the butter and oil in a pan and sauté the onion until transparent. Add the celery, and a flat teaspoonful of salt and a good grinding of pepper. Cook gently, stirring, until the celery is well-coated in the onion mixture. Add the stock and simmer until the celery is completely soft. Liquidise, or pass through a mouli. You can add a tablespoonful of single cream to this soup when you are heating it up, but it is not necessary.

CHICKEN SANDWICHES

1 chicken
1 small onion
8 oz/250 g butter

1 wholemeal loaf (rectangular, rather
*   than oval or round)*
½ pint/300 ml mayonnaise
salt and pepper

Roast the chicken: for sandwiches, cooking chicken in a chicken-brick is the best way as the chicken remains moist and you won't be using the skin. (If you don't have a chicken-brick, cook it as you normally do.) Peel the onion and put it inside the bird with a knob of butter. Rub a little more butter over the breast and cook. If using a chicken-brick, put it into a cold oven and turn the oven to 180°C/350°F, Gas 4, for about 1¾ hours, but test it after 1 hour 20 minutes. Set aside to cool.

People are divided about whether or not they like crusts on sandwiches. We like them, but if you don't, they are your sandwiches. To make nice thin slices of buttered bread, you need an extremely sharp knife and soft butter which you spread thinly on each slice before you cut it. (You may feel that these remarks are kids' stuff, but we have been on the receiving end of so many badly-made sandwiches that it seems worth going through the process.)

When the chicken is cool, joint and bone it, removing all the skin. Chop the chicken meat on a board and then put it into a large bowl. Now add the mayonnaise, bit by bit: you only want to bind the chicken meat a little, not produce chicken in a cold sauce. Season with salt and pepper. Spread the chicken fairly thickly on one piece of bread, cover with a second and press gently together. If the sandwiches are going to be crustless, this is the moment to remove the crusts. In any case, the rounds must be divided – either into two triangles, or into four.

Unless you are going to store them in plastic boxes with a lid, they should be covered with a damp cloth until wanted.

HAM SANDWICHES

2 lb/1 kg sweet cured ham   *8 oz/250 g butter*
1 wholemeal loaf   *English mustard*

The only difference between making these and making the chicken sandwiches is that the bread should be buttered more thickly, and that one slice should be thinly spread with mustard, and the other covered with the ham (which should be preferably cut off the bone, but certainly not be slippery slices from a polythene packet).

CUCUMBER SANDWICHES

2 cucumbers   *½ lb/250 g double cream cheese (Crème*
1 wholemeal loaf   *d'Isigny is very good)*
          curry powder

Peel the cucumbers and then slice them as thinly as possible. Spread cream cheese on the unbuttered bread and sprinkle one piece with a very little curry powder. Lay cucumber on alternate slices and put together.

MONA'S FRUIT CAKE

7 oz/210 g caster sugar
6 oz/180 g margarine
2 tablespoons milk
3 eggs, beaten
2 oz/60 g glacé cherries

8 oz/250 g plain flour
½ teaspoon baking powder
½ teaspoon salt
½ teaspoon mixed spice
18 oz/550 g mixed dried fruit

Turn on the oven to 180°C/350°F, Gas 4.

Cream the sugar and margarine and add the milk and beaten eggs. Chop the cherries in half and roll them in some of the flour. Sift the baking powder into the rest of the flour and add to the creamed mixture with the salt and mixed spice. Finally add the dried fruit and cherries.

Line the bottom and sides of an 8-in/20-cm round or the equivalent square cake tin with greased greaseproof paper and fill it with the mixture; bake in the oven for about 2¼ hours. Test after 2 hours with a skewer; if it comes out clean, the cake is cooked. Allow it to cool in its tin before turning it onto a cake rack.

LEMON CURD SPONGE CAKE

butter
4 oz/125 g self-raising flour
4½ oz/140 g caster sugar

3 eggs
grated rind of 1 lemon
1 oz/30 g icing sugar for top of cake

For the lemon curd:
1 oz/30 g butter
3 oz/90 g granulated sugar

juice and grated rind of 1 lemon
2 egg yolks, beaten

Turn on the oven to 180°C/350°F, Gas 4.

Butter a 7-inch/17.5 cm cake tin and dust it with a mixture of 1 teaspoonful flour and 1 teaspoonful sugar. Break the eggs into a basin, add the rest of the sugar and beat over a saucepan of hot water until warm; then remove from the heat and whisk until quite cold and thick. Sieve the flour, add the rind, and stir lightly into the beaten eggs. Put the mixture into the cake tin and bake for 1 hour.

While the cake is baking, make the lemon curd. Put the butter, sugar, lemon rind and juice into a double saucepan, and when the sugar has dissolved, gradually add the thoroughly beaten egg yolks. Stir until the mixture thickens. (If you want to do this fast, take the top half of the saucepan and put it on a direct flame, but you must stir continuously to prevent the eggs scrambling.) The mixture thickens more as it cools.

When the cake is cool, cut it in half carefully, spread with lemon curd and put it back together. Dust the top with icing sugar.

DAMP GINGERBREAD

6 oz/180 g butter
10 oz/300 g plain flour
3 oz/90 g almonds, roughly chopped
6 oz/180 g dark brown sugar
6 oz/180 g sultanas
¾ teaspoon bicarbonate of soda

1½ teaspoons ground ginger
1½ teaspoons ground cinnamon
4 oz/125 g black treacle (see page 86 for measuring)
2 eggs, beaten
a little warm milk

Turn on the oven to 180°C/350°F, Gas 4.

Cream the butter. Add the dry ingredients and the treacle, then the well-beaten eggs, and a little milk if the mixture seems too stiff to mix. Pour the mixture into a rectangular (10 × 6-inch/25 × 15-cm) tin lined with buttered greaseproof paper and bake in the oven for about 2 hours.

FLAPJACKS

1 lb/500 g dark brown sugar
1 lb/500 g margarine

2 tablespoons golden syrup (see page 86 for measuring)
1½ lb/750 g rolled oats

Turn on the oven to 180°C/350°F, Gas 4.

Melt the sugar and margarine in a saucepan and add the golden syrup. Then add the oats, and stir well. Press this mixture down into a greased and floured baking tin – 10 × 12 inches/25 × 30 cm – and cook in the oven for 35 minutes.

MULLED WINE

Serves 8

1 bottle decent red wine
1 tablespoon sugar
½ sherry glass curaçao or *1 sherry glass*
   port

1 cinnamon stick
a little grated nutmeg

Don't make the mistake of thinking that really awful plonk, heated, will stop being really awful plonk.

Heat the wine with the rest of the ingredients, but do not boil. A good way to keep it hot is to strain it back into wine bottles and stand them in buckets of hot water.

SUMMER PUNCH

Mix 1 bottle of white wine with an equal quantity of soda water. Add a good dash of brandy and sweeten to taste.

The best way to do this is to make a sugar syrup by boiling water and sugar together (10 oz/300 g granulated sugar to 1 pint/625 ml water). When it is cool, you can add cut up peaches, nectarines, strawberries, greengages, cherries (score them down their crease first), orange and lemon slices, or any other fruit in season that you like. This is not very alcoholic, but people do tend to drink quite a lot of it. The base of 1 bottle of wine should do 8 people.

---

20 *Holiday Cooking*

From the moment of starting a family, women have very little prospect of a grown-up holiday, which in many ways means that for her the holiday isn't one at all: a change, but hardly a rest. Added to this is the incontrovertible fact that self-catering holidays cost less than staying in a hotel or boarding house and for most people with young families, finances dictate the holiday. But there are advantages. Trying to keep a four-year-old sitting through an hotel meal can be quite as tiring as making him or her something you know he will eat, with premises other than an hotel dining-room to riot in after he has been charged up by the meal. But if you don't want to be a domestic slave while everybody else bathes, basks and generally enjoy themselves, it is as well to make some plans and devise a routine that gives you some spare time.

One main cooked meal a day is enough and, depending upon the age of your family, you can make it lunch or dinner. Breakfast can be continental: rolls, croissants, bread, toast etc. with butter and jam; cereals, if insisted upon, hot drinks and fresh fruit. The secondary meal – picnic lunch or snack supper can be food bought from delicatessens; cheeses, salamis, ham, quiche, pâté, crusty bread and whatever fruit is abundantly available and consequently cheap. The main meal should have one substantial course with a large salad or a cooked green vegetable. In France and Italy, there are cake or pastry shops even in quite small villages where treats can easily be bought.

As most family holidays take place in August and as many families now go abroad, we are assuming that it will be hot, and if that is a fact about your holiday, it will be well worth taking a cold bag or two with you. The fridges in rented accommodation are seldom large enough: you can save on your shopping expeditions if you can shop for two days and for this you need ample cool storage space.

We also suggest that you take your own sharp knife, or knives with you; we have neither of us ever encountered a rented kitchen where there was a knife that would cut anything sturdier than butter with ease. If you are contemplating regular picnics, then containers for transporting food and a thermos or two are also desirable and, of course, the cold bags come in here as well.

Unless you really hate getting up in the mornings, early shopping is a good idea: it is not so hot or so crowded and the whole process will be quicker and easier. Make the family do their share of clearing up and organise the working part of your day so that you will have one long, clear period when you are not expected to do anything. If you are cooking lunch, then it should be from three o'clock until the children's supper time. If you are cooking dinner, it should be from eleven in the morning – by which time you will have shopped and put a picnic lunch together – until six in the evening. Of course, all this does depend upon the age or ages of your family, but in principle it is a good rough schedule.

Finally, the menu for this section is also only a guideline: if your family are keen on pasta, there are several other sauces that you could make for it in this book. If your holiday is by the sea and fish is easily obtainable, there are a number of other fish dishes – and so on. Holiday cooking is to some extent dictated by where you are; not so much because you wouldn't be able to get the ingredients of the dishes we suggest, as that there may be specialities of the region or a seasonal glut of some fruit or vegetable it would be sensible to use.

Egg in a Bun

Swiss Eggs and Ham

Cold Omelettes

Pan Bagna

Hot Pasta with Cold Tomato Sauce

Baked Fish with Anchovy Sauce

Paella

Coq au Vin

A Simple Cassoulet

Meat Loaf

Bollito Misto

Fried Aubergines with Skordalia

Fruit Fools

German Fritters

EGG IN A BUN

Serves 4

4 round bread rolls (the soft kind are the   *1 oz/30 g grated cheese*
    best)   *4 eggs, separated*
2 oz/60 g butter   *salt and pepper*

Turn on the oven to 180°C/350°F, Gas 4.

Cut the tops of the buns, scoop out the soft part, butter the inside and put them in the oven for about 5 minutes to make them crisp. Then put half the grated cheese inside each bun. Put one egg yolk in each bun. Season the eggs. Turn up the oven to 200°C/400°F, Gas 6.

Whisk the egg whites stiffly, add the rest of the grated cheese to the whites and put the mixture on top of the yolks. Bake the buns in the oven until the whites are set.

Note: This recipe comes from Fortune Stanley's book, *English Country House Cooking*, as does the recipe for Swiss Eggs and Ham which follows.

SWISS EGGS AND HAM

Serves 4

4 tablespoons double cream   *4 eggs*
8 oz/250 g cooked ham, chopped   *salt and pepper*
2 oz/60 g grated cheese

Turn on the oven to 200°C/400°F, Gas 6.

Into an ovenproof dish, pour 3 tablespoonsful cream, the chopped ham and half the cheese. Stir and bake in the oven for 5 minutes. Turn the oven down to 180°C/350°F, Gas 4.

Break the eggs into the dish, season, add 1 tablespoonful cream and sprinkle with the rest of the cheese. Bake in the oven 5–10 minutes, until the whites are set.

COLD OMELETTES

Middle-Eastern and Iberian cold omelettes tend to be solid affairs ideal for picnics or served in wedges with salad for lunch. French omelettes, altogether more delicate affairs, are also good served cold, wrapped round a bland creamy cheese, fresh vegetable purée, or shellfish, such as crab, in mayonnaise. A completely plain flat omelette can be cut into strips when cold and used as a garnish or a salad ingredient. An example of each kind of recipe is given below but holidays are the time for improvisation and imagination, so use them also as starting points.

VEGETABLE OMELETTE

Serves 4–6

3 tablespoons vegetable oil
1 large onion, peeled and chopped
2 cloves garlic, peeled and crushed
2 leeks, washed and cut into rings or *a handful of fresh spinach, roughly chopped*
4 oz/125 g broad beans or *peas, podded*
2 tomatoes, skinned, de-seeded and chopped

1 green chilli, de-seeded and cut into threads (optional, but surprisingly nice)
salt and pepper
grated nutmeg
2 oz/60 g fresh parsley, finely chopped
6 eggs
1½ oz/45 g butter

Heat the oil and sauté the vegetables until soft, adding a little water if they are sticking. Season with salt, pepper and a little nutmeg. Stir in the parsley.

Beat the eggs in a large bowl. Add the cooked vegetables, (make sure they are not so hot that they cook the eggs). Melt the butter in a large frying pan about 10 inches/25 cm in diameter. Pour in the egg mixture and cook gently until the bottom is set. Slide under a heated grill to brown the top. If you have no grill, cook the omelette in a suitable pan in a moderate oven until just set. Serve cold in wedges.

TORTILLA

The simplicity of this makes it perhaps the nicest of all omelettes – wonderful for picnics.

Serves 4–6

4 fl oz/125 ml olive oil
3 onions, peeled and chopped
3 large potatoes, peeled and diced

salt and pepper
6 eggs

Heat the oil in a large heavy-bottomed pan and cook the onions and potatoes, stirring intermittently for about 20 minutes or until they are tender. Season with salt and pepper. Beat the eggs in a bowl. Lift out the vegetables and stir into the eggs. Pour off remaining oil into a cup. Clean the pan. Return the oil, adding more if you think you need it for frying the omelette.

Heat the oil, then pour in the egg mixture. Press down gently and cook until the egg is set. Slide under the grill and cook the top. If you have no grill, you can turn the omelette and slip it back into the pan top-side down or alternatively cook the omelette in a suitable dish in a moderate oven until the eggs are set through.

This is good hot, warm, or cool, but perhaps best of all warm.

FRENCH OMELETTES

For each omelette:
1 large egg   *salt and pepper*
½ oz/15 g butter

Possible fillings:
1 tablespoon fromage blanc or *other soft cheese, mixed with fresh herbs and a small clove of garlic, crushed*
1 tomato, skinned, de-seeded and chopped, mixed with chopped basil, salt, pepper and a small pinch of sugar
a few prawns mixed with a little mayonnaise and some cayenne pepper
crabmeat – treated the same as above
chopped bacon crisply cooked, mixed with shredded lettuce and dressed with a light vinaigrette
some sliced mushrooms sautéed in butter to which you add a spoonful of cream
left-over vegetables such as peas or broad beans, puréed

Beat the egg with a teaspoon of water. Season with salt and pepper. Melt the butter in a 6 inch/15 cm diameter omelette pan. Pour in the egg and cook until set. Spoon your choice of filling on one side of the omelette – being quite restrained with the filling. Turn the omelette out onto a serving dish. Repeat as many times as you have guests. Serve with salad and good bread, and perhaps some slices of salami.

COLD OMELETTE AS GARNISH

2 eggs   *tiny pinch sugar*
salt   *1 dessertspoon vegetable oil*

Beat the eggs so that they are well amalgamated, but not frothy. Season with salt and sugar. Heat the oil in a pan and pour in the egg mixture.

Turn the heat to low, cover (using foil if necessary), and cook gently for
about 5 minutes, until the egg is set. Turn the omelette over to seal the
other side. Take out the omelette and cool.

Cut into strips and use either in a salad, as a garnish for soup (in
which case make the omelette thin), as a garnish for rice dishes or
dressed with a vinaigrette or a light mayonnaise and mixed with spring
onions and parsley to make a version of egg salad.

PAN BAGNA

For this sustaining pressed sandwich, use either a French loaf or round
flat soft bread cut horizontally which is, in fact, the sort of container that
would be used in Provence.

Serves 4

1 loaf (see *above*)
¼ pint/150 ml virgin olive oil
2–3 tablespoons wine vinegar
salt and pepper
1 clove garlic, peeled and crushed
2 large 'Mediterranean' tomatoes, sliced

1 large Spanish onion
1 green or *red pepper, de-seeded and*
   thinly sliced
1 small tin anchovy fillets
2 oz/60 g black olives, stoned

Slice the loaf in half horizontally. Make up a vinaigrette with the oil,
wine vinegar to taste, salt, pepper and garlic. Sprinkle the cut sides of
the bread liberally with the vinaigrette.

Arrange the sliced tomatoes, onion and pepper on the bottom half of
the bread. Garnish with the anchovy fillets and olives. Place the top half
of the bread on the sandwich, wrap it tightly in aluminium foil and leave
for 1–2 hours with weights on top; this helps the flavours to meld and
the sandwich to form a solid mass easy to slice and serve.

Pan Bagna is traditionally eaten while playing *boules*.

HOT PASTA WITH COLD TOMATO SAUCE

This is one of the best of all summer dishes using that herb that
encapsulates the scent of summer – basil. The sauce should be mixed

with the pasta at the moment of serving, and the dish served quickly before the sauce warms or the pasta cools.

Serves 4–6

4 tomatoes, skinned and chopped or 2
   'beef' tomatoes, skinned and chopped
6 spring onions, cleaned and finely
   chopped
1 tablespoon finely chopped parsley

10–12 fresh basil leaves, roughly
   chopped
3 tablespoons virgin olive oil
1 tablespoon red wine vinegar
salt and freshly-ground black pepper

Mix the above ingredients together, if possible letting them sit awhile for the flavours to meld. Cook 1 lb/500 g fresh pasta until it is *al dente*. Drain, pile into a hot dish and add the sauce at the table.

BAKED FISH WITH ANCHOVY SAUCE

Since it is even possible nowadays to buy fresh fish in English seaside resorts, it is useful to know about this anchovy sauce, which has an interesting, positive relationship of result for the effort entailed. Most whole white fish, such as cod, haddock, grey mullet or, if you are lucky enough to find it, sea bass, stand up well to being roasted in the oven.

Serves 4

1 whole fish weighing about 2–3
   lb/1–1.5 kg
herbs (fennel, dill or parsley)
1 bay leaf
a slice of lemon

sea salt and freshly-ground black pepper
olive oil
1 small tin anchovy fillets
2 oz/60 g butter
½ pint/300 ml double cream

Ask the fishmonger to clean the fish, leaving on the head and tail.

Turn on the oven to 220°C/425°F, Gas 7.

Using a small sharp knife, make three diagonal slashes on each side of the fish, cutting practically down to the bone. Tuck herbs and the bay leaf, plus a slice of lemon into the body cavity. Rub sea salt and freshly-ground black pepper into the surfaces of the fish, making sure that some topples into the slashes. Trickle olive oil over the fish and place in a roasting pan; then put it into the pre-heated oven. An average-size fish should be cooked in approximately 25–30 minutes. The cuts in the sides will enable you to see if the flesh is opaque to the bone.

To make the sauce, open the tin of anchovies and rinse about 5 fillets in warm water to remove excess salt. Melt the butter in a frying pan or sauté pan. Add the anchovies and stir round until they break up and more or less disintegrate. Add the cream, bring to the boil and stir.

Add some freshly-ground black pepper and taste to see if the sauce could stand the addition of another anchovy. The flavour should be robust. Carefully lift the fish (whose skin should be brown and crisp) onto a serving dish and serve the sauce separately.

Plain boiled potatoes are the best accompaniment.

PAELLA

There are many versions of paella and no doubt much Spanish argy-bargy about which are authentic. The right sort of rice (from Valencia) is an important factor. It is a round, stubby variety, in shape like pudding rice but nothing like it in texture. Italian Arborio risotto rice is a good substitute if you cannot get Spanish rice. Paella should be cooked in quantity so as to accommodate a variety of ingredients, and therefore a large pan is essential. Paella is often cooked outside on an open fire, which of course contributes to the flavour, and if your pan is large, it is a good heat source. If the pan overlaps a gas or electric ring by a long way, keep gently turning the rice sides to middle to ensure even cooking.

The ingredients below are a guideline. Feel free to add or subtract, within reason. If your funds do not run to saffron, then substitute 1 teaspoon ground turmeric as a sunny yellow colour is essential.

Serves 6

1 small roasting chicken, chopped into small pieces
1 pint/625 ml mussels, scrubbed and checked for duds
2 tablespoons white wine
1 lb/500 g small squid (optional)
6 tablespoons olive oil
1 large Spanish onion, peeled and chopped
3 cloves garlic, peeled and crushed
6 oz/180 g bacon in a piece or salt pork

8 oz/250 g tomatoes, skinned and chopped
4 oz/125 g French beans or shelled peas
1 green or red pepper, grilled, peeled and cut into strips
1 lb/500 g Valencia rice (see above)
1 pint/625 ml unshelled prawns
1 teaspoon saffron strands or turmeric
pimentón/paprika
salt and pepper

Use the chicken carcass plus giblets (if any) to make 2 pints/1.1 litres of good stock, adding in if you have them to hand, a carrot, stalk of celery and a bouquet garni.

Open the mussels by heating them with the white wine (or water) in a heavy pan with the lid on. Remove and strain the accumulated liquid and save it. Clean the squid if you are using it and cut the bodies into rings and separate the tentacles.

Heat the oil and sauté the onion. Add the chicken pieces and garlic. Cook slowly, turning and moving until golden, then remove the chicken. Cut the bacon or salt pork into small cubes and sauté them until lightly browned. Return the chicken pieces; add the squid and cook for 5 minutes. Next add the tomatoes, beans or peas and the pepper. Add 6 fl oz/180 ml chicken stock and simmer for 10 minutes. Combine the rest of the chicken stock with the mussel liquid and measure out 1¾ pints/1 litre.

Add the rice to the pan and stir. Add the prawns (peeled or unpeeled, depending on preference), the opened mussels still in their shells and salt and pepper. Start adding the stock as you would for risotto, i.e. letting some be absorbed before adding more. After the first addition of stock, scatter in the saffron or turmeric. Cook until the rice absorbs no more stock and is tender.

Sprinkle a little paprika or pimentón (the same thing really) on top and let the paella sit for a few minutes in a warm place before serving. It should not be boiling hot.

COQ AU VIN

Should you happen to be holidaying where wine is cheap, it is the moment to steer a bottle in the direction of a coq au vin. Of course a red Burgundy is the correct ingredient but you can fudge a little as long as you use a fairly decent bottle; plonk will just spoil a good chicken. If you are making this dish in Burgundy, use a few tablespoons of Marc de Bourgogne in addition; otherwise see if you have some duty-free cognac left.

There are many recipes for coq au vin, most of them requiring too many processes for relaxed cooking, so we have adapted a gracefully simple method given by Elizabeth David in *French Country Cooking*. To assuage holiday appetites, make sure there are plenty of triangles of fried bread as an accompaniment.

Serves 6

1 plump chicken
salt and pepper
lemon juice
2 fl oz/60 ml vegetable oil
2 oz/60 g butter
4 oz/125 g piece bacon or *salt pork, cut into cubes*
1 small glass brandy
1 bottle red wine (see above)
the giblets of the bird, excluding the liver

15–20 button onions or *small shallots*
butter for frying vegetables
sugar
12 oz/375 g button mushrooms
BEURRE MANIÉ *made from 1 level tablespoon flour worked into 1 oz/30 g softened butter*
slices of white country bread
oil for frying
fresh parsley, chopped

Season the bird inside and out with salt, pepper and lemon juice. In a deep, thick-bottomed pan, melt the oil and butter. Fry the cubes of bacon, remove, and then carefully brown the bird on all sides. Pour on the brandy. When it is warm, set it alight and then let the flames die down.

Return the bacon to the pan, stir round and add the bottle of wine. Add the giblets of the bird, excluding the liver, cover the pan and simmer very gently for about 1 hour. Near the end of the cooking time, peel the onions and sauté in a little butter. Sprinkle on some sugar and let it caramelise and add a splash of red wine. In a clean pan, sauté the mushrooms (wiped clean, if necessary) in some more butter.

Remove the giblets from the chicken pan and discard; remove the chicken to a serving dish and keep warm. Add the glazed onions and cooked mushrooms to the pan, then reduce the liquid by boiling. If it needs additional thickening, add the *beurre manié* piece by piece and simmer until you have a glossy sauce. Pour it over the chicken and serve with triangles of bread fried in hot oil, the corners of them dipped into finely-chopped parsley.

A SIMPLE CASSOULET

Cassoulet is another fine way of feeding numbers and numerous people with keen appetites is usually a feature of holiday catering. A true cassoulet worthy of the appellation Castelnaudary or Carcassonne takes time and attention. This is a pared-down approach, but nonetheless good. In France it is easy to buy *confit* of duck or goose, but if you happen not to be in France, never mind. Aim for something that gives unctuousness, even if it is only a good quality sausage. Any left-over haricot beans are a splendid basis for a soup, e.g. minestrone. Or should your rented accommodation run to a liquidiser, they can be whizzed into a cream and spiked with garlic.

Serves 6–8

2 lb/1 kg dried white haricot beans
½ lb/250 g gammon or *bacon*
1 tablespoon vegetable oil
3 onions, peeled and sliced
2 tomatoes, peeled and chopped
1 heaped teaspoon honey or *syrup* or *treacle*
5 cloves garlic, peeled and slivered
1 bay leaf

a generous pinch of thyme or *oregano* or *rosemary*
stock – either homemade, or from a cube
1 duck or *1 chicken*
1 lb/500 g good sausages, e.g. Toulouse sausage or any interesting boiling sausage
1 leg confit *of duck* or *goose, if available*
fresh breadcrumbs

Soak the beans overnight or, alternatively, bring them to the boil, boil for 5 minutes and leave for 1 hour to swell. Then cook them in fresh water for 1 hour until they are three-quarters cooked. Turn on the oven to 180°C/350°F, Gas 4.

Cut the bacon or gammon into cubes. Using 1 tablespoon of oil if it is gammon, sauté the cubes and then add the onions and let them soften. Add the tomatoes, honey, garlic and herbs. Pour on the stock just to cover and simmer. Meanwhile roast the chicken or duck until nearly done.

Towards the end of the cooking time of the chicken or duck, add the sausages to brown in the roasting pan. When they are done, turn down the oven to 140°C/275°F, Gas 1. Rub a large earthenware pot with garlic. If you have some *confit*, place it, with some of the fat adhering, in the bottom of the pot. Slice the browned sausage into chunks, then add the chicken or duck, carved into 8–10 pieces, and sausage chunks to the pot. Cover with the beans and give the pot a good shake to make them settle. Pour on the stock which should be at simmering point.

Place in the cooled oven; after half an hour, strew breadcrumbs over the top of the dish and cook for 1 hour more. A crust should form on the top. If necessary, raise the heat at the end to brown the crust. A good deal of wine goes well with this dish.

MEAT LOAF

The best meat loaf is made with a mixture of meats, i.e. beef, lamb and pork. It can be made with beef alone, but it then tends to lack unctuousness. Many supermarkets now sell minced lamb and pork, or a winning smile at the butcher should persuade him to mince these meats for you. Whilst meat loaf should never be a receptacle for left-overs, it can accommodate a variety of vegetables and also grains such as kasha, cous-cous or even corn flakes.

The recipe below contains our suggestions, but if you have other ideas – for example, chopped green pepper or cracked wheat in place of bread crumbs – you should feel free to experiment. Meat loaf is good either hot with a spicy tomato sauce as an accompaniment, or cold with chutney or Cumberland sauce.

Serves 6–8

1 lb/500 g minced beef ⎫ *(or 2 lb/1 kg*
½ lb/250 g minced lamb ⎬ *beef alone)*
½ lb/250 g minced pork ⎭
2 eggs
6 oz/180 g fresh breadcrumbs, brown or
   white
2 carrots, peeled and grated

2 oz/60 g mushrooms, cleaned and
   chopped
2 onions, peeled and finely chopped
2 cloves garlic, peeled and chopped
½ aubergine, cut into small cubes
   (optional)
a dash of soya sauce or *Tabasco*
salt and freshly-ground black pepper

Turn on the oven to 180°C/350°F, Gas 4. If you are using aubergine, which actualy adds a nice texture, salt the cubes and let them sweat out their bitterness. Pat dry.

Mix all the ingredients – use your hands for the best results – and then press the mixture into a loaf tin or a casserole of suitable size. Give the top a slightly rounded shape. Bake in the oven for 1–1½ hours. Pour off any accumulated fat and serve. If you prefer to serve it cold, wrap it in foil, and weight it with a couple of tins until quite cool. Refrigerate.

An alternative method is to sauté the vegetables until soft before you mix them with the meats; drain off any fat first. If you are using aubergine, it is a good idea.

BOLLITO MISTO

A *bollito misto*, properly made and served from a trolley in an Italian restaurant is a grand thing indeed. For the purposes of holiday cooking, it is an easy way of feeding numbers, requiring unsophisticated equipment and bequeathing you with ideal leftovers of cold meat from which to make salads or sandwiches. A classical *bollito misto* contains beef or veal, chicken, tongue and a *zampone*, a superior sausage with a casing made from a pig's trotter. On holiday, use what is to hand, but aim for a contrast of white meat, dark meat and something spicy and interesting such as a high meat-content sausage. The sauces are what make this dish special.

Serves 8–10

2 carrots, peeled	*2 lb/1 kg beef for boiling, e.g., brisket or*
1 onion, peeled	*chuck steak in a piece*
2 tomatoes	*1 small salted tongue (optional)*
1 bay leaf	*2 pig's trotters or 1 calf's foot (optional)*
parsley	*1 chicken*
salt and pepper	*1 large country sausage or several smaller*
	ones

Bring enough water to cover the meats (excluding the sausage) to the boil with the vegetables, herbs and seasonings. Add the beef and the tongue, and trotters if you are using them. Let them all simmer and skim off any scum. After 2 hours, remove the tongue and peel away the skin; trim off any fat and gristle and return to the pan. Add the chicken, and top up with more water if necessary. Simmer for 45 minutes to 1 hour, then turn off the heat. Next poach the sausage in a separate pan. To serve, slice the meat, arrange it prettily on a dish and hand round with the sauces below. Plain boiled potatoes are a good accompaniment.

Note: Slice only as much meat as you want for one serving and return the rest to keep it moist and flavoursome in the broth. The broth will give you wonderful stock for soups.

SALSA VERDE

2½ tablespoons finely chopped parsley	*1 teaspoon Dijon mustard*
2 tablespoons finely chopped capers	*1 teaspoon red wine vinegar*
6 anchovy fillets, mashed	*8 tablespoons olive oil*
1 clove garlic, peeled and crushed	

Put the first five ingredients into a bowl and mix thoroughly. Stir in the vinegar. Slowly add the oil, beating all the while. Taste and check if you want to add salt or more vinegar. You can, of course, add other fresh herbs according to your supplies.

SALSA ROSSA

3 onions, peeled and thinly sliced
4 tablespoons vegetable oil
2 green peppers
1 lb/500 g ripe tomatoes, peeled and
   chopped or 1 14 oz/435 g tin
   Italian tomatoes

a drop of chilli sauce or 1 small green or
   red chilli, de-seeded and finely sliced
a pinch of sugar
salt and pepper

Cook the onion in the oil until soft. Remove the seeds and core from the peppers; chop them finely and add to the onions. Cook until softened. Add the tomatoes, chilli, a pinch of sugar and salt and pepper. Cook gently for 30 minutes. Serve warm.

FRIED AUBERGINES WITH SKORDALIA

This Greek mode of serving aubergines is perfect holiday food. The sooner you eat the aubergines after they are fried, the better. They do not hang around gracefully. You could, if you wish, substitute mashed potato for the breadcrumbs in the recipe. Many Greek women would, but we like the rough texture donated by the crumbs.

Serves 4 as a substantial first course

1 large or 2 medium aubergines
4 plump cloves garlic
1 fat slice stale white bread
3 oz/90 g ground almonds
olive oil

salt and pepper
lemon juice
seasoned flour
more olive oil or vegetable oil

Aubergine slices must be salted and left to bead with perspiration to remove bitterness and stop them mopping up quantities of oil. So wipe the aubergine, trim off the calyx and cut into ¼-inch/0.6-cm slices. Lay in a colander and sprinkle with salt.

The sauce can be made with a pestle and mortar, but a liquidiser or food processor speeds it up immeasurably. Peel and crush the garlic cloves. Trim the bread of its crusts, soak it in water and squeeze tightly in your hand. Put the garlic and bread into the machine for a brief whizz. Add the almonds and blend.

Slowly add the olive oil as if for mayonnaise until you have a homogeneous thick sauce. Season with salt, pepper, and lemon juice to taste. If it looks a bit porridgey, the texture and colour can be improved with a little milk or thin cream. Pile into a pretty bowl.

Wipe the aubergines with kitchen paper, then shake them in a bag with seasoned flour. Heat the oil to a depth of about $\frac{1}{4}$ inch/o.6 cm in a frying pan; vegetable oil can be used for economy. Fry the aubergine slices, turning them once, until golden. Drain on kitchen paper. You will have to do this in batches, keeping them warm the while.

Serve immediately with the skordalia sauce.

FRUIT FOOLS

Since the main holiday is a time when there is a good variety of fruit available, and all children love puddings even when they don't much like raw fruit, fools make an easy and popular dessert.

Most soft fruit is good for a fool, but some are used puréed raw and some need to be cooked. Strawberries, raspberries and blackberries should not be cooked, but apples, apricots, gooseberries, blackcurrants and red or white currants should be stewed first, until just soft.

Stew the fruit gently in a very little water (e.g., 3 tablespoonsful water to 1 lb/500 g apricot or gooseberries or any currants). To this water, you should add sugar. As taste about sweetness varies so much, as well as the varying tartness of the fruit you may choose, it is impossible to give an exact quantity of sugar. We would suggest 2 tablespoonsful sugar for 1 lb/500 g of apricots and probably 3 tablespoonsful for gooseberries. Use what you think fit, and then taste the syrup when the fruit has stewed. If there isn't enough sugar, add more. If too much, pour off a little of the syrup and add the juice of a lemon. If the fruit has made a great deal of juice in the cooking, pour off most of the syrup before you purée the fruit.

When the fruit is cold, add slightly whipped cream. The proportions should be $\frac{1}{2}$ pint/300 ml to 1 pint/625 ml of fruit purée. If you like, you can add half whipped cream and half creamy yoghurt to the mixture. If you are somewhere where cream is difficult or impossible to obtain, you can do the whole thing with yoghurt. Put the fool in the fridge for at least 1 hour before serving. This will make enough fool for 6–8 people.

GERMAN FRITTERS

Serves 6

1 egg + 2 egg yolks
2 tablespoons top of the milk
2 oz/60 g butter
3 tablespoons sunflower seed oil

12 slices white bread, with the crusts cut
*   off*
raspberry jam
caster sugar

Mix the eggs and beat them with the milk. Heat the butter and oil in a pan. When very hot, dip slices of bread in the egg mixture, drain for a second and fry quickly, until light brown and crisp. Put on kitchen paper to drain, and then spread raspberry jam on half the slices, put the other slices on top and dust each sandwich with caster sugar.

Index